Caste-Based Exclusion

Edited by

Jagan Karade

RAWAT PUBLICATIONS

Jaipur • New Delhi • Bangalore • Hyderabad • Guwahati • Kolkata

ISBN 978-81-316-0706-0

Published by
Prem Rawat for **Rawat Publications**
Satyam Apts, Sector 3, Jawahar Nagar, Jaipur 302 004 (India)
Phone: 0141 265 1748 / 7006 Fax: 0141 265 1748
E-mail: info@rawatbooks.com
Website: www.rawatbooks.com

New Delhi Office
4858/24, Ansari Road, Daryaganj, New Delhi 110 002
Phone: 011 2326 3290

Also at *Bangalore, Hyderabad, Guwahati* and *Kolkata*

Typeset by Rawat Computers, Jaipur

Printed at Nice Printing Press, New Delhi

Dedicated to

all Bhimsainiks of Mahad Satyagrah

who fought against

caste discrimination in modern India

Contents

Acknowledgement

It gives me immense pleasure to present the book, *Caste-Based Exclusion*, which has been a continued practice and it evolves in different forms in the socio-political and cultural life of the Dalits. This volume focuses on these issues and explores the roots of this inhuman practice that brought a blot on humanity in India. On these issues many writers and eminent personalities helped me to give shape to this book and for this I thank them immensely. I thank all those who directly or indirectly rendered their help and cooperation in this venture of success. I would like to express my deep sense of gratitude to the contributors of the articles in support.

It is my duty to thank the eminent personalities like Dr Bhalchandra Mungekar (Former Vice Chancellor, University of Mumbai and Member, Rajya Sabha, Government of India), Dr Uttamrao Bhoite (Former Vice Chancellor, Yashwantrao Chavan Maharashtra Open University, Nashik and Bharati Vidhyapeeth, Pune), and my research guide, Dr P.G. Jogdand (Mumbai University, Mumbai) for their guidance and support. I would also like to thank Dr D.N. Dhanagare (Pune), Dr Nandu Ram, Dr Anand Kumar (JNU, New Delhi), Dr Pradip Kumar, Dr Smita Patil (IGNOU, New Delhi), Dr Ishwar Modi (Jaipur), Dr R. Indira (Mysore), Dr Nirakar Malik (Assam), Dr Pradeep Aaglave (Nagpur), Dr B.K. Nagla (Haryana) and Dr M.H. Makwana (Gujarat).

I offer my special thanks to Dr N.J. Pawar (Vice-Chancellor) and Dr Ashok Bhoite (Pro-Vice-Chancellor), Shivaji University, Kolhapur for their encouragement. I thank Dr D.V. Muley (Registrar, Shivaji University, Kolhapur) and the faculty members especially, Dr R.B. Patil, Dr R.N. Salve, Dr P.B. Desai and Dr P.M. Mane who always supported me. I am obliged to Dr Praveen Jadhav, Sanjay Khilare and Sunil Ogale for their strong motivation. I would also like to acknowledge my deepest gratitude to Mr Shankar Bhoir (Pune), Dr Manish Wankhede (Nagpur) and Dr Richard Pais (Mangalore) for taking pains in the pre-publication work.

My family members, mother Indumati, wife Dr Sujata, children Utkarsha and Ujjwal are the sources of my energy and always encouraged my ideas. I cannot forget the kind words of my father-in-law, Advocate S.G. Sudarshani along with Mrs Sudarshani constantly supporting me and my family on all occasions.

Finally, I express my gratitude to Rawat Publications and their associates, without whose help this book could not have been completed.

Jagan Karade
Kolhapur

Contributors

Bibhuti Bhushan Malik is the Director of Dr Ambedkar Studies Centre and Associate Professor of Sociology, at Babasaheb Bhimrao Ambedkar University (a Central University), Lucknow. He has completed his M.A., M.Phil. and Ph.D. from the Centre for the Study of Social Systems at the Jawaharlal Nehru University (JNU), New Delhi. He was awarded Junior Research Fellowship (JRF) as well as Senior Research Fellowship (SRF) by the University Grants Commission, New Delhi for his research work. He started his academic career as a Lecturer at Dayalbagh Educational Institute (Deemed University) Dayalbagh, Agra. He also worked as Reader in Sociology at M.G. Kashi Vidyapeeth, Varanasi. He has contributed a number of articles and research papers in English and Hindi in various national and international journals. His area of specialization is Sociology of Ecology and Environment, Sociology of Development, Sociology of Weaker Sections, Dalits and Ambedkar Studies. He has published a book, *Poverty in India: Fundamental Issues: A Social Science Perspective and Social Ecology of Forest Resources*. At present, Dr Malik is engaged in a major research project funded by the University Grants Commission (UGC), New Delhi. (email: bbmalik57@gmail.com)

B.S. Waghmare is working as Professor, Department of Political Science, Dr Babasaheb Ambedkar Marathawada University, Aurangabad. He has completed his M.A. and Ph.D. from Marathawada University, Aurangabad and M.Phil. from JNU, Delhi. He has been teaching Political Science for the last three decades. His two books and more than 15 articles have been published in edited books and reputed research journals. He has completed one minor and one major research project, which were funded by UGC, New Delhi. He attended and presented research papers in various national, international seminars, conferences and workshops. He is a member of various committees of Dr Babasaheb Ambedkar Marathawada University, Aurangabad. At present he is engaged in a major research project funded by UGC, New Delhi. (email: bhujangw@rediffmail.com)

Desraj Sabharwal is working as an Associate Professor, Department of Sociology, M.D. University, Rohtak, Haryana. He joined as Lecturer in 1993 in the Sociology Department, M.D. University, Rohtak. He earned his Doctorate from the same university. His area of specialization is Sociology of Marginalized Communities and Sociology of Peasantry. He is engaged in research on Dalits and Peasantry and has published many papers in journals and books. (email: desraj.sabharwal@yahoo.in)

Jagan Karade is an Associate Professor in the Department of Sociology, Shivaji University, Kolhapur. He is an ICSSR Fellow. He obtained his M.A. and M.Phil. from Shivaji University, Kolhapur and Ph.D. from University of Mumbai, Mumbai. He is the author of three books entitled *Reservation Policy and Reality, Nationalistic Dr Ambedkar* and *Occupational Mobility among Scheduled Castes* and three edited books entitled *The Effects of Religious Conversion, Globalization and Indian Challenges* and *Development of Scheduled Castes and Scheduled Tribes in India.* His several articles are published in reputed journals and edited books. He has completed a major research project which was funded by UGC, New Delhi. Dr Karade is Member, Management Council, Indian Sociological Society. At present he is engaged in a major research project funded by ICSSR, New Delhi. (e-mail: jagankarade@yahoo.co.in)

Meherjyoti Sangle is an Assistant Professor, P.G. Department of History, SNDT Women's University, Mumbai. She did her graduation in Microbiology and Bio-Medical Techniques before obtaining a Graduate and Master's degree in History. She has been teaching and doing research in Historiography, Indian History, Women's History, Gender Studies and History of Health and Medicine in Colonial Period. She has co-edited a book *Historiography: Past and Present*. She completed the UGC minor research project on *Medical Schools in Western India: Imperial*

Necessities and Indigenous Response (1875–1920) in 2005. She has received UGC Teacher Fellowship for Ph.D. for three years and has recently submitted thesis for degree of Ph.D. on *Women's Health Care and Women Physicians in the Bombay Presidency (1886–1947)*. (email: meherjyoti2002@yahoo.co.in)

Praveen Jadhav is the Head and Professor, Department of Economics, Tilak Maharashtra University, Pune. He is the author of four books, *Socio-Economic Status of Scheduled Castes, Ambedkar's People in India, Environmental Economics* and *Deprived Communities in Contemporary India*. His 25 articles are published in reputed journals and newsletters. At present he is engaged in a major research project funded by UGC, New Delhi. (email: praveenjadhav7@yahoo.co.in)

Ramesh Kamble has been teaching sociology for the last two decades. His areas of interest are: contemporary theoretical perspectives in sociology; social construction of identities, especially gender, caste and class; critical studies and globalization. Presently, he is working on two research themes: Archiving Dalit Panther Movement and Theorizing Humiliation, which is funded by UGC, New Delhi. (email: kambleramesh@hotmail.com)

Shankar Gaikwad is working as an Associate Professor in Department of Sociology, Dr Babasaheb Ambedkar Marathawada University, Aurangabad. He obtained M.A., B.G.L., Ph.D. degrees from the same university. He is teaching for the last two decades. Before commencing the teaching career, he served in the Maharashtra State Services as District Inspector of Land Records during the years 1981–86. His two books and nine articles have been published in edited books and research journals. He attended and presented 35 research papers in international, national and regional seminars and conferences. He has completed two major research projects funded by UGC, New Delhi. He has availed Inter University Associateship in three spells at Indian Institute of Advanced Studies, Shimla. (email: slgaikwad_54@yahoo.co.in)

Vilas Adhav is working as a Professor in Department of Adult, Continuing Education and Extension, University of Pune, Pune. He has published ten books in local language and his 15 articles have been published in edited books and research journals. He has participated in national and international seminars and workshops and presented research papers. He has received several awards at national and international levels. (email: adhavvb@yahoo.com)

Vishal Jadhav is an Assistant Professor of Sociology, Tilak Maharashtra University, Pune. He obtained his M.A., M.Phil and Ph.D from Pune University, Pune and was a Visiting Fellow to the Institute of Development Studies (IDS), University of Sussex, 2003 and 2004. He has been awarded the Dudley Seers Memorial Award for best article in *Journal of Development Studies* (2006) and was selected for the International Sociological Association's doctoral workshop held at Moscow, 2008. (email: gharja@rediffmail.com)

Y.S. Alone is working as Professor, School of Arts and Aesthetics, Jawaharlal Nehru University, New Delhi since 2007. Previously, he worked at the Department of Archaeology, Deccan College Post Graduate Research Institute (Deemed University), Pune and Department of Fine Arts, Kurukshetra University, Kurukshetra. He has published several research papers and chapters in edited volumes on Ancient Indian Art. His research interest includes ancient Indian art including Buddhist art and modern Indian art and popular visual culture, as well as general social sciences. He has presented research papers at national and international art-history and social sciences seminars, conferences at many places in India and abroad. He is a member of editorial board of the journal *The Journal of South Asian Archaeology: Ancient Asia.* (email: aloneys@yahoo.com)

1 Economics of Dalits and Academic Discrimination

Praveen K. Jadhav

Dalits have been placed at the bottom in the Indian social structure. They had been kept in severe social, economic and cultural poverty over a long period of time. They did not have means of production. They were working as service providers. The caste hierarchy had divided the services of Dalits as the most inferior. Besides that, inhuman treatment, exploitation, concept of pollution, untouchability, atrocities, etc. were attached to Dalits for hundreds of years. Dr B.R. Ambedkar, the leader of Dalits fought for their rights. He was able to provide certain rights to Dalits in pre- and post-independence period. The Constitution of India also has given certain safeguards to Dalits. In spite of that, large majority of Dalits are suffering from social evils, especially in rural areas. In consideration of social and economic history of Dalits, it has attracted many scholars throughout the world. Many sociologist scholars have studied Dalits from various approaches. Indian and foreign sociologists have contributed their research with respect to Dalits in India. Unfortunately, economists in India have not considered Dalits as a research topic in their branch. Economics of Dalits does exist and could be interesting and challenging; besides that, excluding rare exception, none of the Indian economists has considered Dalits as a research topic. In this article, the focus is given on economics of Dalits and discrimination that existed in the academic system.

Meaning of Dalits

Dalit, this term or the word has different meanings given by different scholars. Some scholars and activists considered this term in a more confined and defined way, whereas, others have explored it in wider and broader ways. The word Dalit is of common usage in Marathi, Hindi, Gujarati and many other Indian languages. The word Dalit was first used in the new context in Marathi language by Neo-Buddhist activists, the followers of Babasaheb Ambedkar in the early 1970s. It refers to those who have been broken, ground down by those above them in a deliberate way. There is, in the word itself, an inherent denial of pollution, karma and justified caste hierarchy (Zelliot, 1978: 77). Shah (2001: 17–18) writes that, 'Dalits are the poor and downtrodden. Generally, Dalit includes those termed in administrative parlance as Scheduled Castes (SCs), Scheduled Tribes (STs) and Other Backward Castes (OBCs). However, in day-to-day usage in political discourse, the term is so far mainly confined to Scheduled Castes'. Dhasal (1973) has given the meaning of Dalit in a more extensive way. According to Dhasal (1973), the term Dalit means 'Scheduled Castes, Scheduled Tribes, Buddhists, Workers, Landless Labourers and Nomadic Tribals'. Whereas most of the scholars confined Dalits to the 'ex-untouchables' or the 'Scheduled Castes'. These two meanings have a wide scope including major part of the society, which are socially and economically poor. However, some other scholars have different opinions in this regard.

According to Phadke (1977: 33), the term Dalit means that caste which was socially excluded by the 'Hindu' caste system. Mande (1979: 24) argued that, Dalit means those, who were denied the human rights of living by the social system. In more simple words it can be stated that, Dalits are nothing but 'ex-untouchables'. This meaning seems to be more historical, practical and realistic. In this article, the meaning of Dalits is confined to the ex-untouchables (or Sudras), who are now known as Scheduled Castes. The 'Sudras' (or Dalits) were classified as inferior and the last *Varna* to other three *Varnas*, in the ancient social system in India. Along with this several social, economic and political restrictions were imposed on them. This classified Sudras (or Dalits) include various caste groups, which have suffered social and economic deprivation over a long period of time. They had to live in severe poverty outside the village.

These untouchables or castes were officially defined as 'depressed castes' in 1932 and they were systematically listed in the

1931-Census of India. The Simon Commission in 1935 first coined the term Scheduled Castes. All the untouchable castes, which were listed in 1931-Census of India, came to be known as the 'Scheduled Castes' (SCs) through the Government of India Act of 1935. In the meantime, the government published a list of Scheduled Castes under the Government of India (Scheduled Castes) Order, 1936. The Government of India in post-independence period carried forward the same idea. According to the Constitution of India, under article 341(1), the President of India after consultation with the Governor may specify, 'the castes, races, tribes or parts of groups within castes or races, which shall be deemed to be Scheduled Castes'. Accordingly, the President has notified the Scheduled Castes in an order called 'Constitution (Scheduled Castes) Order–1950 and the Scheduled Castes and Scheduled Tribes List (Modification) Order–1956' (Kamble, 1982: 20–21). In this article the terminology, Dalits, is used as synonymous for 'Scheduled Castes'.

Meaning of Economics

'Economics' has been defined by many economists in various ways. One famous definition given by Robbins (1932: 15) is quoted here. According to him 'Economics is a science, which studies human behaviour as a relationship between ends and scarce resources which have alternative resources'. This applies to both the behaviour of the individual and of the society as a whole. Professor Boulding argued that 'Economics is a study of mankind in the ordinary business life'. Jacob Vinor defined it as 'Economics is what economists do' (quoted in Ahuja, 2001: 5). There are many definitions that describe 'economics' in various ways, however all the definitions have focused on some basic economic problems. Ahuja (2001: 5) puts these economic problems as below:

1. What goods are produced and in what quantities by the productive resources which the economy possesses?
2. How are the different goods produced? That is, what production methods are employed for the production of various goods and services?
3. How is the total output of goods and services of a society distributed among its people?

4. Are the use of productive resources economically efficient?
5. Whether all available productive resources within a society are being fully utilized?
6. Is the economy's productive capacity increasing, declining or remaining static over a frame of time?

The central economic problems of the society are concerned to all its social groups. The productive resources, their capacity and their distribution among the people – these issues have been part and parcel of economics. Economics must be explored for the welfare of the society, which includes all individuals. In case of Indian society, the individuals are divided on their social background and hence their share in resources is limited. Economics or economists must be able to explore the realistic picture of society along with its evaluation. In the modern times especially after 1929, along with Micro and Macro Economics, other branches of economics also have developed up to a considerable level. Some of them are – 'Economics of Industries', 'Economics of Agriculture', 'Labour Economics', 'Economics of Insurance', 'Economics of Resources', 'Economics of Money and Banking', 'Economics of Infrastructure', etc. In each branch and sub-branch of economics, the role of economics or economists is to determine the maximum social welfare. Unfortunately, in the context of Indian society, economics has dealt with the social welfare of 'elite' groups. Economists or economics in India has neglected the economics of a large section of society, which has been living at the bottom with severe economic poverty over a long period of time. Economics has not given any solution to economic problems of these people.

Economics of 'Dalits'

The ultimate goal of economics is social welfare and maximum satisfaction of both, the individuals and the society, as a whole. This has been the central theme of economics. Dalits are an important part of society, constituting significant share in the total population. Besides that, economics in India has never considered Dalits as a basic part of study. As a whole, Scheduled Castes, Scheduled Tribes and Other Tribes constitute around 30 per cent of Indian population. This huge population was never brought under the ambit of economics. Economics could not give solution to these segments of the society. This is because economics in India is nothing but economics of *elite* group. It explored only the cream of the society and rest of the people had no economics. This approach has brought about a huge setback to Indian economy and Indian society. Large section of the society remained in severe economic poverty and deprivation. Economists were silent over these issues. The million dollar question is that, whom should we blame? The branch of 'economics' has been living in compartments in India for several years. The traditional 'economists' in India did not try to interlink this branch with 'sociology' and 'psychology'. This negligence brought the isolated status to this branch of 'economics'. The base line of this basic subject in relation to Indian society is that, 'economics in India has emerged from the caste hierarchy'. The study of the Indian economy in multidimensional approach must be linked with 'sociology', 'culture' and 'psychology', whereas this has not been done in general.

The 'economic discrimination', 'economic inequality', 'economics of resources', 'labour discrimination', 'culture and economics', 'economics of land', 'segmentation of labour', etc. – all these issues have deep roots in the 'caste hierarchy'. Although these are the economic issues but have been determined not by economic factors. In each branch of economics, there is a second side and this side is being neglected conveniently by economists. It is true that, the intercaste economic inequality has emerged from the caste hierarchy; however, most of the economists do not consider the 'Economics of castes' as branch of economics. When there is some academic innovation in this regard (caste economics), the 'established' economists place this branch under 'sociology' and they neglect the real issues in a comfortable way. So far, these economists have never tried to promote the 'Economics of Dalits' or 'Economics of caste' in a systematic way.

The 'economists' in India wish to study the 'Banking', 'Money', 'International Trade', 'Labour Economics', 'Indian Economy', 'Growth of Development' and even the 'Micro-credit system'. But they did not cross the line of these studies and go to the real roots. According to ground reality, in the context of Indian economy, every branch of economics has socio-psychological aspects. These are the *backstage* issues, which are neglected by the economists.

The economic structure in India has been built on the 'social system' that existed for hundreds of years. The economic activities, distribution of resources, wage determination, etc. are determined on the basis of social system. The caste hierarchy has brought the economic inequality in all aspects. This cannot be hidden. This cannot be neglected. We must accept this reality in order to end the evils of caste hierarchy. Accordingly development plans can be designed. The understanding of this economic structure and academic experiments in this regard may bring solution. Unfortunately, most of the Indian economists still do not consider the 'Caste hierarchy' as the origin of the economic inequality between various social groups. Thus, the economists are involved in activities as beating around the bush. It is really surprising that, why the eminent and intellectual Indian economists have not given attention towards these basic issues? Did they not understand? Did they not see? Or were they not capable? I do not find any of these possibilities, and then the question is that why they did not study?

Contribution of Foreign Scholars

Sociology and Economics of Castes has been an interesting field of research for many foreign scholars. They have contributed their best. There has been series of scholars, who studied Dalits in pre- and post-Independence period. In this regard, the pioneer work has been done by two famous scholars in pre-Independence period. Enthoven (*The Tribes and Castes of Bombay*, 1919) and Russel and Hiralal (*Tribes and Castes of Central Provinces*, 1916) have contributed through their remarkable work. They have systematically listed various castes and tribes in selected regions of India, which include all those castes, which are now known as Dalits. Even in the contemporary period, these two famous contributions remained relevant. Some other scholars are – Dubois (1857), Kroeber (1950), Hutton (1961), Beteille (1971) and others.

In the recent period, the famous foreign scholar Gail Omvedt has given her remarkable contribution to Dalit studies. Some of her contributions are – *Dalits and the Democratic Revolution: Dr Ambedkar and the Dalit Movement in Colonial India* (1994), *Dalit Visions: The Anti-Caste Movement and the Construction of an Indian Identity* (1994), *Buddhism in India: Challenging*

Brahmanism and Caste (2003) and *Ambedkar: Towards an Enlightened India* (2004). In a similar way, there are few more foreign scholars, who have considered Dalits as a part of their study (Zelliot, 1978; Detlef, 2003 and others).

In the context of caste economics or Dalit economics, some of the eminent foreign scholars have contributed to the field of caste economics. It was really surprising and appreciable that these foreign scholars have given much attention towards the caste-based economics. For them, it was difficult to understand the *Indian Caste Hierarchy* or the *Varna System*, besides that they have considered the caste economics as the important issue. Their contribution must be appreciated. In this regard, I must quote some of the eminent scholars as – Cohn 'The Changing Status of Depressed Class', 1955 and Akerlof 'The Economics of Caste and the Rat Race and Woeful Tales', 1976. Thus it can be stated that, the foreign scholars have considered Dalits as an important issue of study, especially in sociological approach. Few of them have explored in 'economic' approach.

'Dalit' Studies and 'Dalit' Scholars

Dalit studies are made by Dalit scholars, with rare exceptions. This is perfectly true in case of sociology and economics of Dalits. Non-Dalits do not consider this as an issue of research. The survey of literature with respect to Dalit studies supports this argument. Especially in Maharashtra, Dalit academicians have studied Dalits. Initially, the issue of Dalits (depressed castes) was understood by Dr Ambedkar. According to Ambedkar (1936) 'the caste system is the root of the economic inequality'. After Independence, educational mobility of Dalits brought various socio-economic changes. Many Dalit academicians did research on various issues of Dalits in India. Some of them (especially from Maharashtra) are – Kamble (1979) *Caste and Philosophy in Pre-Buddhist India*, Kamble (1982) *The Scheduled Castes*, Dahiwale (1986) *Occupational Mobility among the Persons from Ex-Untouchable Castes in Kolhapur City*, Jogdand (1989) *The Protest Movement and Social Change: A Study of Dalit Movement in Maharashtra*, Gaikwad (1991) *Protective Discrimination Policy and Social Change*, Kurne (1997) *Ethnic Identity and Social Mobility: A Case Study of the Buddhists in Pune*, Gaikwad

(2001) *The Neo-Buddhists Elites: A Study of Their Role, Status and Mobility*, Naik (2003) *Thoughts and Philosophy of Dr B.R. Ambedkar*, Jadhav (2005) *Socio-Economic Status of Scheduled Castes* and Karade (2009) *Occupational Mobility among Scheduled Castes*. Besides these studies, there are several other studies on Dalits conducted by Dalit scholars. This is perfectly true in case of Maharashtra. In other states of India, this trend is more or less the same. On the contrary, there are very few non-Dalit intellectuals like Thorat and Deshpande (1999), Kakade (1998), Rege (2006) and others who have considered Dalits as a field of study.

In the context of economics of Dalits; most of the economists or intellectuals have neglected Dalits, as a part of their study. Indian economists, who are part of non-Dalits, have neglected the social and economic reality of Indian society. It is very unfortunate that, a large section of the society has been living in severe economic poverty and with various economic problems, yet they have been neglected by the economists. The poverty and deprivation of Dalits was sustained for longer period due to the caste hierarchy, which has been highlighted by the non-Dalit intellectual economists. This should have been their central part of study. But this did not happen.

In the recent period some of the economists (in India) have dealt with the issue of 'caste' and 'economics'. They have given empirical evidences to the relationship between the intercaste economic equality and the caste hierarchy. They have proved that, 'economics of discrimination' and 'labour discrimination' in India are determined by the 'caste hierarchy' even today. In this effort Thorat (Thorat and Deshpande, 1999; Thorat and Negi, 2005; Thorat and Attewal, 2007; Thorat and Kumar, 2008; Thorat and Newman, 2010) have played a gigantic role. He has explored the grassroot economic problems of Dalits and other weaker sections of Indian society. It is a fact that, merely 'Labour Economics' does not explore the reality of Indian labour system. There exists discrimination on the caste background of the labour force. This must come out, and the student of economics must know this reality. Such discrimination and difference could be found in every branch of economics with respect to Indian society. But, this is being neglected conveniently by the economists.

As a whole, considering some exception, it is observed that, the non-Dalit academicians (Indian) did not deal with the issues related to castes and Dalits; on the contrary the Dalit academicians have studied the issues related with the Dalits. Is it not an academic injustice? Is it not an academic discrimination? Is it not the academic 'untouchability'? If not, then, why did not the Indian eminent and intellectual 'economists' develop this branch of economics? Was it not their responsibility? Were the academic activities also influenced by the caste hierarchy? Was it the responsibility of only Dalits to explore their problems? Had Dr Ambedkar not been born and not spent his lifetime fighting against the social-caste evils, then what would have been the situation of the Dalits in Indian society?

'Dalit' Studies: A Paradox

It is clear from the observation that, it has been the trend that, Dalit studies are being conducted mainly by Dalit academicians. Non-Dalit academicians do not consider this study as an issue of research. In the context of economics, it is clear that, non-Dalit economists never considered Dalit studies as central part of research. However, there are some Dalit academicians from economics, who wish to conduct and have conducted such kind of research for their doctoral degrees. Many a time, such academic creation is not recognized by the academic system. The established academic system thinks that the study of Dalits is part of sociology and not economics. Thus, this has blocked further studies in this regard. Dalit academicians want to study various issues of Dalits, but they are unable to get research guidance for such subjects. In fact, they are being discouraged to conduct studies on Dalit economics. On the one hand, non-Dalit scholars are not willing to study the economics of Dalits and on the other, Dalit scholars are being discouraged by non-Dalit scholars to conduct such study. Ultimately, the academic system runs on the thoughts of non-Dalit scholars. The recognition for academic output is also in the hands of non-Dalit scholars. Thus, this approach of academic system has led to a paradox in the process of Dalit studies.

Economics Beyond Economics

In Indian academic system, there has been the study of various branches of economics, which starts from 'Money' to 'Trade' and from 'Individual' to 'Society'. All branches are being studied. These branches are more traditional. Of course, these are essential branches of economics, but there is a need to look *beyond* such 'economics'. There is lot of 'economics' *beyond* the 'economics' that existed in India. Although the ultimate goal of 'economics' is maximum welfare of the society, economics in India was never thought of in a realistic way. Therefore, there is a need to develop such branches of economics, which are directly and indirectly related to the society and the groups of society. It is a fact that the Indian society has been divided into various social groups. There has been heterogeneity in Indian society. Indian economists must think of this reality and accordingly, there is a need to develop the branches of economics. In many foreign countries, there has been expansion of the branch of 'economics' to its various branches of 'sociology', 'culture', 'psychology', 'philosophy', etc. Some of the new branches of economics are – 'Social Economics', 'Cultural Economics', 'Economic Psychology', 'Economic Philosophy', 'Identity Economics', 'Gender Economics', 'Resource Economics' and other similar branches are being studied separately. These branches of economics are more *applied* in nature and are linked directly with the social welfare. Along with traditional economics (Micro Economics, Macro Economics, Public Finance, Money and Banking, etc.), these interdisciplinary branches of economics have developed into a significant level in foreign countries. Unfortunately in India, these branches have been neglected and no efforts are being made to develop such branches. This has resulted in various grassroot economic problems of weaker sections of Indian society, especially the Dalits. The intellectuals from economics should go beyond the traditional economics for the sake of 'India'. But the established academic system does not bend. Well! May be they are also victims of the social system. They are living in that academic system which has been created by social-cultural philosophy of the caste hierarchy. But yet there is time to think – they must think about this reality, otherwise, they will be protecting the economic injustice to Dalits, like their forefathers.

Economics of Tribes: Some Neglected Issues

Indian society has been divided into various castes and religions. 'Scheduled Castes', 'Scheduled Tribes', 'Nomadic Tribes', 'Other Backward Castes', etc. are some of the sections of the society. There is a need to study the economics of all tribes separately. The tribes have been far away from the main stream for hundreds of years. The present position is the same. The social, economic and cultural position of some tribes in India has been worst. The Indian scholars have neglected this section of the society also. Economists in India never thought about this ground reality. As a result of that, economic problems of these tribes could not be solved. There is a need to explore the tribes with respect to economics. The micro-level studies of each tribe may give solution to their economic problems.

Conclusion

Indian society has been divided into various categories based on the castes. A large section of the society has been living in severe poverty and deprivation. This worst situation of theirs continued over a long period of time. The caste hierarchy has resulted in economic poverty and deprivation of various communities. This is a fact that, even today, the social and economic position of Dalits and *Tribals* is influenced by caste hierarchy. They are living with severe economic problems. These problems have been unsolved for hundreds of years. The intellectuals from economics must consider this reality seriously and conduct various studies in this regard. Such effort may bring some constructive solution. Therefore, the understanding of 'economics' in India must be changed. 'Economics' must be linked with social and economic reality of the society. The researches in Economics of Dalits and Economics of *Tribals* will explore various economic problems and will give constructive solutions. The economists, policy makers and academicians in India must think positively. In fact, there is a need to introduce such subjects in Indian syllabus at graduation and post-graduation levels. The government must also give proper incentives for such studies. As a whole, the social and economic condition of Dalits would be improved along with the academic expansion of this branch of economics.

References

Ahuja, H.L. (2001), *Advanced Economic Theory*, S. Chand and Company, New Delhi.

Akerlof, G. (1976), 'The Economics of Caste and of the Rat Race and Other Woeful Tales', *Quarterly Journal of Economics*, Vol. 90, pp. 599–617.

Ambedkar, B.R. (1924, republished in 1983), Speech delivered at 'Barshi', Dhamma Deep Publications, Barshi. Quoted in Deepak Wankhede (2009), *Geographical Thoughts of Dr B.R. Ambedkar*, Gautam Book Store, Jaipur.

——. (1936, reprinted in 1987), 'Philosophy of Hinduism', in Vasant Moon (ed.), *Dr Babasaheb Ambedkar: Writings and Speeches*, Vol. 3, Department of Education, Government of Maharashtra, Bombay, pp. 1–94.

——. (1946), *Who Were the Shudras?*, Thacker and Co. Ltd., Bombay.

Cohn, Bernard S. (1955), 'The Changing Status of a Depressed Class', in McKim Marriot (ed.), *Village India: Studies in the Little Community*, University of Chicago Press, Chicago, pp. 53–77.

Dahiwale, S.M. (1986), *Occupational Mobility among the Persons from Ex-Untouchable Castes in Kolhapur City*, Ph.D. Thesis (Sociology), Dr Babasaheb Ambedkar Marathwada University, Aurangabad.

Dhasal, Namdeo (1973), 'Aamhi', Diwali Special Issue, Mumbai. Quoted in A. Kusare Kulkarni (1991), *Dalit Swakathane: Sahitya Roop*, Vijay Prakashan, Nagpur.

Enthoven, R.E. (1919, reprinted in 1990), *The Tribes and Castes of Bombay Presidency*, Asian Educational Services, Bombay.

Gaikwad, Narendra (2001), *The Neo-Buddhists Elites: A Study of Their Role, Status and Mobility*, Ph.D. Thesis (Sociology), Dr Babasaheb Ambedkar Marathwada University, Aurangabad.

Gaikwad, Shankar (1991), *Protective Discrimination Policy and Social Change*, Ph.D. Thesis (Sociology), Dr Babasaheb Ambedkar Marathwada University, Aurangabad.

Hutton, J.H. (1961), *Caste in India: Its Nature, Function and Origin*, Low Price Publications, New Delhi.

Jadhav, Praveen (2005), *Socio-Economic Status of Scheduled Castes: Comparative Study with Respect to Kolhapur District*, Ph.D. Thesis submitted to Tilak Maharashtra Vidyapeeth, Pune.

Jogdand, Pralhad (1989), *The Protest Movement and Social Change: A Study of Dalit Movement in Maharashtra*, Ph.D. Thesis (Sociology), Dr Babasaheb Ambedkar Marathwada University, Aurangabad.

Kakade, Suresh (1998), *Political Sub-Culture of Neo-Buddhists: A Case Study of Political Attitudes of Neo-Buddhists in Maharashtra*, Research Project submitted to Tilak Maharashtra Vidyapeeth, Pune.

Kamble, B.R. (1979), *Caste and Philosophy in Pre-Buddhist India*, National Publishing House, New Delhi.

Kamble, N.D. (1982), *The Scheduled Castes*, Ashish Publishing House, New Delhi.

Kantowsky, Detlef (2003), *Buddhists in India Today: Description, Pictures and Documents*, Manohar Publications, New Delhi (English translation by Hans-Georg Tuersing).

Karade, Jagan (2009), *Occupational Mobility among Scheduled Castes*, Cambridge Scholars Publishing, United Kingdom.

Kroeber, A.L. (1950), 'Caste', in Edwin R.A. Seligman and Alvin Saunders Johnson (eds), *Encyclopedia of Social Sciences*, Macmillan, New York.

Kurne, Anjali (1997), *Ethnic Identity and Social Mobility: A Case Study of the Buddhists in Pune*, Ph.D. Thesis (Anthropology), University of Pune, Pune.

Mande, Prabhakar (1979), *Dalit Sahityache Niralepan*, Dhara Prakashan, Aurangabad.

Naik, C.D. (2003), *Thoughts and Philosophy of Dr B.R. Ambedkar*, Sarup and Sons, New Delhi.

Omvedt, Gail (2004), *Ambedkar: Towards an Enlightened India*, Penguin, Delhi.

——. (2003), *Buddhism in India: Challenging Brahmanism and Caste*, Sage Publications, New Delhi.

——. (1994), *Dalit Visions: The Anti-Caste Movement and the Construction of an Indian Identity*, Orient Longman, New Delhi.

——. (1994a), *Dalits and the Democratic Revolution: Dr Ambedkar and the Dalit Movement in Colonial India*, Sage Publications, New Delhi.

Phadke, Bhalchandra (1977), *Dalit Sahitya: Vedana and Vidroh*, Srividya Prakashan, Pune.

Rege, Sharmila (2006), *Writing Caste/Writing Gender: Narrating Dalit Women's Testimonies*, Zubaan Publications, New Delhi.

Robbins, L. (1932), *Essays on the Nature and Significance of Economic Science*, Macmillan, London. Quoted in H.L. Ahuja (2001), *Advanced Economic Theory*, S. Chand and Company, New Delhi.

Russel, R.V. and R.B. Hiralal (1916, reprinted in 1975), *Tribes and Castes of Central Provinces*, Cosmo Publications, New Delhi.

Shah, Ghanshyam (2001), 'Introduction: Dalit Politics', in Ghanshyam Shah (ed.), *Dalit Identity and Politics*, Sage Publications, New Delhi.

Thorat, Sukhadeo and R.S. Deshpande (1999), 'Caste and Labour Market Discrimination', *Indian Journal of Labour Economics*, Vol. 42, No. 4, October-December.

Thorat, Sukhadeo and Prashant Negi (2005), *Reservations and Private Sector: Quest for Equal Opportunity and Growth*, Rawat Publications, Jaipur.

Thorat, Sukhadeo, Venkatesan and others (2006), 'Human Poverty and Socially Disadvantaged Groups in India', Discussion Paper, UNDP, Human Development Resource Centre, Delhi.

Thorat, Sukhadeo and P. Attewal (2007), 'The Legacy of Social Exclusion: A Correspondence Study of Job Discrimination in India', *Economic and Political Weekly*, Vol. 42, No. 41.

Thorat, Sukhadeo and Narendra Kumar (2008), *In Search of Inclusive Policy: Addressing Graded Inequality*, Rawat Publications, Jaipur.

Thorat, Sukhadeo and Katherine Newman (2010), *Blocked by Caste: Economic Discrimination in Modern India*, Oxford University Press, New Delhi.

Zelliot, Eleanor (1978), 'Dalit New Cultural Context for an Old Marathi World', *Contribution to Asian Studies*, Vol. 11, pp. 77–78. Quoted in Ghanshyam Shah (ed.) (2001), *Dalit Identity and Politics*, Sage Publications, New Delhi.

2 Understanding Dalit Movements

Trajectories and Concerns

Ramesh Kamble

I

On 29 September 2006, in Khairlanji, a village in the district Bhandara of the Maharashtra State of India, Surekha Bhotmange, along with her teenage daughter Priyanka and sons, Sudhir and Roshan were publicly humiliated and brutally murdered by the caste Hindu villagers. Surekha and her daughter were paraded naked throughout the village and gang raped before being brutally killed in broad daylight by a mob of the caste Hindus from their own village. This incident came to light only after a month when Dalit organizations protested vociferously about the apathy, and about serious intentional neglect on the part of State agencies in arresting the violence, callous attitude with which the State agencies reacted towards the nature of violence involved and serious neglect in carrying out investigation procedures, including postmortem of the dead bodies, so as to suppress the evidence, resulting in denial of justice. In fact, a report by the Centre for Equity and Social Justice, a unit of Yashwantrao Chavan Academy of Development Administration, an institution working under the Government itself, stated that 'there seems to be a deep-rooted social conspiracy towards facilitating the crime and subsequent suppressing of evidence on the part of the certain communal forces as well as various elements from politics and administration' (YASHADA, November 2007: 30).

If the mob of caste Hindus committed most indignant atrocities on a Dalit family in Khairlanji, and the forces in politics and

State administration helped in suppressing the evidence in the case, the sate terror in suppressing the subsequent Dalit protest too, is characterized by cruelty and brutality. The fact-finding team efforts initiated by People's Civil Rights Movement activists have shown that the State administration, especially the Police department, unleashed brutal atrocities against Dalit protesters who were angry at the apathy and intentional neglect exhibited by the State administration in responding to the Dalit atrocity. Instead of responding sensitively to the Dalit disenchantment and their legitimate demands for justice, the State administration unleashed brutal violence and justified its cruelty by claiming the involvement of 'Naxalite hand' in Dalit protests. Through this, the State administration succeeded in crushing Dalit struggle against atrocities, in terrorizing Dalits, if they exhibit any signs of autonomous and critical consciousness that questions and challenges the indifferent State, unresponsive to demands for justice, and in legitimizing its brutal oppression by concern for law and order. Of course, though the *Naxal* angle was later underplayed, the police repression continued supposedly to restore the law and order situation. Moreover, even after the protests were violently curbed, police brutality did not cease to exist. Despite the fact that police attacks resulted in severely injuring Dalit women and children in *lathi* charge and firing that killed a Dalit boy, Dinesh Wankhede, the police charged most of the arrested under sections 307 (attempt to murder), 148, 149, (rioting with deadly weapons) of the IPC (PUCL and others, January 2007: 19). This indeed suggests State's brutal attempt to suppress Dalit protests against the atrocities they suffer. Thus, the State's complicity in both the crime against the Dalit family and the State brutality in suppressing Dalit struggle against the atrocity are the glaring truths of the Khairlanji incident and the protests that followed. Again, Dalit protesters had to face the State's cruelty as well as the attack by the caste Hindu hooligans who had come on the streets, apparently to restore the law and order situation. In the history of Maharashtra, for that matter even in the country, there is no example of such 'civil society' activism fighting the oppressed sections (instead of aligning with them) and helping the State administration.

Moreover, if the caste Hindus and state administration had a role in denying justice to Dalits in Khairlanji, the role of media too was not free from traditional caste prejudices and biases. Though the media helped in raising the issue into prominence (although one month after the incidence had taken place), initially it viewed that the event, as resulting out of an illicit relationship that the local caste Hindu community supposedly sought the police intervention and arrests. With this, media thus helped reiterate and justify patriarchal biases against women who become victims of sexual violence. Moreover, it is only later, following the Dalit protests, that the media saw the incidence as a caste atrocity. What is more, while the media showed sensitivity to the atrocity on the Dalits in Khairlanji, it also construed the Dalit protests as a threat to law and order, thus leading in some way to, implicitly, justifying the police brutality against Dalit protesters resisting the caste atrocity and the State complicity. Some members of electronic media even went so far as to dub the Dalit protest as the 'form of caste violence the country has rarely seen before' (*Times Now*, *News-hour*), without realizing that the caste violence has always been violence – torching, lynching, brutally murdering Dalits, publicly humiliating Dalit women, terrorizing Dalits if they protest – directed against the members of oppressed Dalit castes by the dominant upper castes. In short, experiences of atrocities show that Dalits not only continue to be subjected to brutal atrocities by caste Hindus, they also continue to confront not only unresponsive, indifferent but also oppressive State agencies; and the castiest forces now join hands with the State agencies in curbing Dalit resistance and contestations against the State. Similarly the media agencies too, barring a few exceptions, share the traditional caste and class prejudices and exhibit indifference against Dalit atrocities, and what is more important join with the dominant interests in justifying the oppression against Dalits.

II

There are many reasons to start this paper with a brief description of Khairlanji and the post-Khairlanji events. Firstly, unlike the other 'socially backward' caste-ridden States in the rest of the country, the Maharashtra society and politics is seen to have been influenced by the legacy and vision of saints, social reformers and the non-Brahmin leaders such as Chatrapati Shahu Maharaj, Jotirao Phule and Dr Babasaheb Ambedkar. Moreover, Maharashtra has been a birthplace of radical Dalit movement in the country that has inspired radical Dalit assertions in the rest of the country. And yet the Khairlanji and post-Khairlanji events indicate as to how Dalit struggle for dignity, equality and respect is unfolding in the backdrop of the society (which has remained largely oblivious to the above-mentioned influences and legacy). Beneath the apparent façade of progressive social environment, find a deep-rooted ethos of rigid caste hierarchal power structure and deep-seated resentment to Dalits claims for equal treatment. Thus, from the post-seventies onwards any significant attempt on the part of Dalits to disturb the traditional caste hierarchal 'balance' has met with inhuman brutality, suppression and intolerance. The Maharashtra society – which has witnessed radical Ambedkarite movement in colonial and post-colonial India and its subsequent radical expression in the Dalit Panther movement and Dalit literature during the seventies – seems to have remained indifferent to the changes ushered in by these movements. Continuous atrocities against Dalits indicate that any attempt on their part to assert for equal humanity and thereby contest the traditional hierarchies has been brutally resisted by the upper castes. Of course, even a cursory glance at atrocities against Dalits show that the forms of assertion that have evoked inhuman social and societal violence need not be an active assertion as equal subjects; taking up education, wearing clean clothes, taking up jobs in non-traditional set-ups, riding bicycle or a vehicle, assuming self respect and dignity, all has been construed as threat to the traditional hierarchical caste order. The event in Khairlanji and brutal suppression of subsequent Dalit protests suggest that Dalits could not be 'included' in the mainstream of the society, provided they meekly accept their lowly status, or strive for empowerment only within the boundaries dictated by the dominant caste order rather than assert for their rights as independent autonomous subjects.

Secondly, the Khairlanji events also show the nature of challenges the Dalit movements and politics is facing in Maharashtra. The events show the futility of the conventional 'mainstream' Dalit politics in articulating Dalit quest for justice, equality and dignity. The events show, as to how the gradual weaning away of Dalit movement into the 'accommodative politics' severely hamper Dalit struggle. The Dalit politics is so accommodated in the 'mainstream' power concerns and is incapable of raising issues of consequence, or assertions that disturbs the interests of the dominant castes. Hence, the Dalit people's revolt against the State complicity in the Khairlanji atrocity was also a revolt against the accommodative politics of the mainstream Dalit politics. The contemporary mainstream Dalit politics in the State, which though has emerged from Dalit Panther movement during the seventies, has been added on to the politics of the dominant interest. Hence, it exists so as it does not disturb the dominant control and the interests of ruling classes.

Thirdly, Khairlanji and post-Khairlanji protests also draw our attention to the limitations, or even futility, of the policies and efforts of 'empowerment' of the marginalized Dalits. The events suggest that even if policies for Dalit inclusion and empowerment are to be implemented sincerely (which is yet to happen) and even if Dalits achieve socio-economic mobility, their right to life with dignity would not be guaranteed in 'democratic' India. The 'inclusion' and 'empowerment' such politics has thus ushered in, is not an independent of ruling class interests. If Dalit empowerment leads to disturbing the interests of the ruling classes, or if such empowerment offsets the traditional hierarchies, attempts of Dalit empowerment are faced with inhuman atrocities. Thus Dalits would always have to exist under the patronizing and repressive regimes of both the State and non-state actors. The police brutality in repressing the post-Khairlanji Dalit people's struggle shows that the State does not treat its citizens equally. While taking to streets and vandalism of some other sections of society is 'tolerated', treated leniently, Dalits occupying public space for protests against the atrocities they suffer are brutally crushed.

Fourthly, these events have shown that the Dalits are 'alone' in their quest for life with dignity. The failure of social and political movements, such as mainstream women's movements or movements of workers and peasants, in taking due note of the heinous crimes against the Dalit family or in contesting State complicity in the crime could not be explained otherwise. Hence, the non-state actors and civil society initiatives have seen the Khairlanji atrocities as ultimately a Dalit issue and not as the one that poses challenge to the democratic ethos of India. Thus, women's movements that exhibited serious concern over barbaric communal politics in Gujarat, and self-critical stance while engaging with women's involvement in crimes against minorities, have remained inexplicably silent over the Khairlanji issue. While Dalit organizations have waged struggles against communalism and have forcefully campaigned for the implementation of Mandal commission for the OBC reservations, the silence and apathy of women's movements and OBC politics and the civil society initiatives regarding cases of atrocities against Dalits is painfully conspicuous. The *mookmorchas* (silent marches) by peace and harmony activists, involving sometimes even school children, college students, and elderly citizens, which have tried to bring sanity in barbaric social character of Indian society amid communal violence or environmental crises, were glaringly absent or have remained '*Mook*' about Khairlanji and post-Khairlanji violence.

Fifthly, the Khairlanji events show the utter shallowness of institutions of democratic governance in India. While the world and even academic scholars celebrate the biggest functioning democracy of the world, the view largely is based only on the voting patterns in the elections; the undemocratic and autocratic social ethos that underlies this biggest democracy is conveniently overlooked. Due to the deep-rooted castiet social ethos in Indian society neither the elaborate legal provisions, such as Prevention of Atrocities Act, for securing Dalits' rights to life, nor the policy provisions aimed at their social mobility have delivered justice. Moreover, Human Rights Commissions or Commission for Scheduled Castes has proved to be ineffective institutional structures as far as Dalit's quest for life and dignity is concerned. This discussion shows that despite hundred years of Dalit struggle and sixty years of democratic governance, Dalits continue to suffer humiliation on account of untouchability, social discrimination at multiple levels; neither the promises of democracy are fulfilled nor the institutional attempts and programmes have delivered justice, dignity and socio-economic development to them. Instead, the agencies of governance neglect their duties in safeguarding Dalits;

they rather attempt to shield the oppressors, thereby denying the Constitutional promise of justice and equal citizenship.

These questions have serious implications for understanding Dalit social experience and movements, the complex of caste ethos/power/dominance and democracy in India, and the response (or lack of it) of the non-state actors in addressing oppression suffered by Dalits.

In this background, this paper tries to map ideological and political trajectories of Dalit movements and attempts to articulate their most pressing concerns. I suggest that the trajectories of Dalit movement and politics could be understood in terms of dynamics of 'Politics of Identity', 'Politics of Issues', and 'Politics of Accommodation'. I would argue that politics of unfair 'inclusion' and 'accommodation' has led to gradual weaning of efficacy of Dalit movement in addressing concerns of ensuring freedom, dignity and equal citizenship for Dalits. Dalits' experiences of brutal atrocities, which have gradually assumed most heinous forms, pose a serious challenge for both Dalit struggle for dignity and equal democratic space and sections of Indian society and polity that wishes to be committed to the politics of emancipation. As an attempt of understanding and explaining reasons for brutal atrocitics against Dalits, I have suggested the twin concept of 'shame and rage'. The argument here is that the diligent pursuit of educational and economic mobility by Dalits, their efforts to claim equal citizenship through Constitutional provisions, and their quest for dignity, 'shame' the sections of the upper castes which continue to be rooted in the caste power relations; these sections, in turn, react with 'rage' against the Dalits. Moreover, Dalit attempts for mobility threatens the primacy of the traditional hierarchal order and thereby undermines the 'superior caste status' claims of the dominant upper castes. Lastly, the paper attempts to articulate the possibility of the politics of emancipation in which emancipator concerns of the Dalit movement and politics are seen to be inseparably linked to the politics of the broad category of the marginalized, namely, landless labourers, and workers engaged in unjust and oppressive working conditions and women confronting multiple vulnerabilities. But before we engage into these issues it would be pertinent to start with a brief discussion on the category of Dalit and the status of Dalits in Indian society.

III

The Category 'Dalit'

The category of Dalit has become an important context for understanding contemporary Indian society, economy, polity and culture. Scholars have sought to make Dalit as an analytical category through which history, culture, society, economy and polity are examined. Of course this is a recent development, initiated primarily by Dalit scholars or scholars sensitive to the issues of justice, dignity and critical analysis of processes of 'othering' in India. Conventionality, however, sociological and anthropological studies have focused on caste and the nature of social stratification and processes of change in Indian society. One attempts here to explain the nature of caste, the nature of changes taking place in caste society, processes of mobility and its implications for understanding changes in aspects of dominance, hierarchy and varied contextual embedding of these aspects of caste society. Of course, the engagement with village society has led to making the world of communities, including Untouchables as concerns of sociological analysis. However, it is only very recently that the category Dalit has been 'included' in social science research and pedagogy. Again, here too the category Dalit existed either as an 'add-on' to conventional concerns of sociological engagements or it has now been in the form of Dalit studies in the academic institutional settings. The concern of these studies has largely been Dalit social movement, social mobility, examination of state policies and measures, which is of importance. Further we cannot undermine the recently emerging body of nuance knowledge of Dalit social experience in which Dalit's attempts of gaining subjectivity in transformation and in contesting knowledge claims of the dominant knowledge/power regimes. But the orientation present in this academic 'visibility' has largely been of adding Dalit, or now in ever more popular gender studies, adding Dalit women to the conventional forms of analyses and academic structures (again some of the critical literature is written in the form of 'status reports' at the behest of NGO initiatives). This has led to partial or inadequate understanding of the category Dalit. One of the forms of erroneous understanding of the category Dalit is evident in the conceptualization of the term 'Dalit' in literature in the area. The growing body of literature on Dalits has tried to search the origin of the term Dalit in its Sanskritic etymological roots that is, as broken, crushed and victimized. This not only provides partial but even erroneous view of the term, it also undermines a century long Dalit struggle against the oppressive social order, Dalit attempts of transforming social order, social discourse as well as Dalit subjectivity in everyday life contestations: Dalits were/are victims no doubts, but they too have fought relentlessly against their victimization.

Hence, it is necessary to see that the term Dalit has emerged to prominence in the unfolding of Dalit movement during the 1970s, and indicated both Dalit quest for human identity and their struggle against oppressive caste social order. In other words, the term Dalit emerged in Dalit struggle aimed at transforming their identity as well as oppressive social order that legitimized and reiterated inequality, discrimination and exploitation as markers of social life. Moreover, though the term gained currency in Dalit Panther movement in Maharashtra, it has now become source of Dalit identity assertion in other parts, most notably in northern and southern states of the country too.

Furthermore, though Dalit movement shares a broad concern for asserting Dalits right to life, livelihood and dignity and process of democratization, these concerns are rooted in regional specificities of oppressive and exploitative structures. Hence, we now speak of plurality in terms of issues, imaginations and meanings associated with the term Dalit. Of course, this is not to obfuscate the fact of common experiences of discrimination, atrocities and exploitation faced by Dalits but to point out, to nuance and situational unfolding of the category Dalit.

Status of Dalits in Indian Society

This attempt of understanding Dalit movement has to be placed in the background of Dalit social experience in Indian society. A brief discussion of the status of Dalits in Indian society, thus, would be a pertinent starting point.

The Dalits were defined and objectified by the Brahminical social order as *untouchables*. The Order of Caste articulated and legitimized by the Brahminical knowledge-power ideological apparatus, divided society into hierarchically arranged social groups on the basis of the principle of ritual, purity and pollution. Those who claimed to be ritual pure regarded themselves as having superior social status and those considered ritually most impure were rendered the lowest social designation. Thus the social hierarchies, and accompanied social, economic and political locations of the caste groups were developed on the basis of designation of the groups on the purity-pollution scale. The caste of Brahmin though did not have political power, was still considered as having apex position in society due its adhered association with the ritual purity, and had knowledge/power to centre their central position in the caste social organization and also to define the nature of Hindu social universe. The Dalits, who were designated at the lowest due to their status on the 'purity-pollution' scale, were constituted as untouchables, which resulted in their social exclusion vis-à-vis other caste Hindus. But, this social exclusion was not devoid of certain oppressive and exploitative forms of inclusion: Their designation as untouchables rendered Dalits unfit for human association, and at the same time, fit to carry out only menial, unskilled, lowly, impure form of forced labour, dictated by the hereditary social status. Hence the practice of untouchability signified not only asocial segregation but also economic exploitation as Dalits were 'fixed' into lowly, impure, un-paid or ill paid forms of work. This arrangement was legitimized, ensured and sustained through the 'theory of Karma'. The theory of Karma – that the salvation and better treatment is possible (in the next birth that is) only with unconditional loyalty to caste Dharma (caste duty) in this birth, and that the present social designation is the result of *Karma* in the previous birth – helped the continuance of the order of caste, which Dalits too had to accept due to pressures of survival. Dr Ambedkar, an important social thinker of modern India who contributed extensively to academic studies and offered incisive sociological analysis of the Hindu society, points out that:

'The system of Untouchability is a gold mine to the Hindus. In it the 240 millions of Hindus have 60 millions of untouchables (during 1940s) to serve as their retinue to enable the Hindus to maintain pomp and ceremony and to cultivate a feeling of pride and dignity benefiting a master class, which cannot be fostered and sustained unless there is beneath it a servile class to look down upon. In it, the 240 millions of Hindus have 60 millions of Untouchables to be used as forced labourers.... In it, the 240 millions of Hindus have 60 millions of Untouchables to do the dirty work scavengers and sweepers which the Hindu is debarred by his religion to do and which must be done by then non-Hindus who could be no others than Untouchables. In it, the 240 millions of Hindus have 60 millions of Untouchables who can be used as shock-absorbers in slums and dead-weights in bottoms, for in slums it is the Untouchable who is fired the first and the Hindu is fired the last and booms, the Hindus is employed first and the Untouchable is employed the last' (Ambedkar, 1989: 40).

Of course, over the years this situation has changed. The Indian society has undergone various processes of change and the sway of the traditional order does remain as pervasive as it existed some two hundred years ago. The factors such as colonialism, capitalism, industrialization, urbanization and the new legal framework, during colonial rule contributed to change in Indian society. The ushering of the independence from the colonial rule and adoption of democratic Constitution in independent India helped in further changing the Indian society and polity. As a result of modernity (as a value system) and processes of modernization of social structure with new social institutions, Indian society underwent socio-economic change, which also had implications for social status of social groups including Dalits. With possibilities of gainful employment (the possibility of becoming a wage labourer, as opposed to caste designated slave labour) in the capitalist industrial urban context, possibility of education as a source of social change, social consciousness about their imposed inferior status and need to struggle against the oppressive caste order became possible. Thus, apart from the objective conditions mentioned above, the importance of corresponding subjective factors such as Dalit consciousness and movement in articulating Dalit's concerns and struggle against the oppressive social situation cannot be ignored. Whether re-inclusion of Dalits in British army during pre-independence time or realizing constitutional safeguards and legal and policy provisions in post-independent India, or implementation of these provisions and struggle towards democratization of

Indian society, all of this would not have been possible without the assertive Dalit movement.

However, in the independent India, despite Constitutional safeguards and legal and policy efforts, exploitation, oppression and social discrimination, the Dalits' suffering has not changed. Though there have been changes, particularly in education and governmental employment, the bulk of Dalit population in India continues to form a mass of landless agricultural labour and unorganized sector labour; they are desperately poor, marginalized from sources of livelihood and processes of change. The work conditions they find themselves in are new structures of reiterating the patron-client relationships and oppressive conditions of life. Moreover, as Dalits are becoming aware of their rights, asserting for equal humanity and experiencing social change, they are becoming victims of worst atrocities. Thus, on one hand the Indian society is experiencing socio-economic change, achieving new heights of accomplishments in technology of new individual consumerism, this change does not necessarily suggests erosion of influence of the traditional social order and values. Along with modernity, traditional social order – caste based divisions, hierarchy and discrimination – continue to impact social identity. The traditional order continues to decide socio-economic locations, access to resources, mobility opportunities, and even interpersonal relations. It is in this context that we must understand the Dalit assertions for dignity and justice and quest for transforming the social structure on the principles of justice, equality and liberty. Thus, in the next section I have tried to map the journey of Dalit movement in terms of politics of identity, politics of issues and politics of accommodation.

IV

Dalit Movement and Politics of Identity

The initial concern of the Dalit movement for securing dignity and justice was expressed as the Dalit assertion for human rights. Dalits sought to enter Hindu temples in order to assert that as human being they too had equal rights for temple-entry, which was denied to them by the system of Untouchability. The Mahad Temple Entry Satyagraha, the Nasik Kalaram Mandir Satrygraha, and Parwati Temple

Entry in Poona (now Pune) were some examples of these struggles. Another expression came in the form of assertion of Dalit identity, which was to be constructed defiantly outside the framework of Brahmanism, through a rediscovery of Dalit history and culture located in an egalitarian order, real or imaginary, as opposed to the iniquitous Brahminical social order. This ideological assertion reflected in various *adi* movements in India, namely, '*adi*-Dharam' movement in Punjab, and '*adi*-Dravida', '*adi*-Andhra', '*adi*-Kannada' movements in South India which advanced an ideological claim that Dalits were the original inhabitants of this country – à la sons of the soil – and belonged to a superior egalitarian cultural tradition. In Uttar Pradesh, for instance, Dalit groups such as *Mehtars, Bhangis, Chamars, Doms*, and *Jatvas* who claimed that they were Buddhists, questioned caste discrimination against them and asserted that they were the original inhabitants of India who were conquered by deceit and manipulations by the Brahmins coming from outside. In the South the ideological assertion was seen in Iyoti Thass' (Geetha and Rajadurai, 1998: 17) attempts of conversion to Buddhism. From 1870s he had initiated movement of Buddhist conversion among the untouchables.

Of course, apart from this assertion of human identity in the traditional and religious framework, rediscovery of traditions and religiosity, the Dalit movement in later years approached the question of justice in the modern secular context. During the Ambedkarian struggle the ideological basis for Dalit assertion came from ideals of justice, liberty, equality and fraternity that based these ideals. He engaged with the colonial State in the ideological framework of modernity and advanced the untouchables' claims for dignity in the language of rights. This was seen in Ambedkar's continuous critique of Brahmanism, its philosophical foundations, its ideal of *Chaturvanya*, in the language of denial of untouchables and women into the membership of community of equals. Ambedkar's articulation and reconstruction of Buddhism, to which he converted with his five lakh followers in 1956, exhibits both critique of Brahmanism and socially engaged character of Buddhism. For Ambedkar Buddha's *Dhamma* was concerned with reconstruction of society on the principles of justice, equality and reason as guiding principles of social organization. The democratic values that Dr Ambedkar adhered to and the parliamentary form of governance that he advocated had roots in Buddha's *Sangha*.

Further during 1930s, Ambedkar was working towards a broader unity of the oppressed based on their social and economic experiences of marginalization. While speaking before the Great Indian Peninsula (GIP) railway workers he had pointed out that the oppressed in this country have to struggle against two enemies: Brahmanism and Capitalism. Through the Independent Labour Party he had advanced a broad category of the oppressed – Dalits, marginalized peasantry and unorganized sector of working classes.

This ideological legacy was later reinvented during the radical assertion of Dalit youth during early 1970s. Following the Black Panthers of America, these creative writers named themselves as Dalit Panthers. The Panthers that experienced alienation from the ruling class oriented post-Ambedkarite Dalit politics; they were disturbed on the issue of growing atrocities on Dalits in rural areas and sought to radicalize culture and politics as tools of resistance. It is they who gave currency to the term Dalit and also posited it with the new broad content – by referring to untouchables, landless agricultural labours and urban working classes and women. The Panthers stormed the sites of atrocities and sought to reinvent self-respect and struggle as means of addressing problems faced by Dalits. Despite the fact that Panthers were to later split on egoistic expressions of right interpretation of Ambedkarism, *Dhasal* going the Marxist way and *Dhale* sticking to Buddhism seen as opposed to Marx, the movement gave rise to new literature that brought with it expressions of altogether a different world unknown to the middle class Brahmanical taste, and one that depicted pain, oppression and resistance. This literary movement inspired political and literary movements in other parts of the country. This was very briefly seen in Gujarat and later in Karnataka in the form of Dalit Sangharsha Samiti. During the last two decades Dalit Panther is once again being reinvented in Tamil Nadu as aggressive stance towards Dalits atrocities by the dominant landowning backward classes (Gorringe, 2005: 54).

Dalit Movement and Politics of Issues

The Dalit movement in the 1930s saw a shift from temple-entry satyagrahas to right to education, employment and political representation as necessary prerequisites for securing justice. Concluding the temple-entry satyagraha, Dr Ambedkar pointed out that Dalits were not interested in entering temples of a religion that teaches inequality and injustice as part of religious duty and that they carried out temple-entry satyagrahas only to assert their equal humanity. He also pointed out that justice could be ensured only through struggle for education, employment and political representation. Thus, Dalit movement articulated the question of justice and dignity in the context of a modern secular framework, rather than the traditional religious mode. Thus, Dalits campaigned for education of Dalit children, and had to struggle to end discriminatory attitude of teachers and school authorities. However, the question of political representation, the question of separate electorate for Dalits, brought Ambedkar to the bitter and well-known controversy with Gandhi and the Congress. This also shows that perhaps caste Hindu hegemony would have 'tolerated' Dalits entering temples, and occupying a designated space in religious structures, but Dalit assertion for a share in modern resources capable of initiating social change and thereby undermining the authority of Brahminism was visualized as a real threat to Brahminical hegemony.

Thus, the politics of issues, a concern for a share in the resources in modern structures (not mere acceptance and benevolence) as possible mechanism of empowerment and change was the focus of the Dalit movement. Of course, the Dalit concern for politics of issues also saw the other oppressed such as marginalized peasantry and unorganized working class as victims of exploitation and oppression. It is important to note that while other working class struggles, especially in Bombay (now Mumbai), were campaigning for concerns of workers in formal organized sectors, Ambedkar's Independent Labour Party (ILP) focused on unorganized sector working classes. Thus, with the formation and struggles led by the ILP, the Dalit movement exhibited a concern for politics of the issues of the larger marginalized constituency, which also presented a possibility of the broader conception of politics of emancipation.

Further, in addition to these struggles, Ambedkar also stressed on education as a possible vehicle of social change and life with dignity. Towards this end he initiated a People's Education Society that started colleges in Bombay (now Mumbai), and later an institutional campus in Aurangabad (*Nagsenvan*). These institutions, during his lifetime, were best centres of learning. They attracted best teachers and zealous students. It is through these efforts that educated youth, who were to occupy positions in government employment, were trained. In Marathwada, the People's Education (PE) Society's campus was later to become a centre of literary movement in the form of '*Asmitadarsha*'. Of course in contemporary times the glory of PE society has vanished, thanks to the inefficient and irresponsible administration.

Politics of Accommodation

Despite these early concerns with the politics of the issues of the broader marginalized constituency, the post-Ambedkar Dalit movement, with an exception of the Dadasaheb Gaikwad led the satyagraha of landless agricultural labour, came to be entrapped in the politics of accommodation. The educated leaders of the Dalit movement during the post-Ambedkar era pursued the dream of political power as a panacea for addressing the Dalit question. They deliberately vulgarized Ambedkar who had exhorted them to be the ruling community in the particular context of emphasizing the importance of political power as 'a key to all problems'. Running after the mirage of political power through electoral process, necessarily led the Dalit leaders astray from meaningful emancipatory politics of the oppressed and trapped them into the ruling class net. Ruling class politics thus largely subsumed Dalit politics and the Dalit movement. The sole expressions of radical Dalit assertion for dignity and some possibilities of engaging with broader emancipatory struggles of the marginalized could be seen in the agitations launched by Dadasaheb Gaikwad. He led the satyagraha of the *Bhumihinas* or the landless, and worked on concrete issues of marginalization.

Absorbed in the Congress politics of accommodation, the Dalit movement lost its edge as a possible vehicle of the politics of the marginalized. Thus, the Republican Party of India, with a tie up with the Congress, resulted in both accommodation of Dalit politics and marginalization of Dalit politics from its larger focus. This continues to be one of the faces of Dalit politics even today. Indeed, the emergence of Dalit Panthers led to a resurgence of the Dalit consciousness. Dalit youth, inspired by Dalit Panthers, criticized 'accommodated' Dalit leadership that was ineffective in addressing the atrocities the Dalits encountered. They sought to damn the Brahminical social order and dreamt of the radical change leading to a just India. Moreover, as pointed out earlier, Dalit Panthers attempted to provide a broad content to the Dalit category by articulating the concerns of Dalits, landless agricultural labourers, marginalized peasantry, toiling working masses and women, as represented by the term Dalit, and attempted to provide a broader conception of struggle.

However, despite this, Dalit Panthers too were soon to be trapped in the politics of accommodation. Thus, though Dalit Panthers presented an ideologically conscious Dalit rebel, who challenged the existing Dalit leadership for being ineffective in arresting growing atrocities on Dalits and also succumbing to politics of accommodation, they themselves were soon to be accommodated and contained in the gamut of politics of interest. Moreover, despite contributing to the resurgence of Dalit consciousness that gave rise to Dalit revolt in other parts of India, in terms of acquiring political power through electoral politics, Dalit Panthers too were unsuccessful. This marked the shift in the Dalit agenda: from social movement of the marginalized to political formation to achieve political power through electorates for some Dalit castes. Further, this also marks the beginning of politics of interest in Dalit politics and the new equation: The political power is controlled by dominant political parties that represent dominance of the upper and dominant castes even in the democratic set up. And such oppressive power is based on appropriate Dalit votes. Hence, it was felt that Dalits should politically consolidate their votes and also articulate *Bahujanwad* in the realm of electoral politics. Furthermore, it was felt that only through political power that is gaining seats in assemblies and parliament could the Dalits hope to change the oppressive order of *Manuwad*.

Politics of Interests and Politics of Issues

Such a formulation became successful in the form of the Bahujan Samaj Party (BSP) in UP. From an interest group of Dalits working in government and public undertakings, the BSP gradually moved to become a political party with the capacity to achieve electoral success. The electoral efforts of the BSP that had carved out itself from the organization of all Dalits, Other Backward Classes (OBCs) and religious minorities met with considerable success in the northern states. For the first time a Dalit party catapulted to the political mainstream and captured political power in the most populous state of Uttar Pradesh, albeit with support from a party that claimed to share its constituency in Backward Classes (BCs) and Muslims. While this success enthralled Dalits in the State, it emboldened the BSP to pursue political power with utter ideological impunity. This has further reinforced the notion of political power (rather, electoral success) being a panacea for addressing the Dalit question. It is through success in electoral politics that Dalits would emerge as a ruling class; and that it is through such a success alone that Dalits could campaign against their socio-economic marginalization and also fight oppressive Brahminism.

Indeed, these formulations have been successful in installing the first Dalit lady Chief Minister in India, in highly feudal and caste-conscious State of India. It has also led to the creation of certain structures named after leaders like Dr Ambedkar and Jyotirao Phule and Shahu Maharaj. However, change initiated by these efforts has largely been limited to symbolic spaces, that has not altered the oppressive character of the social order, neither has it brought a change in the socio-economic status of the marginalized Dalits. Moreover, the political office too has proved to be elusive in nature. What is the more important question is: has it amounted to a social revolution in UP? Has the upper caste control over political leadership and over the bureaucracy been broken? The bureaucracy is of special significance because the upper-caste *Kayasthas* have been running it since Mughal times. Certainly, over the years, the BSP has emerged as an important player in UP politics. However, BSP's holding of political office in the State has depended on the interests of the ruling castes and classes. The ruling castes and classes have joined hands with the BSP so far as that does not disturb the interests and control of the ruling upper castes and classes. Whenever these ruling castes have felt threatened due to BSP's socio-political overtures, they have tended to pull down BSP-led government in the State. Similarly, the other backward castes joined the BSP or allied with it, as and when that furthered their interests. Of course, the political developments in UP – the rise of the BSP in UP politics – has led social analysts, such as Christophe Jaffrelot, to consider it as silent revolution from below. The possibility of a Dalit woman leading the government of feudal and caste-ridden states like UP, and the possibility of the transfer in political and bureaucratic power that rested in the hands of the upper castes, and the psychological change among Dalits, from victims to rulers, provides a basis for such an assertion. However, these developments have not helped in substantially ending social-economic marginalization of Dalits, nor it has altered the oppressive character of the social order. Despite achieving political power and bureaucratic positions the common Dalit masses continue to suffer atrocities, marginalization and sometimes, due to political pressures, have to 'share' power with the very oppressors they have tried struggling against. The reckless pursuit of political power thus, led the BSP to ally with the very same *Manuwadi* and castiest forces, the fight against whom was its declared *raison d'être*. The BSP politics in Uttar Pradesh shows that Dalits and Brahminical forces have developed a fluid configuration of 'accommodation and resistance' towards each other.

The emergence of the BSP is also paralleled by the political prominence of the fundamentalist formation – the Bharatiya Janata Party (BJP) – that also is hegemonic and appropriating. By harbouring fanatic religiosity, the Brahmin's outfit, the Rashtriya Swayamsevak Sangh (RSS), has finally succeeded in assuming the highest political office in India, and thereby attempting to provide a Brahminical character to society and culture in the country. The political prominence of the BJP, apart from leading to fundamentalism, communalism and casteism as markers of Indian society, has also posed a challenge to both centrist (Congress) and leftist ideological persuasions. These political outfits (that are also dominated by the upper castes and upper class groups) threatened by RSS fundamentalist and communalist politics are seeking new alliances. Thus Congress, which earlier practised politics of accommodation, now seeks the support of Dalits to fight communalism; and Left ideologues, which refused to see beyond class, have become aware of caste as a marker of oppression and exploitation in India. Hence, this has resulted in formulation of politics of *collective* interest.

Another form of politics of collective interest is witnessed in the BJP and the Shiv-Sena enlisting support of some Dalit caste groups, especially in Maharashtra. Dalit groups such as *Charmkars* and *Matangs*, harbouring the feeling of being ignored, if not rejected, by the leadership of Republican parties, and with the view of getting a share in political power, have joined these forces. This has resulted in some members of these communities being elected to legislatures and even occupying ministerial births. Further, apart from the possibility of a share in political power, the BJP and Shiv-Sena's occupation with Hindutva too found ready association among some of these Dalit castes. Thus, this too has led to the formation of politics of collective interest.

Politics of Interests and the Language of the Dalit-Hindutva Unity

In addition to the politics of collective interests, the politics of individual interests too has found a space in this formation. Often in political parties such as the BJP, Congress, Left parties and now even Shiv-Sena, political activists either come from stable independent economic background, or the parties create sources of empowering political activists. Some of these parties even have full-time activists whose day-to-day needs are taken care by the party structures. As a result, activists are not all the time pressed for day-to-day survival, and are free and committed to work for party's ideological persuasions. Compared to this, activists in Dalit politics have been drawn from the Dalit movement. The activists of Dalit movement in Maharashtra, many of whom are drawn from Dalit Panthers, have generally been drawn from very humble economic background. As youths inspired by Ambedkarite consciousness, and participating in struggle against Dalit atrocities, these activists left college and other professional education incomplete, and hence are without any source for day-to-day existence. Further, activists in Dalit struggle have often been elder sons of homes that have spent meagre family earnings on their education. When dreams of changing the order become more distant and the inability to help even their families that need them is an immediate and continuous experience, these activists tend to get frustrated. In addition to this the lack of any political recognition, despite long participation in the struggle leads them to a feeling of dejection. The author personally knows many such activists who have undergone this experience. Of course this fate of activists is indeed true of other social movements too. Many communists, for instance, too have faced this. The communist movement had sizable number of activists, women and men, who have remained unsung and gone into oblivion. However, the point here is about the politics of recognition. While the contribution to the left movement is recognized as a contribution to the people's cause, that of Dalit movement seen as to the specific issues. Moreover, Dalit masses too, because of being powerless in all spheres of life, have tended to socially recognise those who assume some political office, be that power more rhetorical than real. As a result, Dalit activists have experienced non-recognition from both broader structures of recognition and Dalit masses. Of course, on the other hand, like other political formations such as Congress or Hindutva parties, Dalit politics too has attracted people who harbour the wish to pursue political careers. When, despite working for the party for long time, they become unsuccessful in getting elected to a political office, they tend to look for new areas for political habitation.

Of course though the move of unity of Dalit-Hindutva sounds alluring to 'dissenting' and politically 'eager' voices among Dalit communities, its implications for long-term politics are full of perils rather than promises. For, though 'empowering' some with political office, it has dangers of new patron-client formation, ironically, emerging even in urban and modern conditions. Moreover, it also has serious implications for recovery of Dalit subjectivity and autonomy, not only in the realm of the politics but identity, culture and economy. In recent history, one such formation of Dalit-Hindutva alliance was sought. But the unity with Bhimshakti was the need of the 'hour' for the new Shiv-Sena; it was Shiv-Sena's project that sought to decide the nature, development and outcome of the project. Such a move is dictated by the compulsions of politics of number encountered by the Shiv Sena and the BJP, and it is these forces that determine and direct the discourse and the agenda. Thus, not only is the autonomous voice of the Dalit critique lost in such formulation, but also there is a danger of the Dalit remaining a perennial marginalized 'other' of the Brahminic 'centre'. Hence, the Dalit movement asserting for autonomy of the Dalit voice in the socio-political sphere cannot be a long-term ally to the Hindutva forces.

At this juncture, let us try to understand as to why the developments within the Dalit movement have led to attempts of collaboration with ideological adversaries such as the BJP and Shiv-Sena. It is also necessary to note that the political aspirations of Dalit communities outside the Ambedkarist fold, the perception of the Dalit question shared by forces advancing politics of issues such as the Left, and the feeling of loss of possibilities of sharing political power among Dalit activists, will have to be seen as factors contributing to the attempts of alliances with the ideological adversaries like the BJP and the Shiv-Sena.

Earlier, we noted that the Dalit assertion in the beginning of the twentieth century was expressed in the form of assertion of Dalit humanity in terms of the right to dignity and equal humanity. Thus, various ideological *adi* movements sought to recover Dalit history as rooted in non-Brahminic egalitarian framework. However, the rise of Ambedkarism saw the question of Dalit humanity as rooted in the oppressive and exploitative structures of domination; hence, the Dalit movement during the Ambedkarist phase pursued the politics of issues, and attempted to extend this concern to the politics of issues of the larger marginalized categories. However, in the post-Ambedkar phase the focus of the Dalit movement came to be restricted in achieving spaces of political offices and issues of identity. As a result, the Dalit movement lost connections with the issues confronting both Dalit masses and other marginalized sections. Here, it should be highlighted that the efforts and strength of the Dalit movement was spent on struggling with the traditional issues of the practice of untouchability and caste discrimination. The growing consciousness among Dalit masses, both in rural and urban areas, and assertion against the oppressive caste system gave rise to further cases of atrocities, caste discrimination and social boycott. This resulted in Dalit struggle that was forced to engage with the issues of discrimination resulting from traditional social order. This is also a telling comment on the nature of caste rigidities and prevalence of caste consciousness even in Maharashtra that is seen as a land of rationalist, reformist and even working class movement and consciousness. Indeed the Dalit Panthers did try to infuse a new consciousness and attempted to provide a broader content to the category Dalit. However, in the absence of a stable organized structure, the Dalit Panthers also become willing victims of tactics of the politics of appropriation. Some of its leaders of Dalit Panthers tried to share political space with the Congress, whereas others, that too leading ideologues, have ironically, seen possibilities of politics of masses in formations such as Shiv-Sena. Of course, political parties such as Congress, Shiv-Sena and BJP are keen to share a political space with the Dalits. Such a concern, however, emanates more from claiming Dalit votes rather than commitment to annihilate traditional caste order and ushering of progressive social change. Moreover, it has contributed to the creation of claimants for political power among Dalit communities, which in turn has led to further fragmentation of the Dalit movement and the weakening of the possibility of the politics of issues and politics of emancipation.

On the other hand, political formations claiming allegiance to left ideology and attempting to articulate the politics of issues have shared a problematic relationship with the Dalit movement. Though many Dalit youths are active in Left political formations and Left ideologues they have now 'recognized' caste as context of oppression, Left politics have traditionally seen Dalit movement as sectarian, pro-British and divisive in character. Moreover, ideologically, Left parties have privileged the category of class over that of caste as sites of exploitation and oppression and also as a source of revolutionary politics. Thus, Left formations saw class as a subsuming category and held that the class struggle alone would lead to revolutionary emancipatory politics. There is ground to believe that such a denial of caste as a site of oppression and exploitation was a result of the Left ideologues social location. On the other hand, Dalit activists encountering discrimination ignored the fact that such discrimination was also emanated and reiterated in exploitative and oppressive structures of economic domination.

One of the most serious challenges that the politics of accommodation throws before Dalit movements is the growing atrocity against Dalits. The politics of unfair 'inclusion' (practices of inclusion in which Dalits are denied any say as active agents of change) and politics of 'accommodation', which creates possibilities of 'sharing' of power at the behest of the ruling class interests that do not allow struggle against atrocities, as perpetrators of atrocities could be 'sharing' power with the accommodated Dalit leadership at local levels.

During the last two decades, brutal atrocities have been encountered by Dalits who are gradually assuming self-respect and resisting discrimination at the hands of the dominant castes. The lynching of Dalits in Jajjhar in Haryana, the perpetual ongoing Dalit carnage in Tamil Nadu since the eighties (Viswanathan, 2005), not to mention the caste 'conflicts' in UP and Bihar, have been part of traumatic Dalit public memory.

While the spurt of brutal atrocities against Dalits during the last two decades in Tamil Nadu, Haryana and other parts of the country could be understood on account of relatively recent awakening of assertive Dalit consciousness leading to assertion for social mobility and equal humanity, in Maharashtra, due to a long history of Dalit revolt, Khairlanji kind of atrocities, public humiliation, rape and brutal killing of a Dalit family, were unexpected and hence shocking. Of course in Maharashtra too, we find new spurt of atrocities against Dalits taking place since the nineties in regions such as Marathwada, where, however, the targets of violence are not necessarily erstwhile *Mahars*, but the *Matangs*. The cruel burning of a *Matang* youth Dilip Shendage and hacking of Dadarao Dongre came forth as new phase in atrocities against Dalits.

V

The Dynamics of 'Shame and Rage': Understanding Atrocities Against Dalits

Apart from the usual politics of domination articulated through structures of power, the nature of brutality and inhuman killings unleashed by the dominant castes against Dalits has shocked the Dalits and even other sections of the society. As per the reports, in Khairlanji, Surekha Bhotmange and her daughter Priyanka were publicly stripped, paraded naked and gang raped before being hacked to death. Surekha's two sons, who were forced to rape their sister, were hacked to death and their genitals crushed because they declined to engage in cruel humiliation of their sister. In Bhutegaon, as per the fact finding reports, Dilip Shendage was burnt alive, allegedly at the hands of a local college professor belonging to a dominant caste. The act of lynching of five Dalits in Jajjar in Haryana, while they were engaged in traditional occupation of skinning dead animals, was equally shocking. The ongoing perpetual anti-Dalit violence in Tamil Nadu for reasons such as contesting elections (the *Melavalavu* murders in July 1998), cultivating land, taking-up education, marrying outside caste, converting into other religions, were equally disturbing. Why is such ferocious violence, gruesome brutality, most inhuman cruelty unleashed against Dalits? The reasons could be sought in two forms of explanations: on one hand Dalit attempts at social mobility, educational and economic betterment leads to challenging the traditional caste-based social status, and undermining the uncontested dominant status of the upper castes. But on the other hand Dalit articulations of non-traditional equal humanity; their articulation of new autonomous identity is seen as 'shaming' the dominant castes in villages.

In Maharashtra villages of seventies, the symbols of modernity: dressed in trousers and bush shirts and books in hand, the autonomous self-reliant image of individuality and a sense of defiance towards traditional society and values were exhibited only by the Dalit youth taking up education in the nearby cities. Many a times when these youth walked the muddy streets of the village, especially when they passed through the dominant castes' *alis* or lanes, they were treated with both curiosity and scorn. Some of these youth, now equipped with necessary education succeeded in getting positions in local administration, and later had become clerks, officers in government sector organizations, teachers and professors in educational institutions. Thus, when the dominant landowning upper caste patron, rooted in traditional hierarchical caste ethos, saw a self-reliant, tradition-defying, upright self-respecting son of one of his servile agricultural labourers, tension in the 'balance' and 'harmony' of traditional structure and values had started simmering.

Moreover, with educational achievements, a change in economic status of the servile Dalits in the rural areas occurred. With money sent by their sons now living in urban areas, the face of Dalits' hamlets in the village too started changing. Now Dalits too had better houses, modelled after new concrete construction that resembled the houses of the dominant upper castes. This new 'equality' in both social and economic position at least in case of some, if not majority, Dalits undermined the traditional patron-client relationship, and was perceived as threat to the traditional hierarchies; it signified both social and material change among Dalits and gradual weakening of Dalit dependence on the village.

Compared to the Dalit youth, the dominant upper caste youth had remained backward in terms of educational achievements and thus had remained outside the local administration. Moreover, not all sections of the upper castes were economically sound. Sometimes, owing to volatile nature of agriculture, the economic position of the upper castes dwindled, making them economically vulnerable. Compared to them Dalit families had some members working in the cities, hence, could rely on some financial help in crises and therefore were in a little better position than the poorer sections among the caste Hindus. The economic vulnerability, or the gap between superior status in caste hierarchy and economic vulnerability, made caste Hindus hold on more rigidly to the caste hierarchies and traditions. In this background consolidation of caste identity, Dalit youth's social and economic mobility, apart from disturbing the traditional caste-based social relationships, also 'shamed' both the dominant as well as economically vulnerable upper caste youth who had remained backward in terms of modern sources of development and consequent claims of identity.

Of course, though a minuscule section among Dalits experienced change in socio-economic status, that small section did exude signs of defiance. Often, Dalit youth from cities not only brought sense of change; it also brought a new image of Dalit, conscious of self and society. What is more important is that the youth who had the opportunity to go to the cities for education also acted as agents for social change: they inspired and provided support to other Dalit youth in their educational aspirations, made Dalits in the villages conscious of the caste oppression and need to contest it. Dalit youth now started asserting for a space in village social-cultural milieu by celebrating Ambedkar Jayanti, by taking up processions through the village streets, even through the dominant caste alleys and other such symbols of pride and assertion of equality. All this, I suggest, leads to 'shaming' the dominant castes in terms of both socio-economic development and the hold of traditional hierarchical social order. The dominant upper castes react to this 'shame' by 'rage' against Dalits.

Furthermore, from 1970s, in addition to traditional upper castes a new section of backwards among the caste Hindus had started asserting for political space. On the basis of their numbers they succeeded in assuming control of local political office and other institutions. Additionally, the changes in land holding and introduction of new cash cropping, they also become economically sound, even powerful. The 'Other Backward Class' thus control local and regional political institutions, sources of economic development and generally dominate the rural milieu. With political power, land and other economic resources under their control, the new dominant castes (OBCs) now have become rigid proponents of hierarchal caste order, new watchdogs of traditional culture and religiosity. This makes them ardent enemies of Dalits who have become conscious of their rights and asserting for equal humanity. The caste brutal atrocities unleashed against Dalits by the *Telis, Malis* in Maharashtra and *Thevars* in Tamil Nadu, just to name a few examples, makes this clear. Thus, in Maharashtra, Tamil Nadu, Karnataka, Haryana, Gujarat, Bihar and even in UP attempts have been made to crush Dalit's pride and sense of dignity. Along with the poor, vulnerable Dalits, those who have achieved social mobility and were asserting for their rights, attempting to take recourse to constitutional provisions were targets of most heinous atrocities. In Khairlanji, Surekha Bhotmange was trying resolutely to transform social and economic status of her family, and was questioning and resisting the dominant caste men for denial of her rights. Surekha and her daughter Priyanka were thus resisting both Brahminical hierarchies and patriarchy; they were thus questioning both the caste and patriarchal order. This challenge to caste and patriarchy had 'shamed' the dominant castes (*Telis* and *Malis*) who reacted with 'rage'.

Again, not only a section of Dalits who have succeeded gaining placements in higher echelons of bureaucracy exists in continuous processes of accommodation and assertions with the new power elites, they are often pressurized so that interests of the dominant upper caste are not affected. The vulnerability and ineffectiveness of the Dalit officers in acting decisively in favour of the oppressed and in accordance with the law is clearly exhibited in the Khairlanji case.

The above discussion though helps us in explaining reasons for renewed atrocities against Dalits, it also presents a rather pessimistic picture before democratic concerns. This, thus, demands a re-imagination of politics of emancipation. In the last section of this paper I have attempted to articulate such an emancipatory politics.

Reinventing Politics of Emancipation

Let me end this essay by attempting to articulate the concerns of Dalit politics in the times to come. In 1938, while speaking before GIP railway workers in Manmad, Dr Ambedkar had pointed out that Dalit and marginalized sections of this country would have to fight against two adversaries: Brahminism and Capitalism. Dr Ambedkar's attempts to articulate and campaign for these issues through the Independent Labour Party indicated the possible emancipatory politics the Dalits ought to engage with. What is more important in contemporary times is both these adversaries have emerged as formations threatening life with minimum human dignity in social, economic, political and even cultural spheres and have contributed to the process of disenfranchising. The economic changes that have taken place under the process of globalization are adversely affecting lives of agricultural labourers, marginal peasants, workers in unorganized sectors in urban areas and women. As a result of the withdrawal of the state from key social sectors and growing erosion of state support structures from these areas, marginalized people have little hope in managing their own survival, let alone the possibilities of positive change.

The Dalit population comprises the bulk of these categories. Hence Dalit politics of today too has to be focused on the issues of the marginalized sections such as landless agricultural workers, poor peasantry, unorganized sector workers, urban poor and women, and specifically on the issues confronting Dalit women, who have been victims of intersecting ideologies and structures of patriarchy, gender and caste. Though Dalit women have participated in the Dalit movement, issues confronting them have not become central to the Dalit struggle. These ought to be the priorities of Dalit politics in contemporary times. Similarly, like the oppressive processes of globalization, the emergence of *Hindutva* has led to a hegemonic cultural formation assuming the centre that dictates to and polices the 'Other'. This presents a threat to the social and cultural autonomy of the Dalits. This also presents threats to the recent mooring among the non-Brahmin caste-Hindus striving to claim autonomous voices. Of course, these voices though show ideological unity with Dalit movement, the material interests and quest for power make them immediate enemies of Dalits too. This is seen very clearly in recent brutal and gruesome attack on Dalit family in Khairlanji, and has been the ongoing experience of Dalits in Tamil Nadu and other parts of the country). Again, Dalits as critiques of asymmetrical formations and contributors to the alternative egalitarian culture have critically engaged with hegemonic Hindutva. The concern with politics of emancipation could be seen in the Ambedkarian conceptualization of culture of resistance and reconstitution. Through his re-articulation of Buddhism as located in a critical space and ethical reconstruction, Dr Ambedkar sought to recover the subjective agency of the subjugated in critiquing the ideologies and structures of domination on the one hand, and in reconstructing of social order on the foundations of justice, reason and autonomy on the other. In an atmosphere of growing disenfranchising of losing voices, being silenced and made invisible the critical space the 'modernist' imagination of Buddhism offers a possibility for emancipatory politics. Of course, certainly, such a concern warrants a perspective of Buddhism as rooted in 'materiality and ethicality of human life', i.e. as rooted in the 'real' conditions that characterize human existence.

Of course, such an emancipatory agenda cannot be realized unless those offering the politics around these issues, confronting the marginalized sections, for instance, the Left and other progressive forces, become sensitive to the specificities of oppression and exploitation that is resulting from the ideology and structure of caste. They need to realise that social locations dictated by caste not only influence identities and culture but also the economic, social and political dimensions. Caste thus is not mechanically located in the superstructure, but this superstructure often interacts with, and influences, the base. Often those who voice the issues of the marginalized from class and patriarchal (feminist) axes exhibit an ideological arrogance, a sense of superiority in articulation and legitimization of issues. However, the very fact that the issues of identity, ethnicity and communalism have assumed a central place in social discourse prove that homogenized and unproblematic views of class and patriarchy as social markers have been untenable in understanding social processes. The same perhaps holds true in regard to the environmental politics in India, which often is blind to politics and relationship of caste and resources. Thus, broader and collaborative politics based on issues, commitment to the concerns of the marginalized rooted in genuine democratic ethos, a genuine and not procedural democracy, that privileges the issues of justice and human dignity will contribute to the politics of emancipation.

References

Ambedkar, B.R. (1989), 'Untouchability: Social, Economic and Political', in *Dr Babasaheb Ambedkar Speeches and Writings*, Vol. 5, Government of Maharashtra Press, Bombay, p. 40.

Centre for Equity and Social Justice and Dr Babasaheb Ambedkar Research and Training Institute, Department of Social Justice, Government of Maharashtra (November 2009), *Organised Killings of Dalits in Khairlanji Village, Tal. Mohodi, District Bhandara: A Report under the SC/ST (Prevention of Atrocities) Act 1989.*

Geetha, V. and S.V. Rajadurai (1998), *Towards a Non-Brahmin Millennium: From Iyothi Thass to Periyar*, Samya, Kolkata, p. 120.

Gorringe, Hugo (2005), *Untouchable Citizens: Dalit Movements and Democratisation in Tamil Nadu*, Sage Publications, New Delhi.

Jaffrelot, Christophe (October 2002), *India's Silent Revolution: The Rise of the Lower Castes in North India*, Columbia University Press, New York.

PUCL and others (January 2007), *Suppressing the Voice of the Oppressed, State Terror on Protest against the Khairlanji Massacre, a Report to the Nation.*

Viswanathan, S. (2005), *Dalits in the Dravidian Land*, Navayana, Pondicherry.

3 Atrocities on Scheduled Castes in Maharashtra

Some Observations

Shankar Gaikwad

Atrocities on Scheduled Castes (SCs) have become regular phenomena. This has become the most important social problem in contemporary India. Some incidents became widely known, but this is only the tip of the iceberg. Most of the cases are either not reported by victims or officials do not register them. Many of the causes for the same are well known to all. It is not so secret. Whatever cases are reported and become widely known tell many things and compel us to think seriously.

Atrocities on Dalits are not the problem of law and order only. It is something more and different. It should be viewed in a different perspective and different context. The problem is having different dimensions. This problem of Scheduled Castes (ex-untouchables) is differing from other problems prevailing in Indian society. In this connection Dr Ambedkar points out that 'the problem of untouchables is quite unlike the problems of dowry, widow remarriage, age of consent, etc. which the illustrations of what are properly are called social problems.'[1] An atrocity on Dalits is a unique example of social discrimination and denial and hence requires a careful and serious thought. This problem is different from all other social problems, in the sense that it is the strategy of dominant caste people to suppress the lawful and justifiable demands of traditionally lower group in the social hierarchy.

A number of constitutional provisions (especially Articles 15, 17 and 23) and legislations[2] give effect to this provision, especially the Untouchability Offence Act 1955 amended and re-titled as Protection of Civil Rights Act 1955 (PCR) and the Scheduled

Castes and Scheduled Tribes (Prevention of Atrocities) Act 1989 protecting the rights of these disadvantaged sections. With this background, the expectation is that SCs communities would be getting full protection of law and the atrocities against these groups should have lessened. But the ground reality is quite different.

Police statistics[3] averaged over the past five years shows that every week:

- 13 Dalits are murdered.
- 5 Dalits' homes or possessions are burnt.
- 6 Dalits are kidnapped or abducted.

Every day:

- Officially 27 registered atrocities are being committed against Dalits, 3 Dalit women are raped and 11 Dalits are beaten up.

Every 18 minutes:

- A crime is committed against a Dalit.

Prevalence of discrimination against SCs has been clearly recognized and endorsed by the Prime Minister also. Manmohan Singh, the Prime Minister of India, at an International Conference on Dalits and Minorities in New Delhi on 27 November 2006 draws the parallel between social and caste injustices, saying it was modern India's failure that millions of Dalits were still fighting prejudice. He explained: Even after 60 years of constitutional and legal protection and support, there is still social discrimination against Dalits in many parts of our country. Dalits have faced a unique discrimination in our society that is fundamentally different from the problems of minority groups in general. The only parallel to the practice of untouchability was apartheid.[4]

The term 'atrocity' has not been specifically defined. SC and ST (POA) Act 1989 has given the list of acts which constitute atrocity. Kshirsagar[5] defined it as: 'those crimes which are committed against ex-untouchables with the intention to lower down the morale of the victims and damage their self-pride can be called as atrocities'.

While explaining the term atrocity and its reason, Nandu Ram has given comprehensive idea and also stated the reasons of such atrocities. According to him, '… atrocities are to be viewed as social and physical violence committed collectively or individually by those groups, castes and communities or their members who try to have more access to the existing resources and monopolies of their status superiority over others. The targets of such atrocities are those who have traditionally been degraded and deprived and who try to find a place other than that prescribed to them in the social structure. Their efforts are likely to disturb the status quo and intercept the unlimited chances of the privileged ones, hence, violence and atrocities against them'.[6]

An atrocity on SCs has become almost a regular phenomenon of rural life. This does not mean that SCs in urban areas are safe or free from the atrocities. The atrocities committed on these communities may be less in urban areas than that in villages. Moreover, many a times atrocities committed on them in urban areas may not be identical. The incidents that have taken place in these areas are highlighted comparatively early. One important aspect is that village level caste Hindus and police get relatively free hand in manipulating the atrocity cases so that the culprits go scot free. They are mostly responsible for proving the law as an ineffective instrument to check the crimes against SCs.

Many people sought the explanation in the prevailing economic system and tried to give a non-caste colour to the atrocities. While going through the given economic explanation some questions remain unanswered.

Whether all individuals are (irrespective of their castes origin) from low income group and do they equally face such type of atrocities? Whether the oppressors are always the rich or landlords?

The answers to both these questions are in the negative. 'If the oppression is simply on landless agricultural labourers then, why only Dalits become the target? The answer lies in the fact that agricultural labourers belonging to the SCs and other backward classes/castes are not dealt equally by caste Hindu landlords.

These and such type of other questions are persistent and sufficient enough to show that the atrocities on SCs are not merely on account of their poverty but more importantly their low standing in the caste hierarchy. It is not that Dalits are poor, but the prejudices which the castes Hindus have towards them are a big hurdle to treat them as equals. The person who commits atrocity and the victims are always from caste Hindus (CHs) and SCs (ex-untouchable) respectively.

There are many such occasions where the persons who do not have land or economic standing but are higher than SCs in social hierarchy are not less lagging behind in committing atrocities towards SCs.

Generally, all those SCs who are benefitted by or beneficiaries of the various special opportunities and have thereby raised their standard of living are the victims of the atrocities.

The mindset behind observing untouchability[7] and the caste system continues almost unabated both in rural as well as urban areas in many parts of the country. In the villages along with the classic form of untouchability neo-modern forms of untouchability is prevailing. This means the UOA (Untouchability Offence Act) and POA (Prevention of Atrocities Act) have not altered the situation significantly. In highly urban and metropolitan cities it is practised in a disguised form or with sophisticated concealment. In many new or modern institutions (educational, bureaucracy, Panchayati Raj, hospitals, police stations) SCs have to suffer or face the variety of age-old discrimination practices based on the caste.

Caste and untouchability-based discriminations are essentially structural, and it reflects the denial of civil, political, religious and socio-economic rights.

The caste system/structure, especially caste prejudices and untouchability was central to the problem of atrocities inflicted on SCs.

Changing Situation

During the last few years changes have been witnessed in the caste system. As a result of different factors, especially compulsive environment, untouchability is not observed in a strict sense in the public places and to some extent in private life. From this, one should not come to the conclusion that untouchability has completely disappeared and the SCs are getting equal treatment. Whatever changes are observed in respect of showing readiness in treating SCs on equal footing, at least in modern institutions, it is just an adjustment with the situation. This may be because they do not have other alternatives or it is for their convenience.

As a larger proportion of SCs live in rural areas or villages. It is important to see the social structure prevailing there. Very idealistic picture of Indian village community has been given by some foreigners calling it as 'Little republics', and Gandhiji also talked and dreamt about village republic. But Ambedkar has given a very realistic picture of the Indian village and the place of untouchables in it:[8]

'The Indian village is not a single unit, it consists of castes ... The population of the village is divided into two sections (i) touchables and (ii) untouchables.... In this republic there is no place for democracy (no room for *equality, liberty and fraternity*). The Indian village is the very negation of republic. It is a republic; it is a republic of the touchables, by touchables and for the untouchables. The republic is an Empire of Hindus over the untouchables.'

If we look at the rural social structure we do not find any radical/fundamental changes in the parochial and stereotyped attitude of caste Hindus.

In the traditional society the caste, joint family and village community had important place in determining the status where there was little scope for mobility.

After Independence, the SCs were given the privilege and protection by the State. In order to bring about certain changes from their given position, the Protective Discrimination Policy has been implemented. Consequent upon the programmes meant for their social and economic development and the other general programmes, the situation has changed to some extent especially among those who were able to utilize it. This has helped to a great extent for the occupational mobility, especially to leave the traditional occupation and enter in different occupations which are secular in nature. Thus, their mobility is viewed as threat to the traditional social order and honour by the caste Hindus.

The Conflict: The Castes Involved in Conflict

It has been pointed out and is also true that the castes which are at the forefront in atrocities are generally from the dominant caste.[9] The immediate conflict is not between the upper caste (in traditional social hierarchy) and SCs but the conflict is between those middle castes who have been much benefitted by the new economic and political opportunities and the SCs. Interestingly, these middle caste people are claiming equal status from the upper caste but are denying the equal rights to the SCs (who are also trying to get equal status). The dual behaviours of these middle castes (mostly *Shudras*) have been rightly seen in Dr Ambedkar's[10] remarks. He pointed out that:

'If the Hindu social order was based on inequality, it would have been overthrown long ago. But it is based on graded inequality so that the *Shudra* while he is anxious to pull down the *Brahmin*, he is not prepared to see the untouchables raised to his levels.'

Further he talks about the very result of such behaviour. To put the things in his words, it can be cited as:[11] 'The result is that, there is nobody to join the untouchable in his struggle. He is completely isolated. Not only is he isolated he is opposed by the very classes who ought to be his natural allies. This isolation is one more obstacle in the removal of untouchability'.

M.N. Srinivas has also cited the dominant caste groups, social conservativeness and their vested interests in keeping the SCs as the lowest to him:[12] 'While the leaders of the dominant castes are sensitive to economic and political opportunities, they are socially conservative. They do not, for instance, like the condition of Harijans to improve. They have a vested interest in keeping the Harijans poor and ignorant. At the present time, Harijans are their most important source of agricultural labour, and if they become educated and conscious of their rights, that will be a threat to the position of the dominant castes. Anti-Harijan sentiments are freely heard in rural areas. Attempt by Harijans to exercise the rights given to them by the Constitution have led to violent attacks on them by the dominant castes. They have been beaten up and their huts burnt down and, in addition, they have been subjected to economic boycott…'. They (CHs) are not only denying their (SCs) claims but also trying to thwart all such efforts from the SCs. They (CHs) are jealous about the progress/development taking place among the SCs and are not in a mood to tolerate this (including the awakening of the SCs which is viewed as fatal to their interest).

Nature of Atrocities

The nature of atrocities committed on the SCs is varied. They include physical violence against them and their property. Even in the classification or category-wise incidence of crimes against SCs, shown in the Commissions, various reports include these. But we do not get the particular statistics on the crimes committed against them with a view to damage their image in the society which they have to face, and only they can understand its gravity and intensity. These include humiliation, being called by caste names, by associating one to ones group status, denying human rights or doing all sort of tricks intentionally which hurts their personal ego and emerging identities.

In general sense, the atrocities are considered as the physical violence or assault inflicted on the weak (SCs). Besides this, many more things are included in the atrocities. It is worthwhile to quote the views of Kamble.[13] According to him the various types of atrocities/crimes made against the SCs in one or another term include the following, viz. homicide, prohibition, public insulting, humiliation, personal insulting, discrimination in public, degradation in school, harassment, negligence of government officials, delay in reporting, polluting drinking water, molesting and raping, compelling to do menial jobs, burning of houses and localities, burning of crops, looting, forced to work without wages, etc.

How One Should Look at the Problem: The Perspective

Looking at the stated crimes (which have socio-psychological dimensions, besides physical) committed against SCs, the atrocities have not remained purely a rural phenomenon but they can be found in the cities too. There is a difference in respect to the frequency and nature of atrocities in rural and urban places. Those living in urban places mostly do not come across many of the physical violence. The discrimination and atrocities arising out of caste and untouchability prevailing in society still persists with rural-urban difference.

There may be a difference of opinion given by police administration, press, political leaders and oppressors for such atrocities on the SCs. The majority of non-SCs would rather pretend that it does not exist. Their version is that the Constitution forbids its practice and State has made provisions for the removal of untouchability and prevention of atrocity, then where has the question or the problem remained? There is also a false propaganda by people of non-SCs vested interests that Dalit organizations, activists and politicians are making this an issue for their political gain. It is very much important to take into consideration the view point of the people about the atrocities in which they suffer or would be sufferers, rather than depending on the reasons given by the above said authorities. While pointing out the necessity of giving importance to the Dalit sources (who are the weaker ones and sufferers). It has rightly been pointed out:

'The weaker one is, the less the likelihood of a "fair" hearing. After all, the police, political and administrative office, and press reportage and editing are predominantly upper caste, ruling class preserves. The way official records are written, events understood, action taken and reports filed by the government, police and the press are deeply infused with an upper caste bias – Sometimes benevolent, often callous, malignant, or downright criminals, for us therefore fairness would imply a trust of Dalit sources.'[14]

Needless to say, the reasons given by oppressed and oppressor may be different. It is to be viewed from the Dalits' perspective. Nandu Ram[15] is of the opinion that Ambedkar tried, perhaps for the first time in modern period, to present systematically the bottom views about the Indian social reality.

In one study[16] the respondents from the SCs were asked to mention whether they feel that the atrocities on SCs at the hands of non-SCs are lessened or are continued or are increased. The feeling that atrocities have remained unchanged is reported by majority of respondents. Reasons mentioned by the respondents are given below.

Reasons for Increased/Continued Atrocities

1. Various efforts on the parts of SCs to achieve equality.
2. To serve as deterrent check.
3. Not happy over the progress of SCs.
4. Dispute over Gairan lands.
5. State action favouring the SCs.
6. No adequate protection from State against such atrocities.
7. CHs being deprived of cheap labourers.
8. Traditional attitude of CHs.

9. Jealous/casteism/hatred.
10. Lack of powerful and influential leadership among SCs.
11. Revival of traditional values. Increased religious and caste-based organizations among CHs giving boost to traditional values.

It appears from the above that the reasons felt by the respondents are more social or non-economical, taking into consideration the official reasons reported in the Commissioners Report[17] and the reasons given by the respondents in the said study[18] are altogether different.

The CHs' traditional social attitude towards the SCs and the various attempts made on the part of the SCs to move upward from the given position is central to the problem of the atrocities. The social attitude towards this group is determined and fixed onc… . It is said that 'The social attitude towards the untouchable is determined by the very name "Untouchable". There is a fixed attitude towards "untouchables" which is determined by the stink which is embedded in the name of "untouchable"'.[19] It is pertinent to have an attention towards the existing/established social order and the position of the SCs in it. According to Ambedkar[20] 'the established order is the law made by the touchables. The untouchables have nothing to do with it except to obey it and respect it… This established order is hereditary both in status as well as function. Once a touchable, always a touchable once an untouchable, always an untouchable.… The established order is based on an inexorable law of *Karma* or destiny which is fixed once for all and can never be changed.' The discrimination is the result of this attitude of CH and can be well explained by quoting the views of Ambedkar.[21]

'The discrimination against the SCs is merely the reflections of that deep and strong sentiment … So long as the Hindu social order lasts, discriminations against the untouchables continue to exist.'

Generally, the reaction of SCs towards the discriminatory behaviour can be classified in following broad groups from acceptance to protest on organizational level:

1. Submission or acceptance (shown tolerance) to avoid the conflict.
2. Rejection by showing mild protest on individual level.
3. Adopting the legal and constitutional method/measures.

4. Protest on the organizational level.

Their (SCs) insistence for equal and just treatment questioned the traditional behaviour of CH. SCs also know the fact that all things cannot be settled and obtained as a matter of right only through government help. Probably, the reason might be that the people do not bother about the laws prevailing. In this sector, either because such laws are not implemented in its letter and spirit or various caste customs and traditions rooted in it is extremely resistant to change. In such a situation it is not correct to assume that only legal force or law can bring about the change.

Scheduled Castes of Maharashtra

The social structure, especially the caste system is not very much different from other parts of India. According to 2001 Census, Maharashtra had a total population of 98, 81,656. SCs account for 10.2 per cent of the total population.

Table 1 *Distribution of Main Workers Among Scheduled Castes in Broad Industrial (Maharashtra) Categories*

S. No.	*Category of Economic Activities*		*Total No.*	*Percentage*
1.	I	Cultivators	4,99,233	14.40
2.	II	Agricultural labourers	16,68,092	48.08
3.	III	Livestock, forestry, fishing, plantation of orchards and allied activities	37,362	1.08
4.	IV	Mining and quarrying	18,196	0.52
5.	Va	Manufacturing, processing, servicing and repairs: household industries	1,20,340	3.47
6.	Vb	Other than household industries	2,98,935	8.61
7.	VI	Construction	1,41,847	4.09
8.	VII	Trade and commerce	1,44,929	4.17
9.	VIII	Transport, storage and communication	1,24,808	3.60
10.	IX	Other services	4,15,605	11.98
		Total Main Workers	34,69,347	100.00

Source: Computed from the data provided in Census of India 1991.

In Maharashtra, 59 castes have been scheduled under the SC category. *Mahar, Mang/Matang, Chambhar* and *Dhor* are found almost all over the region and together constitutes 91.13 per cent of the total SC population.

SCs are engaged in the occupation of less income comparing to the general population. The distribution of main workers among the SCs in broader industrial categories is given in Table l.

Table 2 *Educational Level among Scheduled Castes in Maharashtra*

S. No.	*Educational Level*	*Total*	*Percentage*
1.	Illiterate	4,73,541	54.07
2.	Literate without educational qualification		
	(a) Non-formal	40,283	0.46
	(b) Formal	10,35,080	11.82
3.	Primary	11,36,035	12.97
4.	Middle	10,49,172	11.98
5.	Matriculation	4,52,168	5.16
6.	Higher secondary	1,55,429	1.77
7.	Non-tech, diploma or certificate not equal to degree	3,104	0.04
8.	Tech. diploma or certificate not equal to degree	30,330	0.35
9.	Graduate degree other than tech. degree	74,248	0.85
10.	P.G. degree other than tech. degree	21,294	0.24
11.	Engineering and technology	4,436	0.05
12.	Medicine	3,803	0.04
13.	Tech. degree or diploma (Agri and Dairy) equal to degree of P.G.	632	0.007
14.	Veterinary	165	0.001
15.	Teaching	16,065	0.18
16.	Others	187	0.002
	Total	87,57,842	100.00

Source: Computed from the data provided in Census of India 1991.

By looking at their economic activities it can be said that the major proportion of their population in which they are engaged is agricultural labourers. The percentage of the SC literates is less than that of the total population in the state. Their low percentage is more pronounced at the higher educational level. The educational level (at various stages) among SCs is not impressive (see Table 2).

One may get some idea about their socio-economic conditions. A large number of them (majority) continue to live in utter poverty and great deprivation.

They are proportionately more in agricultural labour and very less in cultivation activities. Looking at the owning of agricultural land (a major source of economic and political power for CH especially in rural areas. The land ownership among the SCs of Maharashtra is very low. The study shows[22] that in Maharashtra the percentage of SCs landless (16–70%) plus near landlessness (54.80) is 71.50 per cent.

During recent years SCs have made tremendous progress in several spheres of life. Though a combination of several reasons have led to their progress, the influence of the educational, ideological and political campaign of Dr Ambedkar and the inspiration taken from him is the most important contributing factor in it. The progress is partly due to the government measures which attracted a large number of persons from SCs who wanted to improve their socio-economic conditions.

The *Mahars* are certainly benefitted more and are ahead in many respects than *Mangs* and other castes among SCs.[23] There are certain factors and historical reasons for their achievement.[24] A combination of several reasons has led to their progress.

Besides the various factions among the Dalit organizations mostly led by *Mahar* caste, *Mang/Matang, Chambhars* and *Dhors* have their respective caste organizations. The *Mangs* have also begun to organize themselves to fight against the oppression around the teaching of their caste leader, Anna Bhau Sathe. The process of awakening them had begun. They have begun to abandon the traditional '*gaonki*' work. This was viewed as violating the boundaries set by the CHs. So long as they never thought of violating the boundaries set by CH or raising any resentment against CH's socio-economic hegemony they (*Mangs*) were thought of as not crossing the caste limits which was defined passively, and submissively and CHs speaks approvingly for them.[25] The moment they did not remain quiet but began to assert their rights the circumstances turned adverse.

It has been said[26] that 'the *Chamars* in Bihar and UP, *Malas* and *Madigas* in Andhra Pradesh, *Mahars* in Maharashtra are more victims of atrocities than other SCs in these states. Further, it has been also said that in the entire Maharashtra, the *Mahars* became the target of *Savarnas* as they are the most assertive and politically organized people. As a result, the atrocity on the Dalits in Maharashtra, by default, meant atrocity on the Buddhists. It was for the first time that one heard of Matang being significantly targeted by the *Savarnas*.[27]

It is not true that atrocities are inflicted only on the *Mahars*, but all those who are steadfast and set a new trend of agitation and protest against the oppression are also subject to atrocities. The oppressions or discrimination become so intolerable that they realized the importance of their organizational effort in achieving the social aspiration cherished by them. Among the SCs, the castes other than *Mahar,* viz. *Mang, Chambhar* and *Dhor* have remained backward or are lagging behind in many respects. Moreover, the efforts of mobilizing and preparing them to protest against their harassment is limited only to the *Mahars*. The probable explanation is that they were not engaged in realizing and mobilizing the new aspirations.

The castes other than *Mahars* or Buddhists are also the targets of CHs in Maharashtra and this can be very well seen from the given Tables 3, 4 and 5.

In this connection one can safely assume what has been correctly pointed out by Nandu Ram in one of his writings:[28] 'Atrocities are, thus inflicted more on those SCs who are socially mobile and who assert for their rights and respectable status than ones who compromise with the status.'

Table 3 *Major Caste-wise Cases of Atrocities in Marathwada Region Registered Under Act*

S. No.	Caste	95–96	96–97	97–98	98–99	99–2000	2000–01	01–02	02–03	03–04	04–05	05–06	06–07	Total
1.	Mahar	26	52	35	24	09	12	07	11	05	13	23	01	218 (58.44)
2.	Mang	21	24	16	14	07	04	05	10	09	03	07	03	123 (32.98)
3.	Chambhar	03	6	03	02	02	–	02	–	–	01	02	01	022 (05.90)
4.	Dhor	–	02	02	–	01	–	–	–	–	–	1	–	006(01.61)
5.	Others	02		01	–	–	–	–	–	–	01	–	–	004 (01.07)
	Total	52	84	57	40	19	16	14	21	14	18	33	05	373 (100.0)

Source: District Social Welfare Office, Latur.

Table 4 *Atrocities Against Dalits in Marathwada*

S. No.	*Date of Incident*	*Place (Village, Taluka, Dist.)*	*Issue/reason for Incident*	*Form of Atrocity*
1.	11 July 2003	Chaturwadi, Ambajogai, Beed	Gairan land	Burnt down huts of Nagnath Kamble and other Dalits
2.	10 June 2003	Anvi Bangal Badnapur, Jalna	Drinking water	–Threw the vessels and abused –Beating Matang people
3.	21 May 2003	Matmal, Lonar	Entering the Hanuman temple	Dalit bridegroom paraded in the village with shoes on his head. Beat up bridegroom's mother till she fell unconscious
4.	23 July 2003	Asola (lakh), Aundha Nagnath, Beed	Beat the Dalit youth reporting the matter to police station	Imposed social boycott including stopping the supply of drinking water
5.	11 June 2003	Moregaon, Selu, Parbhani	Polluting CH's at the public water tap	–Devasting house –Dragged, humiliated and beat the women
6.	23 July 2003	Karandgaonwadi (Just 4 km from Bhutegaon) Ghanswangi, Jalna	Giving pathway between farms belonging to SC	–Serious injury to 3 Dalit persons –Death of Savarna person
7.	20 July 2003	Shahapur, Degloor, Nanded	Refused to give his Gairan land for building Mahadev temple	Attack by Savarna

Cont'd...

...Cont'd

8.	14 May 2003	Bhutegaon, Ghanswangi, Jalna	While drinking water did not follow the village caste tradition	Burnt alive Dilip Shende belonging to Matang caste
9.	9 July 2003	Murti, Ghanswangi, Jalna	Clash between two minor girls belonging to different castes, one is from SC and other from Savarna daughter abused in the caste name	Physical battle, mother of SC girl succumbed to her wounds (pregnant got axed)
10.	14 July 2003	Sonnakhota, Dharur, Beed	To fetch water from a tanker	Dongre was brutally killed

Source: Violence against Dalit in Marathwada – The Case Cauldron of Maharashtra: A Report of the Fact Finding team. Committee for protection of Democratic Rights, Mumbai.

Note: The word Savarna is used for Caste Hindus which includes all castes from four varnas (Brahmin to Shudra).

Table 5 *Atrocity Cases in Maharashtra During the Year 2008–2009*

S.No.	*Date of Incident*	*Particulars of the Victim (Name, Caste, Age, Occupation)*	*Place (Village, Taluka, Dist.)*	*Form of Atrocity*	*Issue/Cause for the Incident*
1.	1 January 2008	Mrs Pawar Sushilabai, Pardhi, 42	Mungi, Ausa, Latur	Beaten to death	Denying forcible physical relationship with her daughter-in-law
2.	26 May 2008	Keraba Sambhani Kamble, Mang, 58	Wadgaon, Jalkot, Latur	Untouchability, economic boycott	Drinking water from the govt. well, Untouchability treatment to Gairan landholders.
3.	19 March 2008	T.N. Kamble and other Dalit youths, Mahar, 60	Ghansargaon, Renapur, Latur	–Beating, physical hurt –Attack on houses, social boycott	Wearing good clothes and using mobile
4.	16 June 2008	Sahebrao Jonchale Mahar, 40, Taxi driver (pass)	Karanjala, Vasmat Hingoli	Beaten and burnt alive in his own car	Taking recourse to independent means of livelihood.
5.	5 July 2008	Baban Misal, Mang, 32 (Young Dalit Politician)	Sonegaon, Jamkhed, Ahmadnagar	Murder (killed in brutal manner)	Challenged the monopoly of dominant caste Hindu people.
6.	19 January 2009	Diksha and Panchsheela Shinde, 18 and 19, Mahar (Buddhist)	Shindi Village, Beed dist.	Dalit girls (sisters) abused and assaulted ruthlessly, mercilessly beaten and paraded in village	Girls were educating themselves

Cont'd…

...Cont'd

7.	26 January 2009	H.P. Waghmare and family, Mahar (Buddhist), 29	Khadki ghat, Beed,	Mass attack, Dalit houses burnt (4 houses of Waghmare family)	Dalit became head of the village (Sarpanch) and hoisted the National flag
8.	24 February 2009	Rohidas Tupe, Mang, 23	Patri, Aurangabad	Murder (beaten by mob)	Fallen in love with a girl belonging to a dominant caste

Sources: (i) *Atrocities on Dalits in Maharashtra:* Fact Finding Report year 2008–2009, Pune: Manuski Centre (Total 6 cases are cited in the brochure).

(ii) *Maharashtratil Dalitanwaril Anyay Atyacharacha Satyashodhan Ahawal* (16 July 2008 to 2008) (in Marathi) a brochure published by Manvi Hakka Abbiyan, Pune, 2008 (1–18 pages). The information of total 5 atrocity cases is available in this brochure.

The 3 atrocity cases which are cited in Tables 1, 4 and 5 are common both in *Manuski's* and *Manvi Hakka Abhiyan* report and hence is not repeated. Two (at S. No. 2, 3) and three (6 to 8) atrocity cases cited in this table are from *Manuski* and *Manvi Hakka Abhiyan* report respectively.

Root Causes of the Atrocities

CHs wanted some pretext to attack or make crime against SCs simply because of their (SCs) efforts of attaining rights and privileges extended by the government.

If they (CHs) are sincere enough and law abiding citizens or believers in democratic means, they would have preferred resorting to the constitutional and legal measures. But the experience from various incidents show that this does not happen. The CHs are in an aggressive mood. Whatever they are doing, it is with a view to teach a lesson to the SCs and highlight their traditional (lowest) position. Thus, these efforts are also to suppress the emerging new and independent culture among them which is different from their (SCs) forefathers.

We find the dual or rather hypocritical behaviour (double standards) of CHs in applying the rules for misdeeds, misbehaviour or criminal acts – one for forward caste and the other for SCs. If the same mistake is done towards SCs by the forward caste it is not viewed seriously. But similar misbehaviour by SCs are taken very seriously and they are attacked. And this attack is often extreme. The CHs not only attack but they always give the justification that the attack is not on caste ground. They also spread rumours and sometimes find the stories about SCs' misbehaviour, arrogance and criminal acts. The underlying reality is that such incidences/stories are used as instruments for mobilizing the support to provoke majority caste against SCs. Thus, the feeling is created among the non-SCs that SCs deserve such treatment.

Though the immediate cause for eruption of most horrible massacre and killing may be due to the petty cause (which do have legal and other amicable solutions). The real reasons or underlying reality is something different. The real or root causes should be seen in the light of the background in which the tension has accumulated.

The deprived section, especially SCs, who were denied the opportunities since time immemorial, became more conscious about the new social values incorporated in the Constitution. Due to the awareness among the SCs about their rights and privileges they are claiming and struggling for their rightful place in the society. But this claimed status is not accepted or conceded by the dominant section that were privileged and who were benefitted by the old or traditional values and ideologies. These traditional values and ideologies are so deeply internalized that any claim by the disadvantaged section is treated as a threat to the hegemony/supremacy and dominance of CHs and the claim of these SCs are thwarted even by resorting to atrocities.

The caste-based discrimination or the partiality by CHs has become a part of the life of SCs and they could not escape from this unfavourable or indifferent attitude and atmosphere.

Increasing Crimes Against Dalit

Although Maharashtra State is progressive and has a big impact of the thinking and work of Mahatma Phule, H.H. Shahu Chattarapati and Dr Ambedkar, the increasing trend of atrocities (caste- and untouchability-based discrimination) towards SCs people by CHs still prevail on a large scale.

Maharashtra which enjoyed the state of reputation as an advanced state in many respects, including its progressive policies, is not an exception for the spurt in crimes against Dalits.

The official data of the state of Maharashtra indicates a steady increase in the number of atrocities against SCs. In Maharashtra state the atrocity cases reported against SCs in the year 2004, 2005, 2006 and 2008 were 689, 844, 1,001 and 1,103 respectively. In 2008, Kolhapur ranked top in atrocities with 242 cases, followed by Aurangabad and Nashik with 202 and 171 cases respectively.

A cursory look at the cases cited in Tables 4 and 5 in which the atrocities inflicted on SCs and the immediate cause reveals that the small or trivial matters/incidents are trigged off into a large scale violence.

In one of the cases (Table 5) wearing good clothes and using a mobile phone became the cause for the incident of beating and making social boycott which reminds of the case reported[29] on 9 March 1952. That means we do not find much changes in the mindset of CHs in the last 60 years period. Instead of lessening of the crimes, these are increasing and have become more alarming.

In the democratic set-up the CHs dared to oppose and show a strong resentment against SCs who are exercising their social and political rights. Following independent means of livelihood and leading respectable lives by SCs is also treated as an offence in the eyes of CHs. Presently, Government of Maharashtra has started a '*Mahatma Gandhi Tanta Mukati Goan Samiti Yojana*' which also takes care of maintaining the existing caste system at village level, especially in denying the justice to SCs. In one of the cases (at S. No. 3 of Table 5) this Tanta Mukati Committee has played a crucial role by intervening and is responsible for untouchability treatment and imposition of social boycott to SCs.[30]

In analysing the cases given in the Tables it is observed or we can say that most of these cases also broadly come under the category of not allowing (denying) SCs to exercise their civil/social rights. In spite of the existence of POA and PCR Acts, such type of cases are happening. That indicates, the laws in these respects have remained only on paper. To CHs, observance of such laws is not obligatory on their part. This also means that they give more importance to the traditional caste rules and customs rather than State laws. Interestingly the Gairan land which is in the possession of and cultivated by SCs is treated as CHs' property. They are of the opinion that as and when they need it (for any purpose), SCs are supposed to surrender it, otherwise they (SCs) have to bear severe consequences.

In all these cases, CHs should have to restore/follow the legal and constitutional method to get the things settled, as is generally found in the civil society. On the contrary, however, they have taken the law in their own hands. They are in a hurry to teach a lesson to these SCs people, so that they can act according to age-old caste norms, thereby they can be in a position in maintaining the superiority or domination over the SCs.

The division-wise atrocity cases during the year 2000–01 to 2003–04 can be seen in Table 6.

Table 6 *Division-wise Cases Reported Under Prevention of Atrocities (POA) Act*

S. No.	*Division*	*Years*			
		2000–01	*2001–02*	*2002–03*	*2003–04*
1	Mumbai	7.38	03.82	06.90	05.50
2.	Nashik	14.18	31.04	33.55	30.20
3.	Pune	19.97	10.77	19.98	25.83
4.	Amravati	12.39	19.10	16.40	26.00
5.	Nagpur	20.53	14.98	17.43	16.00
6.	Aurangabad	22.23	45.34	50.27	54.52

Source: Yashwantrao Chavan Development Academy, Govt. of Maharashtra (The information pertaining to the period from 2000–2001 onwards is used here).

In respect to these divisions, the percentage of atrocities, except Mumbai and Nagpur divisions, are considerably higher. Taking into consideration the reported cases in each division, the Aurangabad (Marathwada region) division[31] shows higher proportions followed by Nashik division. Thus, taking into consideration, the proportion of the cases reported, it can be said that the atrocities have increased, especially in Aurangabad and Nashik divisions more than twice during a very short period of four years. The atrocities have been increasing continuously. Looking at the convicted, acquittal and pending cases of atrocities, it can be unfortunately said that there is a poor implementation of the Act.

According to one report in the year 2004, the percentage of convicted cases in Maharashtra is lower (6.7%) than that of all-India (conviction of 22.2 %).

It has also been brought to the notice that more than 5,000 atrocities cases (5,204) are pending in the State of Maharashtra (Table 7).

Table 7 *Region-wise Pending Cases of Atrocities Against SC and ST (2010) in Maharashtra*

S. No.	*Region*	*No. of Pending Cases*
1.	Mumbai	069
2.	Konkan	1,001
3.	Nashik	999
4.	Kolhapur	704
5.	Aurangabad	540
6.	Nanded	562
7.	Amravati	726
8.	Nagpur	603
	Total	5,204

Source: Dainik Lokmat Aurangabad dated 27 December 2010, p. 10.

The district-wise position in Marathwada (Table 8).

Table 8 *District and Status-wise Cases of Atrocities in Marathwada Region Registered Under the Act*

S. No.	District	Year	Status of Cases				
		April 95 to Mar 2005	Police	Convicted	Acquittal	Pending	Finalized
1.	Aurangabad	253	05	04	037	171	36
2.	Jalna	451	08	13	115	247	68
3.	Beed	317	02	13	190	080	32
4.	Parbhani	512	02	05	239	221	45
5.	Hingoli	298	07	05	044	213	29
6.	Nanded	619	07	07	183	340	82
7.	Osmanabad	162	01	04	053	093	11
8.	Latur	372	01	06	230	090	45
	Total	2,984	33	57	1,091	1,455	348

Source: Divisional social welfare office, Aurangabad.

It is rather disheartening to note that both volume of cases pending in the Courts and also extremely poor rate of conviction have been reported in Commissions report.[32]

Table 9 *Incidents of Crime Against Scheduled Castes*

S. No.	Crime Head	Years					% Variation in 2005 Over 2004
		2001	2002	2003	2004	2005	
1.	Murder	763	739	581	654	669	2.3
2.	Rape	1,316	1,331	1,089	1,157	1,172	1.3
3.	Kidnapping and Abduction	400	319	232	253	258	2.0
4.	Dacoity	41	29	24	26	26	0.0
5.	Robbery	133	105	70	72	80	11.1
6.	Arson	354	322	204	211	210	–0.5
7.	Hurt	4,547	4,494	3,969	3,824	3,847	0.6
8.	Protection of Civil Rights Act	633	1,018	634	364	291	–20.0
9.	SC/ST (Prevention of Atrocities) Act	13,113	10,770	8,048	8,891	8,497	–4.4
10.	Others	12,201	14,383	1,14,351	11,435	11,077	–3.1
	Total	33,501	33,507	26,252	26,887	26,127	–2.8

Source: Crime in India–2005, National Crime Records Bureau, Ministry of Home Affairs (GoI, 2008: 103). Quoted in India: Social Development Report 2010, p. 56.

If we look at the various incidences of crimes[33] against Scheduled Caste during the period 2001–2005 (Table 9) at national level we get the picture of continued existence of atrocities with greater number. The frequency of cases, under the crime heads of rape, Protection of Civil Rights (PCR) Act and SC/ST Protection of Atrocities (POA) Act points to the persistence of highly rooted caste-based attitude and heinous treatment meted out to SCs, more especially among females.

Crimes against SCs are on the rise and they are becoming victims on an increasing scale in different parts of the country. The only way to cope with the growing problem of crimes against SCs is by bringing about the attitudinal change among the CHs, which is difficult. It cannot be said that even after 63 years of Independence the hearts and minds of the CHs in the countryside and also to some extent in urban areas have undergone change. They (CHs) are not ready to accept SCs as equals.

Many a times it is alleged that the protection of Civil Rights Act is misused by SCs. The charges cannot be denied. But looking at the cases reported and the acquittals of the persons involved, it indicates that majority of the cases are where SCs are brutally assaulted and nothing was done to those who perpetrated the crime.

It has been rightly said that in case of the social problem dealing with the eradication of social evils, an exemplary punishment is essential so that it can work as a deterrent in the sense that administration would not tolerate such crimes and the culprit will not be spared. Recently, Maharashtra Government[34] has decided to invoke tough provisions of the SC/ST (POA) Act 1989 and fine the entire village where the atrocity is reported and consider curtailing development funds entitled to it. Only adoption of enactment and broadening the scope of law does not serve the desired purpose. The continuous oppression over the decades against these sections shows that they are still experiencing the limitations and failure of government machinery in checking violence.

The statistics show that in majority of cases the accused persons under this Act are acquitted. There are many reasons behind it. But one thing is certain and can be cited as one of the most important reason that is non-seriousness and insensitiveness[35] on the part of the State or Government agencies, ineffective or improper implementation of this Act.

A double standard is maintained by the police officials for taking action, one for CHs and other for SCs. They are very reluctant to file a case under SC/ST (POA) Act but very prompt in taking immediate action when a cross complaint is filed against SCs.

The SC/ST (POA) Act has been made more exhaustive and also have tough provisions than the POA/PCR Act to deal with atrocities. Most important aspects of this Act are that the offences registered against the accused have been made non-bailable under this Act.

There is a misunderstanding and many a times it is intentionally propagated that this Act is against the general community. This is circulated with an intention to get support to provoke the general masses against SCs in general and the Act in particular. This Act is against those who commit crime against SCs/STs and not the general community. And, this should be widely propagated.

Whenever the victim goes to register the case under the Atrocities Act, the police official's usual practice is that the cases are registered under normal laws, i.e. IPC and others. Thus, the victim gets no help or intentionally he is being deprived and denied from getting the help as admissible under the SC/ST (POA) Act.

Not only this, in most of the cases implicitly or explicitly, offenders/accused are supported by the State agencies. These State agencies which are involved in the implementation of the Act should have an official eye and not be caste biased.

This may lead the offenders to get encouraged and multiply their attack against the victims. Complainant or the victims themselves start losing confidence and faith in the State agencies for getting justice and safeguarding their rights. They (victims) are in a state of apprehension.

With this very background the SCs felt greatly concerned and laid emphasis on immediate arrest and punishment of the offenders. It is the experience of SCs that no serious effort is made to arrest the culprit. In this connection the demand made by the *Chunduru* SCs can be cited. It has been reported that they were refused to accept the relief measures until such time the *Chunduru* criminals and their cohorts had been awarded an acceptable punishment.[36]

The urban educated are more vocal in exposing the numerous discrimination and atrocities committed against SCs and the ill-treatment meted out to the SCs. They expressed these things by their fiery speeches. Sometimes, this type of activities also become the cause for committing atrocities on the poor, helpless and innocent SC villagers.[37]

'They are giving fiery lectures, demonstrating in cities and here, we have to suffer because the casteists retaliate by committing atrocities against us ...'

The CHs are in aggressive mood and not in a mood to tolerate the growing political and social consciousness among SCs. The SCs are determined to resist any aggression and demand equality and justice in every sphere of life.

The emphasis and demand are for self-respect. The SC villagers are no more lagging behind in such consciousness. In this connection, the question raised by one of the victims of Marathwada can be cited which is important and really thought provoking.

'Sharad Pawar's (then Chief Minister) government is talking much about rehabilitation. They will rebuild our shattered huts; we will work more and may be able to get back our corn, utensils. But our sisters and wives had to lose their dignity by being raped and sexually tortured. Are we going to get this back?'[38]

Conclusion

Dalit or ex-Untouchables or SCs have been the victims of various forms of social discrimination and injustice practised by non-Dalits. It has a long history. There is also a long history of protest and assertion against this practice in different forms. To overcome such discrimination, efforts have been made by the government to remove the social discrimination and disabilities (mostly imposed on SCs). These measures meant that Dalits have definitely achieved certain objectives.

Today, in contemporary India (post-Independence period) all is not well with the Dalits. They are still discriminated in one form or another and are being denied and deprived from their due rights. 'Educate, agitate and organize' the slogan or mantra given by Dr Ambedkar is considered important by SCs as a whole for their overall progress. In this situation these castes are organizing themselves on the basis of caste line with demands to check the crimes, discriminations and injustice against them.

This paper is aimed to discuss the prevailing atrocities/discriminations in Maharashtra. In the light of the main aim, this paper has highlighted and discussed the nature and root causes of discrimination. The study reveals that presently the awareness of problems of their own community and discrimination/atrocities events is increasing among SCs, particularly among the urban youths. They are still handicapped in combating the atrocities (discrimination) inflicted on them.

Political leadership among SCs is 'dependent type of leadership'. Much cannot be expected from them in contributing to the cause of combating continuing atrocities on these groups.

An atrocity on the SCs in Maharashtra is not a new thing. The atrocities are not committed only on the Mahars or Neo-Buddhists among SCs. There are many incidents when other than Mahars among the SCs are being targeted for atrocities. Moreover, an atrocity on the SCs is not merely on account of their poverty, but also because of their low standing in the caste hierarchy. The moment people from this section show resistance to discrimination and begin to assert their rights the circumstances will turn adversely. CHs are not in a position to tolerate this kind of awareness among SCs. This they (CHs) treat as a threat to their traditional position and want to teach lessons to these groups by resorting to atrocities.

Notes

1. Quoted in P.S. Krishnan, 'Synthesising the Gandhi-Ambedkar-Narayanguru-Marx Vision for Dalit Liberation', *Social Change: Journal of the Council for Social Development*, Vol. 41, No. 11, 2011, pp. 1–39.
2. To give effect to the declaration made in Article 17 of the Constitution, Parliament passed the Untouchability (Offences) Act 1955 which came into force on 1 June 1955. After examining the recommendations made by Elayaperumal Committee 1969, the Parliament amended the Act of 1955 and renamed it as the Protection of Civil Rights Act 1955. It came into force w.e.f. 19 November 1976. This Act proved inadequate in curbing the atrocities, especially offences committed on caste grounds. With this background, Parliament passed another Act, viz. the Scheduled Castes and Scheduled Tribes (Prevention of Atrocities) Act 1989. The Act came into force from 30 January 1990. The term 'atrocity' has been defined for the first time in this Act. According to it, atrocity means an offence punishable under section 3. It is not specifi-

cally defined but is given 23 acts, which when committed on members of SCs and STs by non-SCs and non-STs constitute atrocity and are punishable under this Act.

3. N. Paul Divakar, *Untouchability and Violence against Dalits*, 2011, http://www.hurights.or.jp/archives/focus/section2/2007/06/untouchability-and-violence-against-dalits.html
4. *Gaurdian*, 28 December 2006.
5. R.K. Kshirsagar, *Untouchability in India*, Deep and Deep Publications, Delhi, 1986, pp. 223–226.
6. Nandu Ram, *Beyond Ambedkar: Essays on Dalits in India* (Chapter 9: Atrocities on Weaker Sections: Some Developmental Constructs), Har-Anand Publications, New Delhi, 1995, p. 268.
7. A recent study on untouchability (essentially a survey of the practice of untouchability) across rural India conducted by Action Aid in 2001–02 in 565 villages of major 11 states (including Maharashtra) can be cited in this connection. The findings of the study were analysed and this has been published in the form of book titled, *Untouchability in Rural India*.

   The study revealed that apart from being forced to live on the outskirts of the village or colonies outside the village, Dalits suffer several forms of discrimination in public, cultural, personal and business spheres. They also suffer discrimination when dealing with state agencies and officials. It has also been revealed that untouchability is practiced in one form or another in almost 80 per cent of the villages. For more details see Ghanshyam Shah and others, *Untouchability in Rural India*, Sage Publications, New Delhi, 2006.
8. Vasant Moon (ed.), *Dr Babasaheb Ambedkar: Writings and Speeches*, Vol. 5, Education Department, Government of Maharashtra, Mumbai, 1990, p. 26.
9. Bhagwan Das, 'Untouchability, Scheduled Castes and Nation Building', in Jose Kananaikil (ed.), *Scheduled Castes and the Struggle against Inequality*, Indian Social Institute, Delhi, 1983, p. 32. Bhaghwan Das has mentioned that the atrocities are committed by the members of landholding castes in the respective states, for example, Vellas and Thewars (Tamil Nadu), Kappus, Reddis and Kammas (Andhra Pradesh), Bhumihars and Thakurs (Bihar), Jat, Gujars, Ahir and Rajput (UP, MP and Rajasthan), Jats and Rajput (Haryana and Punjab), Kunbis and Maratha (Maharashtra).
10. Moon (ed.), op. cit., p. 116.
11. Ibid.

12. M.N. Srinivas, *Castes in Modern India*, Media Promoters and Publishers, Bombay (now Mumbai), 1983, p. 91.
13. See N.D. Kamble, 'Price for Social Mobility', Paper submitted to the International Seminar on 'Minority Development Strategies in Comparative Perspectives' at Southern Asian Institute, Columbia University, New York, USA on 10–13 November 1983.
14. 'Andhra Pradesh Upper Caste Violence: Study of Chunduru Carnage', *Economic and Political Weekly*, Vol. 26, No. 36, 7 September 1991, p. 2079.
15. Nandu Ram, *Beyond Ambedkar: Essays on Dalits in India* (Chapter 10: Atrocities and Segregation in an Urban Social Structure: Views from the Bottom), Har-Anand Publications, New Delhi, 1995, p. 240. According to him, the views from the bottom, thus are of those whose statuses and power (although conventionally they were not supposed to acquire either economic or political power in the past), were fixed in principle at the lower level in the traditional society. For the details of views from the bottom, i.e. how victims perceive atrocities, see ibid., p. 241.
16. S.L. Gaikwad, *Protective Discrimination Policy and Social Change*, Rawat Publications, Jaipur and New Delhi, 1999. A study has been carried out in Aurangabad city. The study is based on the data collected from 200 SCs persons (respondents) comprising of college-going students (from different colleges) and employees (working in different government offices). In this study the whole problem is studied from the viewpoint of the respondents (who are the major beneficiaries of government measures meant for SCs). The information collected from them was under different sets including the given one (perception regarding the atrocities inflicted on SCs).
17. The causes of the atrocities were classified under land disputes, economic problems, police atrocities, personal enimity and untouchability, etc. For details see Report of the Commissioner for SC/ST, April 1980–March 1981 (3rd report) 1083, p. 148.
18. Gaikwad, op. cit., p. 172.
19. Moon (ed.), op. cit., p. 419.
20. Ibid., p. 25.
21. Ibid., p. 111.
22. Quoted in Manoranjan Mohanty (ed.), *India: Social Development Report*, Council for Social Development, Oxford University Press, New Delhi, 2010, p. 56.

23. For the caste-wise population, economic activities, educational level and employment among major SCs in Maharashtra discussion, see for instance, Gaikwad, op. cit., pp. 41–60. Besides this, their caste-wise (among major SCs) representation in Government services (Class I to IV) in Z.P., Mahapalika and University employment/administration and representatives in various local self bodies in Maharashtra State (Z.P., Panchayat, Municipal Corporation and Municipalities) have been given. For detailed information, see B.S. Waghmare, 'Reservation Policy and the Plight of Matangs in Maharashtra', *The Indian Journal of Political Science*, Vol. LXXI, No. 3, July-September 2010, pp. 923–946.
24. This has been discussed in number of studies. See, for instance, Sunanda Patwardhan, *Change among India's Harijans*, Orient Longman, New Delhi, 1973; Joshep Mathew, *Ideology, Protest and Social Mobility: Case Study of Mahars and Pulays*, Inter-India Publications, Delhi, 1986; and Eleanor Zelliot, 'Learning the Use of Political Means: The Mahars of Maharashtra', in Rajani Kothari (ed.), *Caste in Indian Politics*, Orient Longman, Delhi, 1970, pp. 29–69.
25. S.P. Punalekar cited the example in which CHs spoke approvingly of the Mangs. See S.P. Punalekar, *Aspects of Class and Caste in Social Tensions*, Centre for Social Studies, Surat, 1981, p. 152.
26. Nandu Ram, op. cit., Chapter 10, p. 295. Anand Teltumbade and others, *Violence against Dalits in Marathwada: The Caste Cauldron of Maharashtra* (A report of the fact finding team), Committee for Protection of Democratic Rights, Mumbai, 1989.
27. Different castes among SCs in Maharashtra have different sources of their pride, which often gives them a sense of identity. Mangs recently have begun to organize themselves and Anna Bhau Sathe, an eminent Dalit writer and Lahuji Salve both happen to be Mangs have become the source of their pride. Mangs believe in their own caste organization and also fight for their just demands through democratic means.
28. Nandu Ram, op. cit., p. 295.
29. Quoted in Moon (ed.), op. cit. (Under the heading where wearing a shirt is an offence.), pp. 118–119.
30. The two brochures (from which Table 5 is prepared) give details about events' background, narration of events in brief, its present status, the lawful implementation and some suggestions are also given at the end.
31. For the brief discussion of SCs in Marathwada see, for instance, S.L. Gaikwad, 'Dalit Identity Formation: The Case of Marathwada Region', in Nandu Ram (ed.), *Dalits in Contemporary India: Discrimination and Discontent*, Siddhant Publications, New Delhi, 2008, pp. 175–195.

32. National Commission for SCs and STs (Sixth report 1999–2000 and 2000–2001), Government of India, New Delhi, p. 213.
33. The crimes committed against SCs and STs are shown/ given broadly under the following ten crime heads: Murder, Hurt, Rape, Kidnapping and Abduction, Dacoity, Robbery, Arson, PCR Act and ST (POA) Act, and other offences.
34. The same Government of Maharashtra (GoM) has permitted to withdraw minor cases registered under PCR and SC/ST POA Act. Government of Maharashtra has withdrawn 1,179 atrocity cases on 20 February 1994, i.e. after renaming of Marathwada University after Dr Babasaheb Ambedkar. The reasons are best known to GoM and the SC political leaders whosoever have consented to do it.
35. S.M. Dahiwale has also talked about this insensitiveness in the Khairlanji case. For detail see, S.M. Dahiwale, 'Khairlanji: Insensitivity of Mahars', *Economic and Political Weekly*, Vol. XLVI, No. 31, 2009, pp. 29–33.
36. 'Andhra Pradesh Upper Caste Violence: Study of Chunduru Carnage', op. cit., p. 208.
37. 'The Marathwada Riot: A Report Atyachar Virod Samiti', *Economic and Political Weekly*, Vol. XIV, No. 19, 12 May 1979, p. 847.
38. Ibid.

4 Caste-Based Exclusion and Inclusion of Dalits in Eastern Uttar Pradesh

A Sociological Interpolation

Bibhuti Bhushan Malik

Social exclusion is a multidimensional process of progressive social rupture, detaching groups and individuals from social relations and institutions and preventing them from full participation in the normal, normatively prescribed activities of the society in which they live (Silver, 2007: 15). Social exclusion is a relatively new concept. It is difficult to find a definition that reflects the whole complexity of the phenomenon. Most of the investigations are one-dimensional and are mostly concentrated on the aspects of economic life. Academic studies prove that social exclusion has a more multidimensional character. Social exclusion is a multidimensional concept, related to the relative position of an individual or a group (a region) in the entirety of society. Each type of societal 'disadvantage' can cause social exclusion. Exclusion is conceptualized through different social processes and dimensions of everyday life: economic, cultural, physical or mental disability, geographical (spatial), political and institutional. In other words, social exclusion is the outcome of a complex process and certainly not the result of poverty alone. Therefore, social exclusion should be understood in the framework of a social structure in which four subsystems are playing vital roles and these are: politics (as the democratic distribution system); economics (labour market and other instruments of economic integration); social system (welfare and social integration); and, community and family systems. However, the concept, even viewed as multidimensional, still poses persistent problems. Anthias argues that social inclusion is not only multidimensional in the sense that it is influenced by different processes – economic, political and cultural – but that the concept is also relational because theses different causes 'will affect categories of persons differently depending on whether they are treated in terms of gender, in terms of ethnicity or in terms of class. It is important that social exclusion and inclusion are not considered as a dichotomy: one is normally not totally excluded or included; e.g. one can be (partly) excluded (e.g. from certain political rights on the basis of geographical or ethnical origin) but included for social welfare services. Exclusion and inclusion are also not static phenomena: within a given society, people can become socially excluded or included over the time. Therefore, it is better not to try to provide a comprehensive definition for social exclusion, but to use an approach that identifies 'deprivation factors' (such as income deprivation, employment deprivation, health deprivation and disability, education, training and skills deprivation, housing deprivation, geographic access to services, crime, physical environment).

In this systemic approach, social inclusion results from synergies between different actors in local government and services, public administration, and social partners through participation, partnerships and networking. Therefore, it can be concluded that exclusion processes remain 'systemic', that is exclusion is seen as a dependent only on system failures. Within this perspective, social exclusion is seen as based on the hetero-designation of certain groups or individuals; which are defined as 'the excluded'. Sometimes, studies ignore the human potential to construct 'inclusion' within one or different everyday spheres.

A few concerns are raised about self-designation processes, the influence of identity on inclusion and exclusion boundaries or personal choices, which may intervene in those identities. Therefore, social exclusion depends also on the individual role/feelings: an individual is socially excluded when he cannot give anything to society, in exchange for what the society can give him.

Social exclusion is the denial of equal opportunities imposed by certain groups of society on others, leading to the inability of an individual to participate in the basic political, economic and social functioning of society. Amartya Sen draws attention to various meanings and dimensions of the concept of social exclusion. He draws a distinction between situations where some people are kept out (or left out), and where some people are included (forcibly) on deeply unfavourable terms. The two situations are described as unfavourable exclusion and unfavourable inclusion.

Sen (1985) argues that it is important to distinguish between active exclusion, i.e. fostering of exclusion through deliberate policy interventions by the government or by any other willful agents (to exclude some people from some opportunity), and passive exclusion, which works through the social process in which there are no deliberate attempts to exclude, nevertheless, may result in exclusion from a set of circumstances.

Sen (1985) further distinguishes the constitutive relevance of exclusion from that of instrumental importance. In the former, exclusion or deprivation have an intrinsic importance of their own. For instance, not being able to relate to others and to take part in the life of the community can directly impoverish a person's life, in addition to the further deprivation. This is different from social exclusion which is of instrumental importance, in which the exclusion in itself is not impoverishing but can lead to impoverishment of human life. Mainstream economists have further elaborated the concept of discrimination that operates particularly through markets.

Caste Exclusion and Discrimination

In India, exclusion revolves around the societal interrelations and institutions that exclude, discriminate, isolate and deprive some groups on the basis of group identities like caste and ethnicity. It is caste-based exclusion which forms the basis for various anti-discriminatory policies. Historically, the caste system has regulated the social and economic life of the people in India. The organizational scheme of the caste system is based on the division of people into social groups (or castes) in which the civil, cultural and economic rights of each individual caste are predetermined or ascribed by birth and made hereditary. The assignment of civil, cultural and economic rights is, therefore, unequal and hierarchical.

The most important feature of the caste system, however, is that it provides for a regulatory mechanism to enforce social and economic organization through the instruments of social ostracism (or social and economic penalties) and reinforces it further with justification and support from philosophical elements in the Hindu religion (Lal, 1988; Dr Ambedkar, 1936 and 1987). The caste system is a fundamental characteristic of fixed civil, cultural and economic rights for each caste, with restrictions on change, implying forced exclusion of one caste from the rights of the other caste, or from undertaking the occupations of other castes. Exclusion and discrimination in civil, cultural and particularly in economic spheres such as occupation and labour employment, are therefore internal to the system and a necessary outcome of its governing principles. In the market economy framework, occupational immobility operates through restrictions in various markets such as land, labour, credit, other inputs and services necessary for any economic activity. Labour, being an integral part of the production process of any economic activity, would obviously become part of market discrimination. This implies that the caste system involves the negation of not only equality and freedom, but also of basic human rights, particularly of low-caste untouchables, thus becoming an impediment in their personal development.

The principles of equality and freedom are not the governing principles of the caste system. This is because the underlying principles of the caste system assume particular notions of human rights. Unlike many other human societies, the caste system does not recognize the individual and his/her distinctiveness as the centre of the social purpose. In fact, for the purpose of rights and duties, the unit of Hindu society is not an individual. Even the family is not regarded as a unit in Hindu society, except for the purposes of marriage and inheritance. The primary unit in Hindu society is caste, and hence the rights and privileges (or lack of them) of an individual are on account of him/her being a member of a particular caste (Ambedkar, first published in 1987). Also, due to differential ranking and the hierarchical nature of the caste system, the entitlements to various rights become narrower and narrower as one goes down the hierarchical ladder within the caste system.

Various castes get artfully interlinked and coupled with each other in a manner such that the rights and privileges of the higher castes become the causative reasons for the disadvantage and disability of the lower castes, particularly the untouchables.

As Dr Ambedkar (1987) observed, a caste does not exist in a single number, only in plural. Castes exist as a system of endogenous groups that are interlinked with each other in an unequal measure of rights and relations in all walks of life. Castes at the top of the order enjoy more rights at the expense of those located at the bottom. Therefore, the untouchables located at the bottom of the caste hierarchy have fewer economic and social rights. Since the civil, cultural and economic rights (particularly with respect to occupation and property rights) of each caste are ascribed, and are compulsory, the institution of caste necessarily involves forced exclusion of one caste from the rights of another. The unequal and hierarchical assignment of economic and social rights by ascription obviously restricts freedom of occupation and human development.

Forms of Caste Exclusion and Discrimination

The practice of caste-based exclusion and discrimination thus involves what has been described as living mode exclusion, exclusion in political participation, and exclusion and disadvantage in social and economic opportunities ('Minorities at Risk', UNDP HDR, 2004). Caste/untouchability and ethnicity-based exclusion reflects in the inability of individuals and groups like former *untouchables, adivasis* and similar groups to interact freely and productively with others and to take part in the full economic, social and political life of a community (Bhalla and Lapeyere, 1997). Incomplete citizenship or denial of civil rights (freedom of expression, rule of law, right to justice), political rights (right and means to participate in the exercise of political power), and socio-economic rights (economic security and equality of opportunities) are key dimensions of impoverished lives (Zoninsein, 2001). Caste and untouchability-based exclusion and discrimination can be categorized in the economic, civil, cultural and political spheres as follows:

Firstly, economic exclusion can be practiced in the labour market through denial of jobs; in the capital market through denial of access to capital; in the agricultural land market through denial of sale and purchase or leasing of land; in the input market through denial in sale and purchase of factor inputs; and in the consumer market through denial in the sale and purchase of commodities and consumer goods.

Secondly, discrimination can occur through what Amartya Sen describes as unfavourable inclusion, through differential treatment in the terms and conditions of contract, one of them reflecting in discrimination in the prices charged and received by discriminated groups. Discriminated groups can get lower prices for the goods that they sell, and could pay higher prices for the goods that they buy, as compared with the market price or the price paid by other groups.

Thirdly, an exclusion and discrimination can occur in access to social needs supplied by government or public institutions, or by private institutions in the fields of education, housing and health, including common property resources like water bodies, grazing land and land for common use.

Fourthly, groups (particularly untouchables) may face exclusion and discrimination from participation in certain categories of jobs (the sweeper being excluded from household jobs) because of the notion of purity and pollution, and may be restricted to so-called unclean occupations.

In the civil and cultural spheres, untouchables may face discrimination and exclusion in the use of public services like roads, temples, water bodies, and institutions delivering services like education, health and other public services.

In the political sphere, untouchables could face discrimination in the use of political rights, and participation in the decision-making process. Due to physical (or residential) segregation, and social exclusion on account of the notion of untouchability, they may suffer from a general social exclusion. Since there is a societal mechanism to regulate and enforce the customary norms and rules of the caste system, untouchables generally face opposition in the form of social and economic boycott, violence, and such acts as a general deterrent to their right to development. Caste and untouchability-based exclusion and discrimination are essentially structural in nature and comprehensive and multiple in coverage, involving the denial of equal opportunities.

Methodology

The primary source of data has been collected through extensive fieldwork by administering the interview schedule, focused interview and quasi participatory observation methods. Further, the secondary and documentary source of data has also been used to explain the magnitude of servitude and level of poverty that persists amongst Dalits of Uttar Pradesh. It also ascertains the change brought about by these programmes in the life of Dalits. This study has been undertaken in the most backward areas of eastern Uttar Pradesh, especially in two selected blocks of Varanasi district. The respondents to this study were village-level Dalit workers, labourers and small farmers and mostly the beneficiaries of anti-poverty programmes. For this purpose the beneficiary list has been collected from the block office.

There are eight blocks in Varanasi district, out of which one fourth blocks have been selected purposefully, viz. Kashi Vidyapeeth and Pindra block. Mostly, six villages from three different types of villages have been selected from each block. Three different types of villages are selected on the basis of following criteria: (1) the village of high incidence and magnitude of poverty, (2) the village of middle incidence and magnitude of poverty and (3) the village of lowest incidence and magnitude of poverty. In these blocks there are around 300 villages, out of which 12 villages were selected for this study on the basis of above criteria. Random sampling was used to choose 441 households from 12 villages of Varanasi district of eastern Uttar Pradesh These household respondents were interviewed through household interview schedule. The villages and the respondents selected are presented in Table 1. To explore a sociological perspective, qualitative analysis has been made. This has been done by understanding and involved interactive process.

Results and Discussion

Feeling of Togetherness or Closeness

Table 1 *Distribution of the Respondents on the Basis of the Feeling of Togetherness or Closeness*

Feeling of Togetherness or Closeness		
	Frequency	*Percentage*
Very distant	44	9.98
Somewhat distant	74	16.78
Neither distanced nor closed	117	26.53
Somewhat close	108	24.49
Very close	98	22.22
Total	441	100

Table 1 represents the frequency distribution of the respondents on the basis of the feeling of togetherness or closeness. Among the respondents, 44 (9.98%) respondents maintain very distant relationship, 74 (16.78%) respondents maintain somewhat distant relationship with others, 117 (26.53%) respondents are able to maintain neither *so distant* nor *so closed*, 108 (24.49%) respondents are of the view that they are somewhat close with each other and the rest 98 (22.22%) respondents viewed that they are very close to each other. So, it is evident that majority of the respondents, i.e. 117 (26.53%) are in the midst of distance and closeness.

From the above discussion it can be laid that the feeling of togetherness and oneness usually develops amongst the minds of the Dalits due to the feelings of oneness towards their own caste, i.e. casteism through which the concept of caste identity came into their mind. This is vividly explained in the following Table 2. Let us examine the caste identity amongst the respondents.

Table 2 *Distribution of the Respondents on the Basis of Caste Identity*

Differences on the Basis of Caste Identity		
	Frequency	*Percentage*
Very distant	82	18.59
Somewhat distant	148	33.56
Neither distanced nor closed	97	22.00
Somewhat close	61	13.83
Very close	53	12.02
Total	441	100

Figure 1 *Frequency Distribution of Respondents*

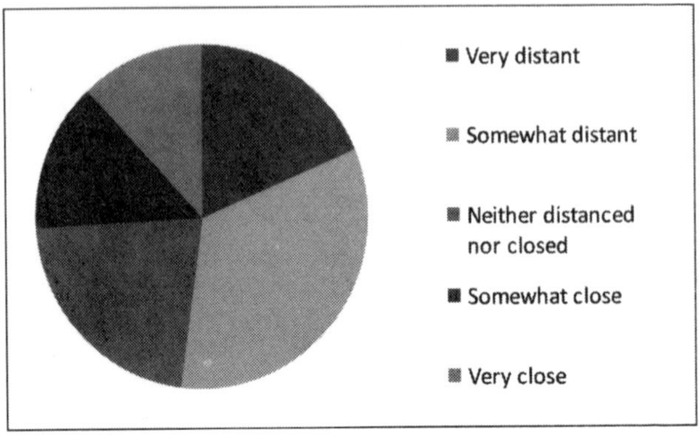

Table 2 and Figure 1 depict the frequency distribution of the respondents on the basis of caste identity. Among the respondents, 82 (18.59%) respondents maintain very distant relationship, 148 (33.56%) respondents maintain somewhat distant relationship with others, 97 (22.00%) respondents are able to maintain neither so distant nor so closed, 61 (13.83%) respondents are of the view that they are somewhat close with each other and the rest 63 (12.02%) respondents viewed that they are very close to each other. So, it is evident that majority of the respondents, i.e. 148 (33.56%) maintain somewhat distant relationship with others.

Caste identity and the feelings of casteism obviously create some kind of differential outlook amongst the respondents since they are entangled with caste conservatism. But that does not mean that caste differences are observed in all cases. The ratio relating to the caste differences can be viewed in the following Table 3.

Table 3 *Distribution of the Respondents on the Basis of Caste Differences*

Caste Differences		
	Frequency	*Percentage*
Yes	302	68.48
No	100	22.68
Sometimes	39	8.84
Total	441	100

Table 3 depicts the frequency distribution of the respondents on the basis of caste differences which create some of the problems amongst them. Among the respondents, 302 (68.48%) respondents agreed with the view that caste differences create many problems in their day-to-day lives, 100 (22.68%) respondents did not agree with this concept and the rest 39 (8.84%) respondents viewed that the caste differential treatment sometimes creates problems amongst themselves. So, majority of the respondents, i.e. 302 (68.48%) viewed that caste differences create various problems in the society.

Table 4 *Distribution of the Respondents on the Basis of Causes of Problems because of Caste Differences*

Which Two Differences Most Often Cause Problems		
	Frequency	*Percentage*
Not Applicable	100	22.68
Difference due to caste hierarchy	87	19.73
Difference in landholding	9	2.04
Difference in wealth/material possession	2	0.45
Difference due to caste hierarchy and landholding	143	32.43
Differences due to caste hierarchy and wealth/material possession	36	8.16
Differences due to caste hierarchy and education	50	11.34
Differences due to caste hierarchy and cleaning	1	0.23
Differences due to caste hierarchy and politics	1	0.23
Difference in landholding and wealth/material possession	1	0.23
Difference in landholding and education	6	1.36
Difference in wealth/material possession and education	1	0.23
Difference in education and cleaning	1	0.23
Difference in education and politics	1	0.23
Unable to answer	2	0.45
Total	441	100

Table 4 depicts the frequency distribution of the respondents on the basis of caste differences which create some problems amongst them. Among the respondents, 100 (22.68%) respondents did not agree with the proposal that caste differentiation does not

Table 5 *Distribution of the Respondents on the Basis of the Disabilities*

	Response		*If Yes*				*Unable to Answer*	*Total*
	Yes	*No*	*Only A Few People*	*Many People, But Less Than Half of the Village/ Neighbourhood*	*More than Half the Village/ Neighbourhood*	*All Schedule Caste People*		
Education/School	35	402	5	3	19	1	9	441
	7.90	91.20	1.13	0.68	4.30	0.23	1.58	100.00
Water	46	391	10	0	27	3	4	441
	10.43	88.66	2.26	0.00	6.12	0.68	0.91	100.00
Health services/clinics	9	427	0	0	8	1	5	441
	2.04	96.82	0.00	0.00	1.81	0.23	1.13	100.00
Justice	14	422	5	5	3	1	5	441
	3.17	95.69	1.13	1.13	0.68	0.23	1.13	100.00
Transport	8	428	2	2	4	0	5	441
	1.81	97.05	0.45	0.45	0.91	0.00	1.13	100.00
Marketplaces	7	430	2	1	4	0	4	441
	1.58	97.50	0.45	0.23	0.91	0.00	0.91	100.00
Public place of worship, temple	89	347	23	9	55	2	5	441
Total	20.18	78.68	5.21	2.04	12.47	0.45	1.13	100.00

create any problems, 143 (32.43%) respondents viewed that due to caste hierarchy and landholding, the caste differentiation is observed, 87 (19.73%) respondents have opined that due to caste hierarchy, the caste differentiation is obvious, 50 (11.34%) respondents viewed that the cause of caste differentiation is the difference between caste hierarchy and education.

The Table 5 presents the frequency distribution of the respondents on the basis of the disabilities observed by the people regarding the use of water, temple, educational institutions, etc. Amongst the respondents, only 7 per cent population agreed that the Scheduled Castes students should go to the public school as against 93 per cent population who did not agree due to caste conservatism, similarly, only 10 per cent population support drawing or use of water from the public well or tap, 97 per cent respondents denied provision for any health services to the Dalits, nearly 97 per cent of population did not agree with regard to the use of justice, market place and transport system as these are used by upper caste members. Hence, it is evident that most of the people blame caste conservatism as leading to constraints on various areas.

Now that most of the people are disentangled from the clutches of the caste-based society and by getting various facilities from governmental and non-governmental levels, they are eager to participate in the community activities so as to develop the society at large. The rate of participation of the people can be viewed from the Table 6.

Table 6 *Distribution of the Respondents on the Basis of their Participation in Community Activities*

Participation of the Respondents in Community Activities		
	Frequency	*Percentage*
Yes	84	19.05
No	214	48.53
I can participate in all activities	102	23.13
Unable to Answer	41	9.30
Total	441	100

Table 6 represents the frequency distribution of the respondents on the basis of their participation in community activities.

Among the respondents 84 (19.05%) respondents agreed with the proposal that they are participating in the community activities, whereas 214 (48.53%) of the population do not get opportunities to participate in community activities, but 23 per cent population are absolutely getting the opportunities to participate in community activities and the rest, nearly 9 per cent, viewed that we are unable to give any final opinion regarding the participation in the community activities.

Table 7 depicts the frequency distribution of the respondents regarding their non-participation of activities on different grounds. Mostly, 68 per cent respondents viewed that the Dalits are not allowed to visit places of worship or temples, 73 per cent populations viewed that on occasions like marriage ceremony they are not given the opportunity to participate, 79 per cent of the higher caste population does not allow their children to play with lower caste's children, 83 per cent of the population is not allowed to speak anything in the Panchayat, 83 per cent of the population opposed sharing the hospital facilities with these distorted people, and 83 per cent of the population is restricted on participation in intellectual activities.

Table 7 *Distribution of the Respondents on the Basis of their Non-Participation in Community Activities*

In which activities are you not allowed to participate	*Yes*	*Other*	*Unable to Answer*	*Total*
Worship places/temples	71 (16.09)	301 (68.25)	69 (15.64)	441 (100.00)
During ceremony and marriages	48 (10.88)	324 (73.46)	69 (15.64)	441 (100.00)
On eating habits	37 (8.39)	335 (75.96)	69 (15.64)	441 (100.00)
Behaviour of untouchability	85 (19.27)	287 (65.07)	69 (15.64)	441 (100.00)
Higher caste people used to give food in a different row	13 (2.94)	359 (81.4)	69 (15.64)	441 (100.00)

Cont'd...

...Cont'd

Not restricted	207	234	69	441
	(46.93)	(53.06)	(15.64)	(100.00)
Unrespected behaviour	8	364	69	441
	(1.81)	(82.53)	(15.64)	(100.00)
Higher caste people do not allow their children to play together	22	350	69	441
	(4.98	79.36)	15.64)	(100.00)
Do not allow to speak in the panchayat	4	368	69	441
	(0.91	83.44)	15.64)	(100.00)
Restriction on going to hospital	6	366	69	441
	(1.36	82.99)	15.64)	(100.00)
Behaviour of untouchability while travelling	5	367	69	441
	(1.13	83.21)	15.64)	(100.00)
Restriction on participation at mental level	5	367	69	441
	(1.13	83.21)	15.64)	(100.00)

Many of the respondents are not ready to cooperate with the community activities due to their conservative outlook and due to the principle of disinterestedness. Apart from that, there are many grounds because of which they are not ready to participate or accommodate such communal interests. All these facts and figures are represented in the Table 8.

Table 8 *Distribution of the Respondents on the Basis of Various Grounds for Non-Participation*

The cause of 'not allowed to participate' (Enumerate: List up)		
	Frequency	*Percentage*
Not Applicable	276	62.59
Caste	20	4.54
Poverty	9	2.04
Caste and Poverty	99	22.45
Caste and Occupation/Unclean Occupation	2	0.45
Caste and lack of education	18	4.08

Cont'd...

...Cont'd

Caste and political affiliation	2	0.45
Poverty and occupation/unclean occupation	3	0.68
Poverty and lack of education	8	1.81
Poverty and religion	1	0.23
Poverty and political affiliation	1	0.23
Occupation/unclean occupation and lack of education	1	0.23
Lack of education and political affiliation	1	0.23
Total	441	100

Table 8 presents the frequency distribution of the respondents on the basis of various grounds on which they are excluded from participating in community activities. Among the respondents, 63 per cent of the population viewed that the proposal is not applicable, whereas 22 per cent population have given importance to caste and poverty by which they are not allowed to participate in community activities, and very negligible persons are focussing on different grounds such as unclean dwelling, lack of education, religion, political affiliation through which they are creating some reasons not to allow to participate in community activities.

Table 9 *Distribution of the Respondents on the Basis of Reasons for Non-Participation in Community Activities*

Not allowed to participate (Enumerate: List up)				
Cause	*Frequency*			
	Yes	*Other*	*Not Applicable*	*Total*
Caste	79	5	357	441
	(17.91)	(1.13)	(80.95)	(100.00)
Poverty	62	22	357	441
	(14.05)	(4.98)	(80.95)	(100.00)
Occupation/Unclean Occupation	4	80	357	441
	(0.91)	(18.14)	(80.95)	(100.00)
Lack of Education	11	73	357	441
	(2.49)	(16.55)	(80.95)	(100.00)

Table 9 presents the frequency distribution of the respondents on the basis of various reasons for which they are excluded from participating in community activities. Among the respondents, 81 per cent population does not agree that due to caste system/poverty/unclean occupation/lack of education they are not allowed to participate; rather, there could be some other constraints by which they are not allowed to participate in community activities.

Conclusion

From the empirical evidence it becomes clear that caste-based exclusion and discrimination of Scheduled Castes in the past and its current continuation (through residual traditional attributes) continues to be one of the main reasons for their lower human development and higher deprivation and poverty. The approach of Indian policy makers to overcome discrimination and addressing social exclusion, includes such policy interventions as legal enforcement of anti-discrimination laws, reservation and referential and general empowering measures that form part of anti-poverty programmes. These policies have brought about positive changes, but the rate of improvement has not been fast enough to reduce the absolute level of deprivation and the gap between the excluded group of Scheduled Castes and tribes and other advanced sections does not reduce distinctively. The continuing exclusion-induced deprivation of disadvantaged groups of Scheduled Castes indicates that addressing social exclusion is often more difficult than addressing poverty. Social and cultural sources of exclusion (in economic, civil and political spheres) are rooted in informal social structures, and institutions of caste and untouchability cover not only the private but also public domain governed by the State.

In this context, the inclusion of excluded groups is different from the social inclusion of materially deprived people. Poverty, even when broadly defined as exclusion from the means necessary for full participation in the normal activities of society, is largely a question of access to resources and services. The social exclusion of groups or individuals within that group is foremost a denial of equal opportunity, respect and recognition of the right to development. Fighting discrimination, therefore, calls for additional policies complementing anti-poverty and economic development programmes. But there is also considerable overlap, and therefore the need to combine and complement, and not divide, programmes against poverty and economic deprivation and policies for equal rights and social inclusion of disadvantaged groups.

References

Action Aid (2000), *Untouchability in Rural India* (by Ghanshyam Shah, Satish Deshpande, Sukhadeo Thorat, Harsh Mander and Amita Baviskar and Research and other Regional Staff), Sage Publications, Delhi.

Agrawal, Girish and Colin Gonsalves (2005), *Dalits and the Law*, Human Rights Law Network, Delhi.

Akder, Halis (1994), 'A Means to Closing Gaps: Disaggregated Human Development Index', UNDP Occasional Paper.

Ambedkar, B.R. (first published in 1987), 'Philosophy of Hinduism', in Vasant Moon (ed.), *Dr Babasaheb Ambedkar: Writings and Speeches*, Vol. 3, Department of Education, Government of Maharashtra, Bombay, pp. 1–94.

——. (first published in 1987), 'The Hindu Social Order: Its Essential Features', in Vasant Moon (ed.), *Dr Babasaheb Ambedkar: Writings and Speeches*, Vol. 3, Department of Education, Government of Maharashtra, Bombay, pp. 95–115.

Arrow, Kenneth J. (1998), 'What has Economics to Say about Racial Discrimination', *The Journal of Economic Perspectives*, Vol. 12, No. 2, pp. 91–100.

Banerjee, Abhijit and Rohini Somanathan (2001), 'Caste, Community and Collective Action: The Political Economy of Public Good Provision in India', Department of Economics, MIT and Department of Economics, University of Michigan.

Banerjee, Biswjit and J.B. Knight (1985), 'Caste Discrimination in Indian Urban Labour Market', *Journal of Developing Economics*, Vol. 17, pp. 277–307.

Birdsall, Nancy and Richard Sabot (eds) (1991), *Unfair Advantage: Labour Market Discrimination in Developing Countries*, World Bank Studies, New York.

Bramley, Glen and Tania Ford (1999), 'Social Exclusion and Lack of Access to Services: Evidence from the 1999 PSE Survey of Britain'.

Buvnic, Mayra (2005), 'Social Exclusion in Latin America', in Mayra Buvinic, Jacqueline Mazza and Ruthanne Deutsch (eds), *Social Inclusion and Economic Development in Latin America*, Inter-American Development Bank, New York.

Darity, Jr. William (1997), 'Reparations', in Samuel L. Myers (ed.), *Civil Rights and Race Relations in the Post Reagan-Bush Era*, Praeger, London.

Darity, Jr. William (ed.) (1997a), *Economics and Discrimination, Vol. I: An Elgar Reference Collection*, Edward Elgar Publishing Ltd., New York.

Darity, Jr. William and Steven Shulman (eds) (1989), *The Question of Discrimination: Racial Inequality in the U.S. Labour Market*, Wesleyan University Press, Middletown, Connecticut.

Deshi, A.K. and H. Singh (1995), 'Education, Labour Market Distortions and Relative Earning of Different Religious-Caste Categories in India', *Canadian Journal of Development Studies*, 21 December.

Haan, Arjan (1997), 'Poverty and Social Exclusion: A Comparison of Debates on Deprivation', Working Paper No. 2, Poverty Research Unit, Sussex University, Brighton.

Holzer, Harry and David Neumark (August 1999), 'Assessing Affirmative Action', NBER Working Paper, No. 7323.

Human Rights Watch (2001), Dalit Human Right Monitor, Sakshi, Hyderabad.

Jomo, K.S. (2003), *Ethnic Discrimination: A Critical Survey of Economic Explanations*, Department of Applied Economics, University of Malaya, Kuala Lumpur, Malaysia.

Khan, Mumtaz Ali (1995), *Human Rights and the Dalits*, Uppal Publishers, Delhi.

Lal, Deepak (1984), *Hindu Equilibrium, Vol. 1: Cultural Stability and Economic Stagnation*, Clarendon Press, Oxford.

Myers, Jr. Samuel L. (ed.) (1997), *Civil Rights and Race Relations in the Post Reagan-Bush Era*, Praeger, London.

National Crime Records Bureau, Crime in India (1999, 2000 and 2001), Ministry of Home Affairs, Government of India, New Delhi.

National Sample Survey Report on Employment and Unemployment Situation among Social Groups in India, 38th, 50th and 55th Rounds, Ministry of Statistics and Programme Implementation, Government of India.

National Sample Survey Report on Land and Livestock Holding Survey, 37th and 48th Rounds, Ministry of Statistics and Programme Implementation, Government of India.

National Sample Survey Reports on Differences in Level of Consumption among Socio-Economic Groups, 38th, 50th and 55th Rounds, Ministry of Statistics and Programme Implementation, Government of India.

Nayak, Vijay and Shailaja Prasad (1984), 'On Levels of Living of Scheduled Castes and Scheduled Tribes', *Economic and Political Weekly*, Vol. 19, No. 30.

National Commission for Scheduled Castes and Scheduled Tribes, Government of India (2003), Sixth Report 1999–2000 and 2000–2001, Delhi.

Radhakrishnan, P. (2002), 'Sensitizing Officials on Dalits and Reservations', *Economic and Political Weekly*, 16 February.

Sen, A. (2000), 'Social Exclusion: Concept, Application and Scrutiny', Asian Development Bank Working Paper.

Scoville, James G.L. (1996), 'Labour Market Underpinnings of a Caste Economy: Failing the Caste Theorem', *The American Journal of Economics and Sociology*, Vol. 55, No. 4, October.

Shah, Ghanshyam (1998), 'Caste and Untouchability: Theory and Practice', Paper presented at the Seminar on 'Ambedkar in Retrospect', Jawaharlal Nehru University, Delhi.

Silver, Hilary (2007), 'Social Exclusion: Comparative Analysis of Europe and Middle East Youth', Middle East Youth Initiative Working Paper, September, p. 15.

Thorat, Sukhadeo (1999), 'Social Security in Unorganized Sector in India: How Secure are the Scheduled Castes?', *Indian Journal of Labour Economics*, Special Issue, September.

——. (2000), 'Caste, Untouchability and Economic and Market Discrimination: Theory, Concept and Consequences', *Artha Vigyan: Journal of Gokhale Institute of Politics and Economics*, Vol. XLIII, Nos 1–2.

——. (2001), 'Ambedkar on Economics of Hindu Social Order: Understanding its Orthodoxy and Legacy', in Walter Fernandes (ed.), *The Emerging Dalit Identity*, Indian Social Institute, Delhi.

——. (2002), 'Oppression and Denial: Dalit Discrimination in 1990s', *Economic and Political Weekly*, February.

——. (2003), 'Caste, Ethnicity and Religion: An Overview Paper on Exclusion/Discrimination and Deprivation', Concept Paper for DFID, Delhi, 3 May.

——. (2004), 'Caste, Exclusion/Discrimination and Deprivation: The Situation of Dalits in India', Concept Paper for DFID, Delhi, 28 May.

——. (2004a), 'Isolation and Deprivations: Economic Situation of Tribals in India', in Sukhadeo Thorat (ed.), *Development Issue in India*, Department of Economics, Dr Babasaheb Marathwada University, Aurangabad, Maharashtra.

——. (2004b), 'Persistence of Poverty: Why Do Scheduled Castes and Scheduled Tribes Stay Chronically Poor?', Paper presented in the Seminar on 'Chronic Poverty in India', IIPA, Delhi and Research Centre for Chronic Studies, London.

——. (2004c), 'On Reservation Policy for Private Sector', *Economic and Political Weekly*, Vol. XXXIX, No. 25, 19 June.

——. (2004d), 'Remedies against Economic Discrimination: International Experience of Reservation Policy in Private Sector', in Bibek Debroy and Shyam Babu (eds), *The Dalit Question: Reforms and Social Justice*, Globus, Delhi.

Thorat, Sukhadeo and S. Venkatesan (2004), *Caste Conflict, Poverty and Human Development in India*, Indian Institute of Dalit Studies, New Delhi.

Thorat, Sukhadeo and R.S. Deshpande (1999), 'Caste and Labour Market Discrimination', *Indian Journal of Labour Economics*, Conference Issue, November.

Thurow, Lester C. (1969), *Poverty and Discrimination*, The Brookings Institution, Washington, DC.

Tripathy, R.B. (1994), *Dalits: A Sub-Human Society*, Ashish Publishing House, Delhi.

UNDP (2000), *Human Development Report 2000*, New York.

——. (2004), *Human Development Report 2004: Cultural Liberty in Today's Diverse World*, New York.

Venkateswarlu, D. (1990), *Harijan: Upper Class Conflict*, Discovery, Delhi.

Zoninsein, Jonas (2001), 'GDP Gains and Long-Term Discrimination against Blacks: The Inverse Relationship', in Charles V. Hamilton et al. (eds), *Beyond Racism: Race and Inequality in Brazil, South Africa and the United States*, Lynne Rienner, Boulder, Co.

5 Problems of Agricultural Marketing of Weaker Section in Maharashtra

Vilas Adhav

Maharashtra has developed as the most progressive industrial state of India. Today, 16 to 17 per cent of the total industrial production originates from Maharashtra. Nevertheless, the fact is that in the process of industrialization agriculture is neglected, but cannot be overlooked. Since 1960, when the State was formed, 42 per cent of the Gross State Domestic Product (GSDP) came from agriculture. Today, the share has gone down to 17–18 per cent. As a consequence, in spite of the second highest per capita income (Punjab being the first), the extent of rural poverty is quite intensive in Maharashtra, almost comparable with Bihar and Orissa (now Odisha). Approximately, 60–65 per cent of the population is dependent on agriculture, whereas agriculture contributes only 18 per cent to the total production in the State. This points out to a higher extent of rural poverty under the surface of prosperity

In Maharashtra, about 37 per cent of the farmers of weaker section are totally landless, 30 per cent own less than one hectare of cultivated land and 11.5 per cent of the families have one to one and half hectare of land. Only 2 per cent of the farmers own more than two and half hectare of land. In short, 67 per cent of the families are landless or own less than one hectare of land. Since the size of the land is small these farmers cannot produce enough surplus for market consumption. This also affects the total production. Therefore, 69 per cent of the families depend on wage labour for sustenance.

Poverty and educational backwardness of SCs has increased the seriousness of their social and economic backwardness. The poverty trap of these weaker sections not only exists but is perpetuated today. Dr Ambedkar had analysed this problem in detail and suggested an alternative strategy. According to him, the origin of poverty amongst the weaker section lies in the economic order based on capitalism, i.e. on private property and individual interests. This order ultimately leads to problems created by exploitation and inequality of the alternative of socialism. He insisted that agriculture, insurance and all important enterprises could be covered under public sector and this transformation should be achieved through a democratic process. Dr Ambedkar's Constitutional Socialism is based on the principle of equality of income, opportunities and just distribution. The main issue is to define and evolve various ways of just distribution. The policies must recognize the importance of providing agricultural capital and just opportunities for earning income by the weaker sections. It is necessary to implement policies based on Dr Ambedkar's views covering issues like reservations for weaker sections in economic planning, increased participation of the State in economic and social sector, thrust on public enterprises, policies for enhanced employment opportunities in public services, optimum wages and reservations as protection against social and economic discrimination. The sad irony of development over the last five decades is that, untouchability and economic discrimination in public and private sectors still persist even though, not sporadically but significantly.

Dr Ambedkar had defined 'deprived castes' in terms of 'Scheduled Castes'. We have also concentrated on this category as a weaker section. This focus is obvious. These caste groups were discriminated by the feudal forces in terms of land labour as well as commodity-based markets. They never had access to land on the basis of production and market. This section of cultivators is pushed into the labour market due to limited yielding capacity of the land and thus is also made to confront the unequal wage order. It is, therefore, essential to examine the existence of discrimination against 'Scheduled Castes' as far as agricultural production and marketing at this stage of liberalization is concerned. Earlier studies on this issue have concentrated on the distinct position of this category in terms of social order and labour market discrimination. Studies examining the availability of markets, therefore, should consider this section as a category of analysis.

The main cause of the social and economic backwardness of the farmers in weaker sections is their seclusion from the mainstream growth through upper caste-based customs and traditions, occupational hierarchy based on the *Varna* and caste system. These traditions and institutes forced them into low skilled manual occupations and perpetuated them into that. This also accounts for their social and economic backwardness. Additionally, bonded labour and disparity in wages, lower living standards and increasing population are some of the discriminating socio-economic factors affecting them adversely. All these issues are reviewed here. Review of research on marketing problems among weaker sections by scholars, economists and thinkers points out that the root cause of discrimination and inequality are equally economic in nature as well as social. The discrimination in the system mentioned above is relatively neglected. This study takes into account shortage of research related to the factors such as input market, product market, labour market, etc.

Agricultural Marketing System and Structure in Maharashtra

Except for Mumbai, the rest of Maharashtra is agriculture based and experience of five decades shows that changes in agriculture do affect the socio-economic and political life of the State in a decisive manner. It is important to design an effective long-term system for the marketing of agricultural produce. The role and participation of farmers from weaker sections in this system, lack of State organized facilities for their marketing convenience etc. are some important issues that have remained neglected till today.

Inadequacy of Infrastructure

1. Regulated markets are the central point of the marketing system. But, the employees and officials of the Market Committees are not fully aware of their roles and responsibilities. There is a dearth of trained expert staff. The devil takes the hindmost; therefore farmers belonging to weaker sections remain at the receiving end.

2. Statistical data are not easily available and those which are available are ill maintained.
3. Media does not provide information related to adequate marketing. This affects right decision about marketing.
4. Experience and research shows that the disciplined machinery for sale and purchase of agriculture produce has not helped the farmers of weaker section.
5. In many places auction is not conducted; there are flaws in accounts, delay in payments and traders do not pay to the farmers in time. All this affects the farmers of the weaker sections more adversely.
6. Marketing Committees are dominated by traders and the State machinery is not sufficiently powerful to control the function of Market Committees.
7. It is necessary to commercialize the functioning of Market Committees.
8. Personnel like Chairman, Vice-Chairman, Secretary etc. hardly have any technical training in things like marketing laws, accounting, etc. It is important to define certain eligibility standards for them or train them properly. It is also important to train the other staff as well. The training facilities are extremely insufficient in comparison to their need. The large campus of any regulated market is busy in huge economic dealings and transactions. They are the backbone of agricultural marketing system; with this in mind sincere efforts must be taken up for their overall improvement.

The co-operative marketing agencies in Maharashtra have fallen behind mainly because they could not reach the farmers of weaker sections. In other words, the farmers from weaker sections lost their faith in these institutions due to blunt discrimination. Normally, they use these co-operatives only to borrow and then to repay the loans for agriculture. Major part of their farm produce is thus sold through traders/middlemen *(adtyas)*.

Unfortunately, marketing co-operatives have not contributed in their might in helping the weaker section farmers in the marketing process.

1. Due to indebtedness the farmers from weaker sections are forced to sell their produce within their village to local landlords and moneylenders.

2. A variety of middlemen such as traders, moneylenders, *adatya*, (wholesale traders) etc. exist in this marketing system. These middlemen are directly responsible for the exploitation of farmers. At times, even the big farmers emerge as middlemen.
3. Due to lack of means of transport on a cheap and adequate basis, the importance of these middlemen has increased.
4. Lack of storage facilities force the farmers to sell their product as early as possible. This leads to a greater supply into the market, since the farmers from weaker sections do not have adequate storage facilities, they cannot wait until they get a good price. Finally, they have to bear the loss.
5. Lack of facilities of standardization of the product where allowance is made far less than FAQ (Fair Average Quality). In Maharashtra, basic and fixed standard for categorizing the produce qualitatively does not exist. Facilities of presale rank grading are not available in every market. Farmers belonging to weaker sections suffer major loss because all the produce which is qualitatively different gets the same price.
6. Lack of standardization of weights and scales, taking advantages of illiteracy among farmers, the middlemen have deceived them for years together and have used faulty weights and scales. In rural areas the precision in measurement is still lacking.
7. Malpractices in the market also rampantly discriminate the weaker sections. Certain amount is taken as a charge of the middlemen's service, porters increase their rates, donations are collected forcefully from the farmers of weaker sections. Sometimes, it takes a form of extortion since the donations are no way related to the farmer's produce brought for sale.

Agriculture in Maharashtra: A Review

Even being one of the rich states of the country (in terms of per capita income) Maharashtra faces a number of problems in agricultural sector, such as low irrigation facilities, low productivity, slow progress in watershed development. It is surprising that though 17 per cent of the total irrigation budget is spent on irrigation in Maharashtra and yet only 16 per cent of total cultivated area is irrigated. In spite of scarcity of water in the state, two-thirds of the irrigated water is consumed for sugarcane alone which is largely grown by farmers from non-weaker groups. It is interesting to note that only 2.6 per cent of the total cultivated area produces sugarcane. On one hand, there is a dire need for irrigation in some regions; canals on the other hand are in about 13 districts where there is excessive use of water because 80 per cent of the irrigation need is met from the underground water. One of the preconditions for consistent growth and development of agriculture is the growth in level of investment in agriculture. In Maharashtra the growth in investment has drastically declined from 30.87 per cent (percentage of total investment) in the Third Five-Year Plan (1961–66) to 4.98 per cent in the Ninth Five-Year Plan (1997–2000).

In order to solve the problems of farmers, greater attention is needed to the development of irrigation. Some of the important points are as follows:

1. Increase public expenditure on agriculture and agro-based industries.
2. Priority should be given to complete all the pending irrigation projects.
3. Avoid excessive use of water in water scarcity areas.
4. Increase efficiency in using water through micro-irrigation development.
5. Minimum 50 per cent of the sugarcane cultivation should be covered under micro-irrigation projects.
6. Encourage cultivation of other high value crops.

The main reason behind slow growth of agriculture in Maharashtra is the slow growth in development of irrigation and watershed development. The state government must increase its public investment with a view to completing pending works. It has to stop sanctioning new projects and must implement the cropping pattern strictly in the irrigated areas. It also has to control the water supply to sugarcane from irrigation canals. All this is important to avoid excessive use of water. Watershed development can be taken up in the regions where rainfed agriculture predominates.

Reviewing the ten plans implemented by Maharashtra State one can note that in the first five plans not a single scheme was undertaken in agricultural development for weaker section farmers. Only during the Sixth Five-Year Plan a scheme was designed to raise the economic level of the weaker sections. In the Tenth Five-Year Plan as well, the agricultural development programme has been designed. But how much useful this scheme was? It cannot be judged confidently due to lack of reliable statistical data about land possession and cultivation by farmers of weaker section. The successful implementation of such schemes will depend more on the efficiency and positive attitude of the administrators. Success can be measured only in terms of actual support given to farmers of weaker sections, but our study noted otherwise.

Entry of Weaker Sections into the Market

The weaker sections own small patches of land. Their size of holding is quite small and, therefore, their access to provision of fertilizers and seeds is limited. This leads to lower productivity and hence lower capital returns. Therefore, they have to work as farm labourers, even at the cost of exploitation in terms of wages. Other farmers get concessions in this process and the farmers from weaker sections are forced to work on less wages, almost like bonded labourers. Discrimination is also evident in terms of division of work. Labourers from other castes are assigned lighter work as well as flexi-time while the weaker sections have to put in long hours of labourious work. Thus, the farmers belonging to the weaker section have to face hardships in the land-production market as well as in the labour market.

The farmers belonging to weaker sections bring small quantities of products in the commercial market, consequently they are heckled and used by the trader. These farmers do not frequent the commercial market and prefer to sell at the farm gate. They come to the market when they are on the brink of an economic crisis. Thus, they do not enjoy the benefits of networking and get low return for the products. Caste factor acts as an important factor in such unfair dealings and trading. If they protest, the traders' unions functioning in the markets ban them. They cannot even take back the products after being offered an unfair price, because they cannot afford to pay for the transportation back home. In fact, while confronting all these factors, the farmers from the weaker section are just passive participants of trading in the market, nor are they empowered to emphasize on getting a fair share in the market.

They are discriminated for their social and economic backwardness and have to face the arrogance, insults, neglect, hatred and exploitation at the hands of rich traders, and have no place in the trading market.

The actual contact between customer and trader is crucial for the existence of the market. The markets are divided into three major groups according to the number of traders.

1. Perfect Competition
2. Monopolistic Competition
3. Imperfect Competition.

This has been taken for granted in the text books. The entry in the market is not really meant for weaker sections. Their participation lessens a theoretical representation of this as attempted.

Market, Market Conditions and Weaker Sections

In Search of Theoretical Scaffolding

When the profit reaches its peak in a competitive market, the established business heads obstruct the entry of new entrepreneurs in the market. A similar strategy is adopted by the established traders, the middlemen through organized trade organizations against the weaker sections try to gain an entry in the market. The characteristics of imperfect competition of oligopoly market apply to the trading market in context of farmers of weaker sections. The established traders not only create barriers to entry for the weaker sections in the market, they actually try to prohibit their entry through various means. Another feature of the monopolistic competition is product differentiation. This is used to give secondary status to the produce of the weaker sections; which is actually of a superior quality. A deliberate distinction is exercised when the actual produce reaches the trader's shop; various deficient factors are 'invented' to give the weaker sections a lower price for their produce.

The productivity on the lands of weaker sections is in a lower quantity hence the very idea of 'relative profit' or 'increase' is impossible and unattainable for them. In addition to this the established traders in the market have their own nexus.

Figure 1 shows two curves denoting the cost/revenue for weaker sections and others. The vertical distance between the

Figure 1 *Cost/Revenue for Weaker Sections and Others*

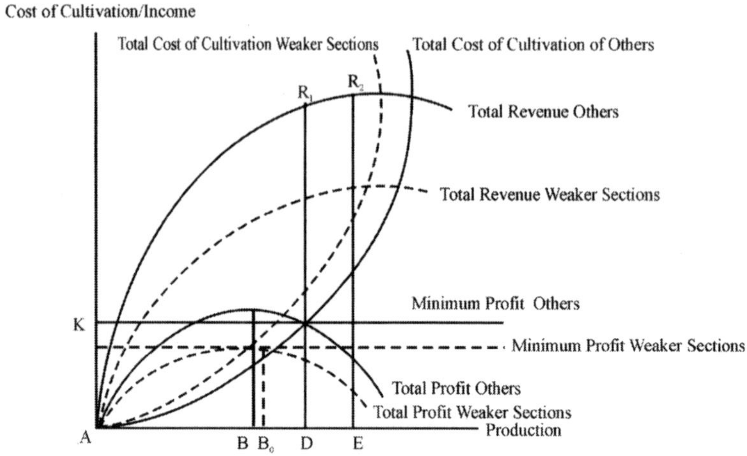

curves of Total Revenue C (T R) and T R weaker sections denotes the profit. The figure shows that the others are endorsed with more profits as compared with that of the weaker sections. On the other hand the weaker sections incur higher cost for land cultivation. The farmers from the weaker section have to incur more cost, as compared with others, for their produce. In spite of spending more, they receive lower profit than others. The analysis explains the dynamics of more expenditure and less profit for weaker sections vis-a-vis others. If the total expenditure and total income of weaker sections is compared with that of others, it is observed that the others get more income by spending less while the weaker sections spend more and earn less. This means that the farmers from the weaker section have to face discrimination in the labour market as well as trading market. The organized sector of established traders get higher net profits and safeguard the interests of each other while the weaker sections get continuously exploited economically. This is quite clear from the Figure 1 above. Due to the principle of retailers, similarly, the farmers from weaker sections never get a secure profit. The strong chain of agents (middle men), traders and others prevent the farmers from getting an access to profit. It is impossible for them to get even the minimum profit, leave alone increased profit as their production capability itself is hampered.

Micro-Level Analysis

Concession and special schemes/facilities were provided to the farmers of the weaker section in post-Independence period. But these facilities were not really planned keeping in view the needs of the section. Age-old traditions and caste hierarchies were certain obstacles in their gaining access to these facilities/schemes. The caste system fixed their low earning occupation and it was a taboo to defy these limitations. So they remained within the confines of the occupations demarcated for them. Apart from this, even today the majority of weaker sections reside in the rural areas which makes it difficult for them to develop skills and means for their progress and development. The skill development in farming is no exception.

Table 1 *Productivity (Per Hectare)*

	Jawar Qnt. Kg	*Wheat Qnt. Kg*	*Bajra Qnt. Kg*	*Hulga Qnt. Kg*	*Maize Qnt. Kg*	*Tur Qnt. Kg*
SC/Weaker Sections	15.54	15.61	11.05	7.00	13.00	6.20
Other	16.40	18.80	13.40	5.50	16.00	5.75
	Matki Qnt. kg	*Gram Qnt. kg*	*Groundnut Qnt. kg*	*Sunflower Qnt. kg*	*Onion Qnt. kg*	*Sugarcane Qnt. kg*
SC/Weaker Sections	6.00	6.75	16.00	7.00	142.00	750.00
Other	5.50	6.75	15.50	7.50	150.00	890.00

Source: Field Survey Data.

The farmers of the weaker section cannot play an effective role in the product market due to their social and economic backwardness. Added to this, they have less capability in terms of investments. They also confront discrimination in land market, due to the discriminatory practices by the landlords. Most of them are forced into the labour market and face exploitation over there. Finally, farmers from the weaker section face discrimination in labour market, land market as well as product market. This has been examined with micro-level analysis.

The micro-level analysis was carried out on the data collected from the area through a detailed survey studies. The production and expenditure pattern of the farmers of the weaker section was collected and analysed. It was seen that factors like small land size, poor irrigation facilities, increased labour wages and rising costs of fertilizers act adversely on these farmer's production process (see Tables 1 and 2). The only crops taken to the market in small quantities are jawar, bajra, wheat, etc. Other crops, vegetables or fruits are not produced and hence are not sold by them. The farmers from the weaker section are forced to sell their product at a lower rate as they are in urgent need of money and due to increased cost, later on are forced to buy the same product at a higher rate, when they require it. This fact also came to light in the survey study.

Table 2 *Cost of Production (Per Hectare)*

	Jawar	*Wheat*	*Bajra*	*Hulga*	*Maize*	*Tur*
SC	7,261	5,610	5,396	3,666	7,375	8,734
Others	7,530	6,430	5,740	2,880	8,077	8,000
	Matki	*Gram*	*Groundnut*	*Sunflower*	*Onion*	*Sugarcane*
SC	4,404	5,651	11,393	7,958	27,205	11,278
Others	4,037	5,460	10,890	8,126	28,738	13,383

Source: Field Survey Data.

The field produce of the farmers from weaker sections was scanty. Some of it is kept for family consumption, thus further cutting down the quantity that can be taken to the market. The market proceeds are used for weekly expenditure of the family. Many of these farmers sell their produce to the local retail/shop instead of going in for wholesale market, as they are in urgent need for ready cash. Thus, they end up as infrequent sellers in the wholesale market due to which they get lower prices than the others (see Table 3). The farmers coming to the market are in a hurry to sell their produce. There are many reasons for this – they have invested for the crop, they have to repay the loans taken from banks and co-operative societies. In addition to this the money is also needed for the next crop. If the loan is not repaid on time, they do not get loans in the next season. Thus, major weakness of these farmers is 'need'. They have to sell their produce at minimal rates to repay the loans taken from the local moneylender, friends, relatives, banks, cooperative societies or the local shopkeeper. They have no other option. They come in contact with the market only in time of need or trouble. Similarly, these farmers have to face many adverse situations like the scanty quantities of crops available for sale, lack of continuity in trading, lack of storage facilities, the escalating transport costs in addition to the ever-present caste factor that puts them at the bottom rung.

Table 3 *Market and Market Access*

	Total Marketed Surplus		*Price Received per Kg*			
	Total Value in ₹		*Jawar*		*Wheat*	
	SC	*Other*	*SC*	*Others*	*SC*	*Other*
I	10,891	12,584	760	906	600	608
II	13,255	15,315	566	585	634	684
III	20,339	23,500	650	712	750	799
IV	45,415	52,474	649	701	675	688
All	89,900	1,02,873	2,625	2,904	2,659	2,779
Avg.	(22,475)	(25,718)	(656)	(726)	(665)	(695)

Source: Field Survey Data.

The farmers from the weaker section often own bad quality land. There is also a dearth of essential infrastructure and even the capital for investments. They find it difficult to plough and cultivate the fields on time as they do not have their own implements. By the time they manage to get hold of this, the lands lose its moisture. This work is adverse for higher productivity. The land is to be furrowed at least (half to one and a quarter ft deep) for good harvest. But these farmers cannot go so deep. These farmers have no access to better and modified techniques of farming. They chiefly grow Jawar and Bajara in their fields. The productivity is low due to many factors including lack of proper and timely cultivation, cow dung manure, fertilizers, pesticides, etc. They are further handicapped by lack of timely availability of enough water supplies. Sometimes, they are also forced to carry out the cultivation of dry land. On the other hand, other rich farmers manage to get more water supplies for their cash crops like sugarcane. This also leads to drying up of the water source, and the crop of the poor farmers fail which results in lower marketable surplus.

Table 4 *Net Income (Per Hectare)*

Size Class	*SC*	*Others*
I	7,279	9,702
II	6,282	6,568
III	7,573	7,918
IV	7,742	8,095
Total	30,876	32,283
Average	(7,719)	(8,071)

Source: Field Survey Data.

The farmers of the weaker sections are thus forced to work on the fields of rich farmers (see Table 4). Sometimes they are also forced to work as bonded labourers. They do not get strong support from banks, funding agencies or cooperative societies, as they are often unable to repay the loans on time. They also find it difficult to offer guarantee for such loans.

In totality, the fragile economic condition of these poor farmers prohibits them from buying good fertilizers, seeds, patricides, etc. from the input market.

Important Findings from the Study on Agricultural Marketing of Weaker Sections

1. When the farmers from the weaker section bring their product to the market, the market price is decided by the licensed traders who are normally from *Marwari*, *Gujar* or *Maratha* community.
2. There is no coordination between the farmers from weaker section and Market Committee representatives. These farmers are supposed to be protected by the rules of the Maharashtra State Agricultural Produce Market Committee (APMC), but it is not so in actual practice. The traders and agents coerce the committee members to take advantage of the market price.
3. The farmers fetch a good price if other wholesale traders come from other cities and towns. Otherwise, the local and retail

traders decide the market price. The nexus between the licensed traders, agents and merchants results in profits for them and loss for the poor farmers.

4. Agri-Produce Market Committees were set up at taluka level in 1963 in accordance with the Maharashtra State Agro-Produce Market Act. But basic tenets of this Act are rarely implemented. The merchants and retailers have unions in the market yard and the farmers lose out on being protected by law as they are not organized as a body. The Taluka Market Committee limits itself to the agents, license fee and market operations. Thus, it does not really work for the benefit of the farmers which was actually the aim behind its formation.
5. After discussions with many farmers, the opinion that emerged was, that open market system should be implemented in its full vigour so as to get the best market price for the produce.
6. Many farmers also opined that as there was no change in cropping pattern, the same crops were produced in greater quantity, and in the face of lower market price they earn less.
7. The farmers were not explained the exact method of auction and they do not have a say in that matter. Even if the produce is of good quality, the market price is decided by the agents and traders with their judgment on quality. Further, only a small advance is given to the farmers for their contingencies. Many farmers keep their produce in the market and go for their other errands. Thus, they have no idea of weighing, auction, etc. The produce is sieved and around 20 kg of grains per quintal go waste. The farmers are paid only the next day after 5 per cent reduction per quintal as deduced for *other expenses*.
8. *Empty gunny bags/sacks*: The farmers buy gunny bags at ₹ 20 per piece but after it is emptied of the grain in the market, it is bought by agents or merchants for ₹ 10–14. Thus, the farmers have to suffer a loss of around ₹ 6 for each gunny bag. Similarly, the bags for carrying onions are purchased for ₹ 8 but after the sales, are bought by merchants at only ₹ 1–2, thus, the farmer incurs a loss of ₹ 5 per bag.
9. The weighing, quality-segregation, cost of produce – these things are not necessarily done in front of the farmers and thus

lack total transparency. The auction method exploits these farmers further. Many farmers were not in favour of this method. They also feel that the Government nominated representatives should be present for the auction so that the proceeding would be carried out in a fair manner. Another fact, worth noting, is when the crop is taken out for sampling; around 0.5 to 1 kg of the crop is wasted.

10. The farmers from weaker sections take around 2 to 5 quintal crop like *jawar, bajara, wheat* for sale to the taluka market. While making entries, the representative of Market Committee, is favourable to upper caste farmers from *Marwari, Maratha, Gujar, Mali* and *Dhangar* communities. The employees, merchants and agents of the Market Committee safeguard the interests of these upper caste communities. They get a fair price as compared to those of the farmers from weaker sections. The farmers from weaker sections are given ₹ 400–500 per quintal for *jawar, bajara,* while the upper caste-middle caste farmers get around ₹ 500–700 per qtl.
11. *Self-Marketing*: Some farmers try to sell their produce at the local level instead of going to taluka market. But the other merchants who purchase the produce at a higher price from taluka place pressurise the farmers to fix the rates in accordance with their dictates. Thus, the farmers do not really have freedom for self marketing.
12. *Wholesale Auction Marketing*: The common customer is not really aware of the daily changes in the prices of crop. The merchants take undue advantage of this fact and sell the produce at higher price even if the prices go down the next day. For example: On a given day, if 'X' crop is ₹ 20 and drops down to ₹ 8 per 1 kilo the next day, if the customer is unaware of the latest conditions of the market, the merchant sells it for ₹ 20 even the next day. Often, the date is not written on the card given by the merchant to the traders. The produce of poor farmers is categorized into lower grade in spite of its good quality. While some farmers use their influence to get their poor quality crop rated in grade one.
13. A few important observations come out from the survey.

(i) In the Taluka Agri-Produce Market, the taluka trade unions farmers, licensed agents, societies have a lot of caste clout and they are unfair while grading the produce of the farmers from the weaker section. The surnames of these farmers are used as markers for this discrimination.

(ii) The Market Committee safeguards the interest of farmers of upper caste. The merchants and agents exploit the poor farmers while fixing the price of the produce.

(iii) The poor farmers do not enjoy any decision-making position in the market; in fact, their participation is very low.

(iv) There is only one person from the weaker section working as commission agent in Phaltan taluka; others work as retail vegetable sellers.

(v) The poor farmers have to invest money which is recovered only after the produce is sold in the market. This entails a long period of waiting for three months (in case of *bajara)*. On the other hand, the traders buy and sell the crop immediately and thus benefit immediately through the Commission. Thus, in this entire process the poor farmer is exploited, becomes poorer and the agents and traders become richer.

The farmers from weaker sections need money for the cultivation, the harvest, seeds, patricides, etc. Since the technicalities of banks and co-operative societies can be time consuming they have to approach the local moneylender or the rich farmers. But this comes at a higher price, that is, higher, interest rates. In spite of this, the produce of their fields is inferior in quality in comparison with cash-rich farmers. Thus they get profit. This was clearly observed in a survey study carried out, comparing the expenditure-production pattern of Jawar-Bajara crop among the farmers from the weaker section and other farmers. The input was compared with the income and it was seen that farmers from weaker sections have to incur more cost on inputs and still get less income due to market-discrimination. On the basis of micro-level analysis it can be safely said that the farmers from weaker sections have to face discrimination in product market, labour market and Input market. The analytical study of the problems of farmers from weaker sections shows that the factors responsible for their economic and social backwardness are local co-operative banks, various Managing Committees, Agricultural Produce Market Committee from the institutional area and moneylenders, agents, traders who were from the non-institutional category. The social location of these farmers is also responsible for their backwardness. The institutional and non-institutional factors combined with social hierarchical discrimination have been responsible for the weaker position of these farmers. This comes out clearly in the study of farmers from weaker sections. These farmers earn negligible value in the commercial trading markets due to their presence. There are chiefly three markets available to them, namely land markets, production market and labour market. The farmers from weaker sections have to face discriminatory treatment in all these three markets.

Recommendations

The economical problems of farmers from the weaker section were located through a detailed survey and analysed for the policy purpose. These farmers face discriminations in unproductive market, input market and labour market. Their economical weakness perpetuates their discrimination in the social sphere. Some recommendations could be made as solutions to elevate their economical and social status, but we are sure that these may be difficult to be taken on the agenda.

1. It is difficult for the weaker farmers to control the market prices but they can keep their cost at the minimum for each of the crop and review it frequently. They can use various ways to cut down the expenses, and these ways can become clear on analysing the use of machines, inputs and labour force. In short, produce can be obtained at relatively lower costs. Alternatively, inputs could be supplied at concessional prices to the cultivators from weaker sections. This will bring down the loss factors, even at discriminated market prices.
2. The farmers from weaker sections don't change their cropping pattern and end up by producing the same crop over and again, thus lowering the returns. Instead of this, they should study the market pattern for various crops and accordingly

cultivate them by rotation. But incentives to grow cash crop with up-to-date technology may help them to increase net income.

3. There is a long chain of agents/middlemen between the farmer of the weaker section and the customer. Many a time through this chain, money is recovered from farmers of weaker sections by unfair means. The Agro-produce markets should devise a concrete action plan which would weaken this chain. Changes should be implemented which would focus on strengthening the economical position of these farmers of the weaker section.
4. If training programmes or guidance programmes are arranged for the farmers from weaker sections it would result in quality consciousness and awareness in them. Multi-service centres could be set up to train and aid them in selecting the crops, grading, division, branding, labelling, packing, etc. A two-way communication could be established between these service centres and the farmers. These centres can also provide extension services. This kind of system needs to be developed.
5. Instead of retail selling in rural areas, the farmers should form a common platform and bring their produce to the cities collectively. This would bring them more profits and lessen the expenses. If State Government implements information-extension services, it would inspire and encourage these farmers and thcy would bc benefitted.

Agricultural Products Guarantee – Surety Scheme

When the production increases and reaches the market in large quantities, the price crashes. The farmers of weaker section cannot take the product back and have to sell it at the then prevailing price. The Market Committee can run product-guarantee scheme at such time. They can keep this produce in the warehouse and can give 70 per cent of the current market rate to them. This can meet their urgent need and they can sell the product later on, thus fetching a profit. This scheme is implemented in some Market Committees of Vidarbha for selected crops. It should be implemented in all market committees for all agricultural produce, taking care to protect them against wastage due to pests and pilferage.

The farmers from weaker sections from rural areas do not approach the market due to their scanty product. The small traders buy their crop and sell it collectively, thus reaping profits for them. The Market Committee can appoint some educated unemployed youths in each village on commission basis. This will lead to a threefold advantage: i) Employment for youth, ii) fair price to the farmers and iii) increased income for market committee.

The idea behind this is since it is impractical to create a permanent post in each village of market surveillance officer; the Market Committee should authorize one unemployed educated youth in each village, and give him commission for procuring the produce on behalf of Market Committee. He could be informed of the daily market prices by telephone. The smaller farmers of the village can contact this authorized person for sale and also other allied market information. The Market Committee can make transportation arrangements periodically to get this produce to the main market.

Broadcasting the Market News

The middlemen are major obstacles in providing the farmer with appropriate market price for his product. The main strength of these agents and middlemen is the current market information which they access through telephone and other means. They are constantly in touch with other agents and traders and get high profits. If the market committee is able to broadcast its daily rates to the farmers they can also benefit from this. Computers have reached almost all the market committees through the programmes of Centre and State governments. Internet facilities are also available at Taluka level. This can be used to build a hi-tech system of information and communication.

Many a times, the produce is not graded. If the Indian farmer wants to find and maintain his place in the age of globalization, then the gradation of produce is mandatory. This will help the customer to buy good quality stuff and also the farmer to get a good market price. The farmers should be encouraged and helped in this direction too.

References

Adhav, Vilas (2005), 'Maharashtratil Durbal Ghatakatil Shetkaryanchya Shetmal Vipanan Samsyancha Abhyas' (Problems of Agricultural Marketing of Weaker Sections in Maharashtra), unpublished Ph.D. Thesis, University of Pune.

Asian Productivity Organisation (APO) (1989), *Marketing Systems for Farm Products in Asia and the Pacific*, Tokyo.

Nadkarni, M.V. (1980), *Marketable Surplus and Market Dependence in a Millet Region*, Allied Publishers, New Delhi.

Narain, Dharam (1961), *Distribution of Marketed Surplus of Agricultural Produce by Size-Level of Holding in India, 1950–1951*, Asia Publishing House, New Delhi.

Patnaik, Utsa (1975), 'Contribution to the Output and Marketable Surplus of Agricultural Products by Cultivating Groups in India, 1960–61', *Economic and Political Weekly*, December.

Singh, S. (1993), 'Marketing Relevance of Guru Panel Report', *Financial Express*, 13 February.

Shroff, Sangeeta (1997), 'Efficiency of State Intervention in Cotton Marketing in India', *Indian Journal of Agricultural Economics*, Vol. 52, No. 2, April-June.

Subbarao, K. (1991), 'Agricultural Marketing', in M.L. Dantwala (ed.), *Indian Agricultural Development Since Independence*, Oxford and IBH Publishing House Co., New Delhi.

6 Evaluation of Some of the Important Government Schemes for Scheduled Tribes

A Special Reference to Education and Economic Empowerment in Maharashtra

Meherjyoti Sangle

Through the ages, the Scheduled Tribes have been exploited by the British policy; adaptation of forest lands and levying heavy revenues on their ancestral profession and forest production. Also throughout the ages, the Indian social system has been socio-culturally exploiting the Dalits. What are the supportive measures taken in independent India for Scheduled Tribes? What is the level of security provided to them by the Indian Constitution? This article evaluates the government policies, schemes and securities of the Scheduled Tribes in Maharashtra.

Multicultural Groups

The largest inhabitation of tribal people is in India. For many centuries, they have been living in remote areas such as forests, hills and mountains. Despite many problems like lack of transport and communications, way of life of tribes in the hills have made them strong, self-reliant and vigilant. In India, castes and tribes have lived in their peculiar way since the beginning. With the advance of time and interactions with other tribes, a confluence of various cultures of the other tribes has been brought about. They come in contact with respect to historical identities, their ethnic values, social, religious morals and economic factors.[1] It is a characteristic seen only in India that despite their social differences the tribes have an institutional and mystic form with a religious background.[2] There are various divisions in social groups in India such as tribe, caste, sect, clan, racial groups and class. Tribes or primitive communities are dominated by the state and Indian policy, and later they became a part of Hindu society.[3] A tribe is a collection of families or groups of families, bearing a common name, members of which occupy the same territory, same language, same profession or occupation, and observe similar socio-cultural values and religious taboos and/or traditions. They have unique and similar political unit that the tribal society follows as the only political organization, either it was headed by clan chiefs or tribal chiefs or by hereditary kings of the community. According to anthropologists, a tribe is a social group with territorial affiliation, endogamous, with no specialization of functions, ruled by tribal officers, hereditary or otherwise, united in language or dialect, recognizing social distance with other tribes or castes, without any social obloquy attaching to them, as it does in the castes structure and conscious of a homogeneity of ethnic and territorial integration.[4]

Transformation Process

Chatterjee says that the process of transformation from primitive communities to higher classes of society is a gradual and a slow process. Number of tribes have changed to higher castes, the process of incorporation of tribes into castes started much earlier since Aryan invasion into India.[5] Tribes gradually started getting assimilated and incorporated into the hierarchy of classes. Risley mentioned four processes through which tribes have assimilated into higher classes as Rajputs, Vaishnabs, and Ramayats. Majority of Koch inhabitants of Rungpore of North Bengal describe themselves as Rajbansis or Bhanga of Kshatriya. Bhumji of Western Bengal, a pure Dravidian race lost their original identity and the more advanced among them who employ Brahmans as family priest.[6] British policies added a number of divisions in society; in addition to this, it applied the 'divide and rule' policy.

British Policy

The entry of missionaries into the remote areas led them to administrating and looking after the tribes and their welfare. In the colonial period, British implemented a number of laws to administer forests and hilly regions but those laws collapsed the normal life of village and tribal communities and their economy. The programme of conservation and preservation of forests resulted in a progressive encroachment on their rights that they had enjoyed for centuries with respect to the use of fuel and timber, forest products and medicinal, herbal plants and hunting. Earlier, British did not understand the lives of the tribal people and hence they enforced many unsuitable policies on them. It was the tribal people who first revolted against the British much before 1857 revolt. In Bihar, Chota Nagpur a series of revolts took place in 1789, 1801, 1807 and 1808 which had to be put down with the help of armed forces. Tribals' lands were granted to retired soldiers at the foot of the hills, thus making a ring fence of loyal military men to encircle the tribals.

Koli (1831–32), Santhal Rebelion (1855, 1869 and 1870) were raised due to oppression of the moneylenders and rapacious landlords. Sardari Agitation (1887), Birsa Movement (1895), many series of revolts continued till the independence for the agitation of lands, forests, hereditary occupations, etc. Because of British policies, tribal people lost their identity and hereditary profession and occupation.

Hutton, who has done a deep study of the problems of tribal people, commented, '... Far from being of immediate benefit to the primitive tribes, the establishment of British Rule in India did most of them much more harm than good...that early days of British Administration did very great detriment to the economic position of tribes through ignorance and neglect of their rights and customs... many changes have been caused incidentally by the penetration of the tribal country, the opening up of communications, the protection of forests and establishments of schools, to say nothing of the openings given in this way to Christian Missions. Many of the results of these changes have caused acute discomfort to the tribes'.[7] S.C. Roy remarked that 'British system of law and administration has impaired the social solidarity of these tribes and weakened the authority of social heads or Panchayats ... and validating tribal customary laws regarding succession and inheritance were proclaimed, the courts often disregarded the customs against inheritance by daughters... ancient tribal custom against such alienation was utterly disregarded'.[8]

The effects were so adverse that G.S. Ghurye says that, 'the acuteness of discomfort was very often so great that it led to apathy indifference, moral deterioration and even a decline in population'.[9] Law and order divided the society by occupation. All Census Reports have mentioned a number of professions. Many tribes had migrated from their original places because British had levied huge revenue taxes on forest land and forest products which directly exploited the birthright of tribes in India. British policy had both weakened Indian social structure as well as strengthened it in some aspects; but they had totally lost the balance of the social system. It was a total disintegration of socio-economic exploitation that hampered its transformation from older social system into a modern social and industrial community.[10]

In 1937, after formation of the government with many Indians, committees were appointed in the provinces of Bihar, Orissa (now Odisha), Bombay (Mumbai), and Madras (Tamil Nadu) to enquire the condition of the tribals. New policy could not be adopted by the government due to Second World War. Most of them were illiterate and isolated. Tribals' rights for their lands, forests were encroached upon and exploited during the British period and handed over to non-tribals. State Committee was appointed in British India, for inquiring the educational, economical and social conditions of the 'Depressed Classes' and of Aborigine Tribes in the Bombay Presidency in 1930. The Committee found that it was very difficult to communicate with the tribals due to geographical difficulties and that was the reason that the problems of the tribals had not been brought to the public domain, in any definite form. Being a large group of illiterates they were not allocated seats in the Legislative Committee and hence, they were not entitled to vote in local committees. The first requirement was that they should get education, become members of Gram Panchayat, and free from social boycotts.[11] On 31 March 1939, D. Symington Committee[12] was appointed to study the conditions of the Bhil Community and other Aborigine and Hill

Tribes into Partially Excluded Areas and to recommend the measures for it, and emphasized on the educational development so that they could get opportunity to participate in the local bodies.

Independent India

Though the British rulers started a number of schemes but they intermingled with political interests and it did not change the life of the tribals or help their development. The independent India has, however, planned to empcwer Scheduled Castes and Scheduled Tribes. Number of Commissions and Committees were appointed to study groups of tribals that highlighted the enormity and complexity of the problem of the Tribal Development of India and recommended the necessity of the smooth integration of the tribals.[13]

Indian Constitution took up the responsibility for tribal welfare for which number of schemes were planned out and implemented. The framers of the Constitution took care to devise a suitable formula which would protect the economic interests of the tribals, safeguard their way of life and ensure their development. Article No. 46 of the Indian Constitution says that the State assures special care for education, social and economic interests of the weaker section of the people and in particular SCs and STs shall protect their social justice and all forms of exploitation. Article 275 emphasizes that grants-in-aid of the revenues of the State and Central Government will take care of it. Article 15, 16 and 19 made possible SCs and STs will consider special attention and get equality in all matters. State Government started these schemes from 1 April 1976. Special Central assistance was provided. The Tribal Sub-Plan (TSP) covers the Scheduled Areas.

Dalits

The word Dalit was popularized by the Dalit Panther Movement, when they adopted this term as an act of confident assertion, rejecting Mahatma Gandhi's nomenclature of *Harijan*, children of God. Dalit Panthers defined this word in their 1972 manifesto as: a member of Scheduled Castes and Tribes, neo-Buddhist, the working people, the landless and poor peasants, women, and all those who are being exploited politically, economically, and in the name of religion'.

Noted Dalit Litterateur Gangadhar Pantawane wrote: '*Dalit* is not a caste; Dalit is a symbol of change and revolution. The Dalit believes in humanism. He rejects existence of god, rebirth, and soul, sacred books that teach discrimination, fate, and heaven because these make him a slave.' While the informed Dalits tend to agree that the ancient beliefs of Hinduism (Brahmanism) are the root cause of their sufferings, most accept a narrower view of membership than the above definitions suggest. Both Dalit and non-Dalit Indians see the term relating only to the Scheduled Castes (the untouchables of the past) and the Scheduled Tribes (the Adivasis or the indigenous people of India).

Scheduled Tribes in India

According to the 2001 Census,[14] the total population of the Scheduled Tribes in India is 84,326,240 persons, constituting 8.2 per cent of the total population of the country. Around 91.7 per cent of them live in rural areas, whereas, only 8.3 per cent inhabit urban areas. The sex ratio of Scheduled Tribes population is 978 females per thousand males which is higher than that of the total population of the country, as well as that of Scheduled Castes.

Madhya Pradesh accounts for the highest percentage of Scheduled Tribes population to total STs population of the country (14.5%) followed by Maharashtra (10.2%), Odisha (9.7%), Gujarat (8.9%), Rajasthan (8.4%), Jharkhand (8.4%) and Chhattisgarh (7.8%). In fact, 68 per cent of the country's Scheduled Tribes population lives in these seven States. The proportion of the Scheduled Tribes to the total population of the States/Union territories is highest in Mizoram (94.5%) and Lakshadweep (94.5%) followed by Nagaland (89.1%) and Meghalaya (85.9%). Within the major states, Chhattisgarh (31.8%) has the highest percentage of Scheduled Tribes population followed by Jharkhand (26.3%) and Odisha (22.1%). These proportions are the lowest in Uttar Pradesh (0.1%), Bihar (0.9%), Tamil Nadu (1.0%) and Kerala (1.1%).[15]

Scheduled Tribes in Maharashtra

In Maharashtra, the population of Scheduled Tribes has increased (Table 1). In 1991, it was 78.937 lakhs and in 2001, the total population of Maharashtra was 968.79 lakhs out of which 85.77 lakhs (8.9%) were Scheduled Tribes (STs). There are 47 tribal groups in the state of which *Katkaria* (*Kathodi*), *Maria Gond* and *Kolam* are recognized as so-called Primitive Tribal Groups. Although tribals are scattered throughout the state, about 54 per cent of them are concentrated in six districts, namely, Thane, Nashik, Nandurbar, Yavatmal, Nagpur and Dhule. About 87.3 per cent of the STs population of Maharashtra lives in rural areas. The Scheduled Areas notified by the Government of India are 5,809 villages and 16 towns in 12 districts, namely, Thane, Pune, Nashik, Dhule, Nandurbar, Jalgaon, Ahmednagar, Nanded, Amravati, Yeotmal, Gadchiroli and Chandrapur.

In addition, the State Government of Maharashtra designated 773 villages in the districts of Raigad, Bhandara, Gondia, Chandrapur, Yeotmal and Pune as Additional Tribal Sub-Plan (ATSP) areas. Other villages having substantial tribal populations have also been included under Modified Area Development Approach (MADA) and Mini-MADA.

According to the Government of Maharashtra, 49 per cent of the tribals live in Scheduled Areas (main TSP area), 2.6 per cent in ATSP areas, and 6.8 per cent in MADA and Mini-MADA areas. The remaining 41.6 per cent of the tribals live outside all these areas. Effectively, 41.6 per cent of the tribals have been denied the special benefits meant for the development of the tribal areas. The area under the Tribal Sub-Plan in Maharashtra is 50,757 sq km as against the total geographical area of 3, 07,313 sq km of the State. This works out to be about 16.5 per cent of the geographical area of the State.

Table 1 *State's Population and the Tribal Population (in lakhs)*

Census Years	*State's Total Population*	*Tribal Population*	*Percentage*
1971	504.12	38.41	7.62
1981	627.84	57.72	9.19
1991	789.37	73.18	9.27
2001	968.79	85.77	8.85

Source: Census Reports 1971–2001.

The main tribes in Maharashtra are the *Bhils,* the *Gonds,* the *Mahadeo Kolis,* the *Gamits, Dongar Koli,* the *Pawars,* the *Thakurs* and the *Varlis*. There are three tribes, viz. the *Kolams* (Yavatmal District), the *Katkaris* (mainly in Thane and Raigad Districts) and the *Madia Gonds* (Gadchiroli District) which have been notified as Primitive Tribes by the Government of India. *Thakurs, Katkaris* are still perhaps the most backward of the tribals in the district. The Koli people are also called *Dongar* or *Raj Koli*. Generally 'Koli' means a fisherman but the Koli people's primary occupation is agriculture. The Mahadev Koli derives their name from their god Mahadev and they live in the Mahadev hills of Maharashtra. They are found mostly in Pune, Ahmednagar and Nashik districts of Maharashtra. They speak Marathi and use the Devanagari script. There are twenty-four exogamous clans among the Mahadev Koli and they use their clan's names as their surnames. They resemble the *Kunbi* and the Maratha communities in matters of dress and appearance.[16]

Their staple food consists of rice, nagli, varai and wheat. Other than agriculture they are also involved in cattle breeding, dairy and poultry farming and wage labour as subsidiary occupations. They live in nuclear families. Bride price plays an important part in the marriage. The marriage ceremony lasts for three to four days. Divorce and remarriage are allowed.

Maharashtra State Co-operative Tribal Development Cooperation is a scheme of Maharashtra State Government established on 22 March 1972 as per the provision of Article 46 of Indian Constitution. This co-operative has been established for multiple services as management of development works in tribal areas. Its objective is to work as an effective implementing agency of the State Government to extend welfare to tribals in the State of Maharashtra. It acts as an effective agency to prevent economic exploitation of tribal farmers, artisans and labourers, to promote economic development of tribals by implementing the direct assistance schemes. According to Annual Budget and Annual Report, the State has allotted the budget for tribal's schemes as given in Table 2.

Education

Literacy is low among the tribals. Whether it is in private employment, school dropout rates, literacy and health indicators,

Table 2 *Annual Budget of Maharashtra State Co-operative Tribal Development Cooperation (amount is in lakhs)*

S. No.	*Details*	*1998–99*	*1999–2000*	*2000–01*	*2001–02*	*2002–03*	*2003–04*	*2004–05*
1.	Allotted Capital	5,000.00	5,000.00	10,000.00	10,000.00	10,000.00	20,000.00	20,000.00
2.	Deposit Capital	1,973.00	2,040.51	2,048.58	2,048.588	2,499.70	2,499.70	2,705.70
3.	Approximate Profit	452.06	144.99	285.78	108.84	72.30	249.14	392.89
4.	Total Expenditure	13,136.80	14,281.89	12,758.44	10,006.05	10,490.96	12,127.14	13,606.33

Source: Maharashtra State Co-operative Tribal Development Cooperation Diary, 2008.
The allotted annual budget has increased by double in 2001–2003 and further doubled in next four years.

access to higher education, or even government jobs, they are at the wrong end of the spectrum. The actual gap between Dalit literacy levels and those of the non-Dalit population grew worse between 1961 and 1981.

Tribals were real inhabitants of India who have been neglected by the civilized people from time immemorial. It is a very hard task to develop them through education in the manners of civilized people advanced in the scientific world. Their stereo-type living has dragged them into the most inferior status. They did not have any chance to develop themselves due to lack of transport and communication means in the interior part of the country where mostly these tribes live.

According to the Census of 1991, the total literacy rate of Maharashtra is 64.87 per cent and the literacy rate of Scheduled Tribes is 36.77 per cent. Out of it, the literate percentage is low. The percentage of female literacy of Scheduled Tribes community is too low compared to males 49.08 per cent and females, 24.03 per cent. In Pune District, total population of STs literacy is 71.10 per cent. Adivasis are 44.27 per cent, where males are 57.95 per cent and females are 29.62 per cent. The percentage of women literacy is nearly half of total population of women in Pune District which is 59.80 per cent. According to 2001 Census, 55.2 per cent of tribals are literate against 76.9 per cent state average. The female literacy rate is 43.1 per cent among STs population as compared to 67.0 per cent among the average of the Maharashtra State. Among literates, 45 per cent have not attained primary education. Only 2.1 per cent of literates are graduates or above. The percentage of literacy among the Mahadev Koli is 30 per cent.[17]

Government started Ashram schools for Pre-primary, Primary, Middle, High-School and Degree level based on *Gurukul* system. Government applied reservation of seats for Post-graduate as well as Professional Technical Colleges and Job-Oriented Courses. Total of 551 Ashram schools are working in the Maharashtra State out of which 428 are in MADA area and 123 are in Mini-MADA area. In 2008–2009, Pune had 230 Ashram schools where 713 teachers were working. During 2009–2010 and 2010–2011 approximately it had 228 and 702 teachers. Middle schools are 5 and 3,146 lakhs were spent during 2008–2009, 10,239 lakhs in 2009–2010 and 11,775 lakhs in 2010–2011.[18]

One of the officers remarked that this system has got excellent success and was especially very useful for girls' education. State encouraged non-government organizations (NGOs) for the Ashram schools. Government hostels are built for tribal boys and girls, and Ashram schools are of English medium. Book banks are started for primary schools – a total of 443 book banks were started in 2010–2011 in Pune.[19] A number of schemes have been running and facilities such as allowances are given to stop dropout of students, allowances are given to the students who take professional training, scholarships to handicapped and below poverty line students. State has provided tuition fee, examination fee, and Insurance policy for students. Donation has been given on accidental death. Even it distributed bicycles to students of both sexes who are in 6th to 9th Standard and who get 45 per cent of marks. Scholarships and prizes are given to the merit holders. Seats are reserved in higher education even in IIT. A study shows[20] that though these students are admitted in higher, renowned educational institutions, they could not cope with other students' talent and did not become social with others, because of number of reasons such as language which is deep rooted in their lifestyle. Dropout percentage is very high and those who could finish their course took extra years to finish their studies. But there are exceptional cases showing excellent results.

Training and Employment

Training is provided for pre-recruitment of army and police and also for direct recruitment to army and police. This scheme has received good response. Training has been given in motor driving schools. Government has taken all financial burden of training for air steward and air hostess in renowned training centres to those who have passed XII Std and whose parents' annual income is within one lakh. The selection criteria for this are that the student should have 50 per cent marks in English and Hindi and their ages should be between 18–26 years and height for girls is 5' 2 inches and for boys 5' 7 inches.

Government of India started scholarships for higher education of ₹ 1,000 per month to students whose parent's income is below one lakh per annum and the student should not have a full-time job.

He or she should have good conduct and attendance. According to sources, this scholarships helped some students to secure their seats in MPSC. For VIII to XII, they have scholarships for handicapped STs students at ₹ 100 per month.

Economic Condition

Tribals have their own rich oral culture. The civilized people have exploited them not only economically but also in all spheres of life. They have been deprived of their legitimate claims. The money-lenders and landlords and opportunists take advantage of their simplicity. During the British period, they became landless. Very few people have got the opportunity to use the permanent pieces of land for cultivation. Due to this, migration percentage is high among these communities. They became labourers on their own land due to unjust laws prepared by British and later followed by Indian Government with little changes. According to Census 1991, 90.89 per cent STs are under poverty line in Maharashtra. It is higher in Thane (*Shahapur*) 96.53 per cent followed by Thane (*Jawhar*) 95.53 per cent. Surprisingly, poverty ratio is less in Dhanora in Gadchiroli whereas 44.27 per cent of STs is in Pune. Out of this 57.95 per cent are males and 29.68 per cent are females who are literate. Out of 10,103 families, 9,042 (89.49 %) families are below poverty line.[21]

Ekadhikar Kharedi Yojana

This scheme destroys the monopoly of private traders who procure notified agricultural commodities and minor forest production. Officers entered inner side of forests and bought forest production (total 23 items) directly from tribals and auctioned these products so that it benefits the tribals. Maharashtra Tribal Maha Mandal opened consumer goods shops in the inner side of the forests and put all their necessary consumer items for tribals. This scheme has become popular among tribals as they get products at a cheap rate directly from traders.

Khavati Loan System

This scheme saves tribals from malpractices of moneylenders. Maharashtra Tribal Economic Condition (Reformation) Act, 1976 controlled and banned the business of moneylenders and private traders in forests and tribal areas. *Khavati* loan system aided tribals for small purposes. During 1976–1977 and 1977–1978, this loan system was started in the districts of Nashik, Dhule, Amarawati and Chandrapur. The State allotted ₹ 3,00,00,000 for this scheme. Food grains, kerosene, clothes, salt, oil, edible oil, turmeric powder, and chili powder have been given in this loan system.

It was more useful to marginal farmers and landless labourers at revised rate of ₹ 2,000 for a unit of 4 family members, ₹ 3,000 for 8 units, ₹ 4,000 for above 8 units. Loan is granted 70 per cent in food grains and 30 per cent in cash. ₹ 6,000 lakh have been spent during 2007–2008.[22]

Economic Empowerment

State Government established *Adivasi Vikas Mahamandal* on 22 March 1972 to empower the tribes economically by training them in Motor Driving, for pre-recruitment of Army, Police and Air Hostess and Air Steward and in computer education such as MS-CIT. It provided a supply of loan for professional training, for self-employment, financial help to their *Sahakari Gruhanirman Institutions*, financial help to put good roof over the house, to maintain hygiene and cleanliness. *Indira Awas Yojana* has provided finance for building toilets and houses.

Shabari Adivasi Finance and Development Mahamandal Limited, Nashik

This scheme includes loans for transport business, lands for farmers, goats, cows and buffaloes for milk business. Central and State Governments have provided loan to distribute the vehicles for transportation and loan has been recurred by the person yearly. Loan has been provided in cash to install hand pump sets for water, new wells, fertilizers, motor-oil engines, electric engines and instruments for land cultivation such as spray, ploughs, pumps, pipelines, long-term loan to spinning mills, etc.

Tribal Social Welfare Department

During 2006–2007, the amount allotted was ₹ 6,497.59 lakhs for Welfare of Women.[23] Tribal Social Welfare Department started to empower their social and economic condition by starting many schemes such as *Dalit Wasti Sudhar Yojana,* Samaj Mandir which emphasized to encourage people for education. The basic necessity has been fulfilled by building houses and toilets with the help of *Gharkul Yojana* and *Indira Vikas Yojana* with the help of loan of ₹ 70,000 for houses from State Government. In all 9,289 houses were funded by this plan during 2000–2011.[24] Solar lamp, Bengo unit, flour mills, Pico-fall machines, sewing machines, etc. have been distributed under this scheme. ₹ 25,000 allotted for Free Stitching training has been given to tribal women for a month who have passed VIII standard. In addition, a sum of ₹ 3,000 has been given for the purchase of stitching machines to tribal women and ₹ 5,500 loan has been given for 333 months.

Abolition of dowry system started on 29 January 1985 and Counseling Centre for Women was started from 2005. ₹ 10,000 has been given to every newly married couple with ₹ 6,000 for *mangal sutra* (symbol of marriage for woman) of 22 carats and remaining ₹ 4,000 for other materials. The condition that has been laid down is that the ages of groom and bride must be 21 aid 18 respectively. *Nav Sanjivan Yojana* used to supply food grains, aid in health matters, etc. Though number of plans and schemes are planned for the empowerment of tribals by the State and Central Governments, Indian society's mentality towards them has not yet changed.

Violence

Though tribals have a tradition of strong local judicial system, often they solve their disputes in local system of Gram Panchayats or Panchayat. The Indian Constitution has given human rights to all citizens including the tribals. However, it has failed to provide effective protection to the hundreds or thousands who have died after torture and ill-treatment. Victims are tortured or brutally beaten to death.

According to the Indian media, news channels and newspapers many cases are never reported especially, when they occur in remote areas. The *Indian Express* commented that 'the victims were picked up at random, illegally confined and tortured to extract confessions till they died. Mock post-mortems hurriedly disposed of.'[25]

Patil ordered CID probe into custodial death,[26] *Pardhi* woman dies in custody and relatives allege torture.[27]

Atrocities

The Scheduled Tribes continue to face widespread violence. Crimes against Scheduled Castes or Dalits have increased. There was an increase of 19.20 per cent in crime against tribals during 2006 as compared to 2005. Crime against tribals in Maharashtra is the highest in India.[28] According to Maharashtra Crime Investigation Department one crime was committed against the tribals every day in 2006. The National Crime Record Bureau recorded 267 cases (4.6% of the total crimes against STs in India) of atrocities committed against the Scheduled Tribes in Maharashtra in 2006.[29] These included 56 rape cases, three abduction cases, eight arson cases and 58 cases registered under the SC/ST (Prevention of Atrocities) Act of 1989, among others. On 11 November 2007, a 17-year-old tribal girl was allegedly gang raped by seven persons in Warud Tehsil in Amravati district.[30]

According to the Maharashtra Crime Investigation Department, two crimes against women took place every hour in the state in 2006. It also stated that Maharashtra recorded one case of dowry death a day, one rape case every six hours, one molestation case every three hours, one case of cruelty by husband and relatives in every two hours and one sexual harassment case every 10 hours.[31]

According to the National Human Rights Commission, as many as 15 encounter deaths were reported from Maharashtra during the period 1 April 2006 to 31 March 2007.[32] On 16 January 2007, Ramdas Gaikwad was allegedly tortured to death in the lock-up in Andheri police station in Mumbai. He was arrested after a case of theft was filed against him and another person by his employer, Mukesh Sharma on 9 January 2007. The accused was remanded to police custody till 17 January 2007. According to Bipin Bihari, Additional Commissioner of Police, West Zone, Ramdas Gaikwad died on the way to hospital when he was being taken to Cooper Hospital at 1.15 pm. The relatives blamed the police for his death. The case has been handed over to the Crime Branch for investigation.[33]

On 18 February 2007, Vinod Chandorkar was picked up by the police of Wadala police station in Mumbai on the basis of a complaint filed by his wife alleging domestic violence. By 7.35 pm of the same day, he had died. The police said he committed suicide in the toilet room but the relatives of the deceased claimed that he was tortured to death. After the opposition parties raised the issue of Vinod Chandorkar's custodial death in the State Assembly, the Deputy Chief Minister and Home Minster of Maharashtra, R.R. Patil ordered an investigation by the Criminal Investigation Department.[34]

On 16 May 2007, Suman Kale, a woman belonging to a de-notified tribe, died in police custody at Ahmednagar, 120 km from Pune. According to the Superintendent of Police of Ahmednagar, Sunil Ramanand Kale was summoned on 12 May 2007 on suspicion of being in possession of stolen jewellery and harbouring dacoits. She was kept at the local crime branch, where her health deteriorated suddenly. The Superintendent of Police claimed that she had consumed poison but failed to explain how she could have access to poison in custody. She died at a private hospital on Savedi road in Ahmednagar where she was admitted on 14 May 2007. *Maharashtra Bhatkya Vimukta Jamati Sangh* President, Kisan Chavan alleged that the deceased was tortured by the police which resulted in her death. Kale's son Saheba also alleged torture. He stated that he was not allowed to meet his mother (the victim) when she was held in custody. There were frequent reports of alleged encounter killings.[35]

On 18 December 2007, Subhash Shivappa Bhosle, a member of Scheduled Tribe/De-notified Tribe of Mangalvedha Town under Solapur district was allegedly killed by the police at Arvali village under Mohol taluka in Solapur district. According to Akhabai, the wife of the deceased, over 200 people gathered to perform a pooja/worship to goddess *Kalobai* at Arvali village on 18 December 2007 evening by sacrificing four goats.[36]

The judiciary was hampered by a significant backlog of cases. There were a total of 3,67,409 cases pending before the Bombay High Court and 40,32,194 cases were pending before the District and subordinate courts in Maharashtra as on 30 September 2007.[37] The lack of adequate number of judges in the courts, among others, led to judicial delay in disposing of the cases.

Land Alienation

Maharashtra has a number of laws, such as the Maharashtra Land Revenue Code, 1966, that prohibits the transfer of tribal land without prior permission of the District Collector. As the Maharashtra Land Revenue Code, 1966 failed, the Government of Maharashtra enacted Maharashtra Land Revenue Code and Tenancy Laws (Amendment) Act, 1974 which provided that no tribal can transfer his land to a non-tribal, by way of sale (including sales in execution of a decree of a Civil Court or an award or order of any Tribunal or authority), gift, exchange, mortgage, lease or otherwise transfer without the previous sanction (a) of the Collector, in the case of mortgage or lease for a period not exceeding five years, and (b) of the Collector, with previous approval of government, in other cases with effect from 6 July 1974.

While poverty affects many communities across the spectrum, it would be correct to say that the Scheduled Castes and Scheduled Tribes are amongst its worst victims. Those millions and millions of Dalits working as agricultural labourers earn between ₹ 12 to ₹ 30 in many parts of the country. This is usually in violation of laws relating to minimum wages for agricultural labourers. In the period of liberalization, the pressure on these groups has become unbearable.

Conclusion

The government implements massive food, livelihood and social security programmes some of which are the largest in the world which theoretically support vulnerable people from even before their birth to their survivors after death. These programmes are, however, plagued by corruption, leakages, errors in selection, delays, poor allocations and little accountability. Overcoming corruption, theft, leakages, inefficiencies, and constraints of costs, are imperative, but still not sufficient, in a highly unequal society like ours, to overcome the barriers that powerless and expelled dispossessed people face to access food and livelihood with dignity. Many tribal people borrowed money for purchasing buffaloes, cows and goats and instruments for farming and within a year sold them. Even same case happened in minor bank system, and savings groups. A number of social groups entered in these Rural Minor

Budget scheme and took away all benefits. Tribal people are ignorant of all these benefits.

Notes

1. J.H. Hutton, *Caste in India*, Oxford University Press, London, 1946, p. 188.
2. K. Kalelkar, *Report of the Backward Classes Commission*, Manager Government of India Press, Shimla, 1955, p. 14.
3. S.K. Chatterjee, *The Scheduled Castes in India*, Vol. I, Gyan Publishing House, New Delhi, 1996, p. 34.
4. D.N. Majumdar, *Caste and Communication in an Indian Village*, Asia Publishing House, 1958.
5. Chatterjee, op. cit., p. 35.
6. H.H. Risley, *The Tribes and Castes of Bengal*, Secretariat Press, Calcutta, 1891, pp. XVI-XVIII.
7. J.H. Hutton, 'Primitive Tribes', in L.S.S. O'Malley (ed.), *Modern India and West*, Oxford University Press, London, 1961, p. 21.
8. A.V. Thakkar, 'The Problems of Aborigins in India', *The Eastern Anthropologist*, Vol. III, No. 1, 1949, p. 30.
9. G.S. Ghurye, *The Scheduled Tribes*, Popular Prakashan, Bombay (now Mumbai), 1963, p. 151.
10. N.V. Sovani, 'Non-Economic Aspects of Economic Development', in Ralph Bralbanti and Joseph J. Spengler (eds.), *Administration and Economic Development in India*, Cambridge University Press, Cambridge, 1963, p. 268.
11. N.P. Bhange, *Tribal Commissions and Committees in India*, Himalaya Publishing House, Bombay, 1993, pp. 405–410.
12. Ibid., pp. 411–420.
13. A.V. Thakar Committee appointed on 18 August 1947; Kaka Kalelkar Commission on 30 March 1956; Renuka Roy Committee on 9 July 1959; Dr Verrier Elwin Committee on 30 March 1960; and so many till D.M. Sukhtankar Committee on 19 June 1992.
14. Census of India, 2001 online. Accessed in October 2010.
15. Ibid.
16. G.S. Ghurye, *Mahadev Kolis: A Scheduled Tribe*, Popular Book Depot, Bombay, 1957.
17. Census of India, 2001 online. Accessed in October 2010.

18. *Annual Reports of Vidhan Sabha*, 2007, 2008, 2009 and 2010, Mumbai.
19. Ibid.
20. Vinay Kirpal, 'High Dropout Rate among SC/ST Students Admitted in IIT, Bombay', *Economic and Political Weekly*, 1978, pp. 165–167 and *A Report of Problems Faced by SC/ ST Students in Institution of Higher Education in IIT, Bombay*, 1984.
21. Census of India, 1991. Accessed online in October 2010.
22. *Annual Budget of Vidhan Sabha*, 2008, Mumbai.
23. *Programme of Budget of Vidhan Sabha, XIth Plan, 2007–2012*, 2008, Mumbai.
24. Ibid.
25. *The Indian Express*, October 1986.
26. *The Free Press Journal*, 18 January 2007.
27. *The Free Press Journal*, 31 March 2007; *The Indian Express*, 17 May 2007; Information received from National Human Rights Commission by Annual Crime Human Right through Right to Information application, 2008, Asian Centre for Human Rights, www.achrweb.org/ihrrg/issue1/ihrrg-jul-sep-2010.pdf, Accessed in October 2010.
28. See http://mahacid.com/from_CD/contents.html 4. See *Annual Report 2006 of the National Crime Records Bureau* 5.
29. Ibid.
30. See http://mahacid.com/from_CD/contents.html 4. See *Annual Report 2007 of the National Crime Records Bureau* 5.
31. See http://mahacid.com/from_CD/contents.html 7. See *Annual Report 2006 of the National Crime Records Bureau* 5.
32. See http://mahacid.com/from_CD/contents.html 4. See *Annual Report 2007 of the National Crime Records Bureau* 5.
33. Ibid.
34. Ibid.
35. See http://mahacid.com/from_CD/contents.html 4. See *Annual Report 2008 of the National Crime Records Bureau* 5.
36. Ibid.
37. Ibid.

7 Atrocities on Dalit in Marathwada

B.S. Waghmare

Against the background of the rich tradition of social reforms in the nineteenth century, the Maharashtra State has been able to establish itself as a progressive State since independence. In the second half of the nineteenth century, Mahatma Jotiba Phule, a great social reformer from Maharashtra upheld the cause of Dalit emancipation and matriarchal social structure and believed in the biological superiority of female. Shahu Maharaja, a king of former princely state of Kolhapur and Dr Bhimrao Ramji Ambedkar undisputed leader of Dalits followed in the footsteps of Phule in the twentieth century and contributed a lot for the upliftment of Dalit and women. Consequently, Mahar Dalits have historically been more politically and socially aware and militant than Dalits in other states. Dr Ambedkar is revered in Maharashtra even more than he is by Scheduled Castes of other States in India. The Maharashtra State is known by the names of Phule, Shahu, and Ambedkar (*Phule, Shahu and Ambedkarancha Maharashtra*) synonymous to progressive ideology looking after the interest of Dalits. At the same time Dalit Movement is also popular for political and social mobilization. This historic effort has had a large impact in the policies of the government providing protection to Dalits. The Maharashtra State since independence remained more sensitive than the Central government on the issues of Dalit advancement which received priority during successive plan periods.

However, this general record, though good, does not wholly reflect the true conditions prevailing in all parts of Maharashtra, so far as the protection and development of Dalit. The progressive image gets shattered by caste riots that sweeps the region often and atrocities committed against Dalit time and again in everyday life, particularly in Marathwada region. The State is mainly divided into four major regions – Western Maharashtra, Konkan, Vidarbha and Marathwada. The western Maharashtra including Konkan was the part of former Bombay Presidency under the British rule; while Vidarbha was with Central provinces and Berar. Marathwada was the part of former princely state of Hyderabad. Though Maharashtra as a State is the result of the policy of the reorganization of states on the linguistic basis, the people in different parts live in different socio-historical conditions. The regional disparities as well as difference in the name of caste and gender have continued to hamper India's development in general, and poverty reduction, social justice and equity and empowerment of Dalits in particular. In contrast to the overall picture of development of Dalits in Maharashtra, the Marathwada region presents a different story altogether. Incidents of violence against Dalits in Marathwada region have figured quite often. They have been routinized and have become regular press material for the front page news in print media as well as audio-visual media in the post-independent India. Despite the fact that State has promised the protection and security in the Constitution (1950), Anti-untouchability Offence Act (1955), Protection of Civil Rights Act (1973) and Prevention of Atrocities Act (1989), the violence continues even after sixty years of independence.[1] The data on atrocities against Dalits shows that during the last decade (1994–2004) more than one lakh incidents of atrocities were registered countrywide under the Prevention of Atrocities Act, 1989 (Venkatesan, 2006). In this context, one pertinent question need to be asked, whether atrocities suffered by Dalits are a result of the traditional caste system or whether it is because of the aspirations and the new consciousness developed among them in the advent of modernization. Dalits knew that their victimization is illegal as per new Constitutional arrangement. Asking them to carry out traditional occupations was thus declared as unlawful.

This article attempts to examine the background conditions – social and economic, prevailing over the years in Marathwada region which directly or indirectly lead to Dalit population's deprivation and exploitation. Secondly, efforts have been undertaken to study the scenario of atrocities against Dalits in Marathwada region over the last fifty years after independence. Thirdly, it has also probed into the details of differences that have widened the gaps between caste Hindus and Dalits in Marathwada region in terms of social relations. Finally, this paper also throws light on Dalit assertion in the region against their suppression.

Marathwada Region

Marathwada region has been characterized as backward and was ruled by Nizam for a pretty long period till 1948. Nizam's rule is notorious for its coercive, oppressive, undemocratic and anti-people character. As a consequence, feudalism gained stronghold in this area and the poor segments like small peasants, landless workers, women and Dalits remained as worst victims of this rule. Generally speaking, visibility of Dalit and women at public places was a taboo. The women even from upper caste/class were asked to observe 'purdah'. There is still a hangover of this oppressive power equation between landed gentry and farmhands.

The lowest segment of society known as Scheduled Castes or Dalits makes up of 11 per cent of the total population of Maharashtra. The region witnesses, quite often, the clashes between the dominant landowning castes in which Dalit women are victimized and the property destroyed. Additionally, the people, students, social activists and political leaders fight against the domination of western Maharashtra for maintaining the regional identity, and having more financial share and development. All of Marathwada gets up in arms because it felt that it was being ignored. The majority of people in the region are emotionally attached to the name of the region. Thus, Marathwada region is a State within the State of Maharashtra, having altogether a different story, which perhaps does not testify to what has been told about the overall development of Dalits. Contrasting situations between Marathwada region and other parts of Maharashtra provide significant context for the study. Marathwada region comprise eight districts, namely – Aurangabad, Jalna, Parbhani, Hingoli, Nanded, Beed, Osmanabad and Latur. All these districts, once part of erstwhile Nizam's Hyderabad state, have peculiar cultural traits, a legacy of the former State. The region is rocky and dry with low and uncertain rainfall, large landholdings and some landless. As per the census of 2001, the total population of Marathwada region is 15.6 million out of which female population is 7.6 million. Irrigation facilities in the state are markedly low. Relatively, western Maharashtra has greater irrigated area compared to Marathwada, Vidarbha or Konkan. Marathwada has 10.6 per cent area of irrigation (Abhange, 1995: 128–137; Deshpande, 1984: 12).

It is revealed from the study that both men and women want more sons than daughters, reasons for which can be sought in the Indian social set up. As per the Census of 2001, the male-female ratio in Maharashtra is 1,000/917. In normal condition, the population should have 1,050 women for every 1,000 men, because of biological superiority of women. When we look into the past to the year 1901, the male-female ratio was 1,000/978. It has been steadily declining ever since, from 934 in 1991 to 922 in 2001. It is evident from this that the deficit of women is steadily increasing in Maharashtra. The picture in Marathwada is still worse. It is a striking finding that sex ratio in Aurangabad and Beed districts of Marathwada is 884 and 898 respectively.

In the 1961–2001, during the forty years since Maharashtra was formed, the rate is more than double from 35.08 per cent to 77.27 per cent. In terms of district level data from the 2001 census, the lowest attainment was in several districts of Marathwada including Jalna, Parbhani, Hingoli, Beed and Nanded. Marathwada has the lowest literacy rate for Scheduled Castes (*Human Development Report, Maharashtra*, 2002: 9). The following Table 1 provides literacy picture of Scheduled Caste population.

Maharashtra's literacy is well above the national average, ranking tenth among major States, with an overall literacy rate of 77.27 per cent. Of course, this is due to the fact that Maharashtra has given special attention in extending educational opportunities to all the sections including lower strata of the society since long past. The literacy percentage of Marathwada remained below the State percentage.

It is from the record of Divisional Commission of Aurangabad that there were cases of death of children due to malnutrition that came to light in September 2001. There might be many more cases

Table 1 *Showing the Districtwise Percentage of Literacy*
(The percentage have been calculated on the total SC population exclusive of the population age group 0–6)

S. No.	State/District	Among the Total SC's Population			Among the Rural SC's Population			Among the Urban SC's Population			Among General Population	
		Persons	Male	Female	Persons	Male	Female	Persons	Male	Female	Male	Female
	Maharashtra	56.46	70 45	41.59	50.27	65.86	33.99	57.07	78.17	54.94	75.56	52.30
											Total	64.87
1.	Aurangabad	50.27	67.59	31.26	41.45	60.15	21.48	62.98	77.98	45.85	72.90	39.60
											Total	56.90
2.	Jalna	35.94	53.06	18.06	32.65	49.96	14.66	56.16	71.87	39.31	64.40	27.30
											Total	46.20
3.	Parbhani	37.77	55.15	19.66	33.00	50.26	15.13	55.71	73.34	36.94	64.90	29.40
											Total	47.60
4.	Beed	41.69	58.27	24.05	37.60	54.16	20.16	61.81	77.94	43.79	66.30	32.30
											Total	49.80
5.	Nanded	40.53	56.90	23 10	36.78	53.15	19.50	58.25	74.28	40.53	64.40	31.00
											Total	48.20
6.	Osmanabad	43.46	58.76	27.18	40.69	56.07	24.35	60.83	75.43	45.06	68.40	39.10
											Total	54.30
7.	Latur	43.88	59.31	27.37	40.78	56.26	24.38	58.18	73.01	41.56	70.50	39.70

of deaths which had not been reported to the Government. In addition to this, there are as many as 5,000 females who were underweight and who suffer from severe anaemia and other diseases, across Marathwada. It is observed that most of these female children have come from Dalit families.

Though the nutritional status of Maharashtra is on increase, the crime and violence against women are reported to be rising to an alarming degree. The National Crime Record Bureau ranks Maharashtra high, in terms of the number of crimes against women: 173.81 crimes per million population. Maharashtra is the fourth highest in the incidents of violence against women. Data on Marathwada region about crimes against women is not available. However, Aurangabad Police Commissioner has provided some data on Aurangabad city which shall be useful for visualizing the trends in the region. It is revealed from the information that the rate of crime against women, such as murder, suicide and domestic violence, is quite high in the limited area of Aurangabad city. The city is considered as the capital of Marathwada region, having headquarters of Deputy Inspector General of Police. One can imagine what might be happening to the women in the remote places of Marathwada region

Marathwada has remained economically backward even in the post-merger years. Large number of population in Marathwada region live on dry farming and 48 per cent male and 52 per cent female are engaged as farm labourers and cultivators. Following Table 2 shows economic conditions of Scheduled Castes in Marathwada.

There is a tremendous gap between Marathwada and western Maharashtra as far as the industrial development, agriculture and roads and railway transport systems are concerned. *Janta Vikas Parishad*, have always been mobilized around the demand of meeting the deficit of development of Marathwada (Ingole, 1984: 89–92). The *Hyderabad Mukti Sangram* had set a force of Congress leaders and masses from Marathwada in politics of Maharashtra in post-independence period. The Hyderabad Congress has proved to be an important platform for gaining the power after police action. Some disciples of the leader of the struggle, Swami Ramanand Teerth has developed as a force in

Table 2 *Showing the Economic Activities Among SC Population in Marathwada*

S. No.	State/District	Main	Marginal	Total	% of distribution of main workers among SC population in each category into broad industrial categories in different districts (in 1991 census)									
					I	II	III	IV	V		VI	VII	VIII	IX
									A	B				
	Maharashtra	39.61	3.21	42.84	14.39	48.08	1.08	0.52	3.47	8.61	4.09	4.18	3.60	11.98
1.	Aurangabad	38.94	2.34	41.28	16.45	47.34	1.09	0.18	1.55	7.76	5.85	3.13	2.40	15.25
2.	Jalna	46.20	3.25	49.45	18.92	64.69	1.02	0.04	2.04	3.81	1.48	1.50	1.30	05.20
3.	Parbhani	44.45	3.13	47.68	09.03	71.53	1.28	0.05	2.80	3.42	1.86	1.50	1.69	06.74
4.	Beed	42.96	4.11	47.07	13.20	67.12	1.49	0.05	1.71	3.27	2.15	1.86	1.69	07.46
5.	Nanded	41.91	4.80	46.71	15.03	68.05	1.09	0.01	1.25	3.38	2.36	1.82	1.50	05.51
6.	Osmanabad	44.33	2.78	47.11	09.23	75.86	1.12	0.03	1.63	2.41	1.62	1.58	0.95	05.57
7.	Latur	41.46	3.54	45.00	07.11	75.77	0.67	0.07	1.00	3.21	2.12	2.56	1.55	05.94

Key: I–Cultivators, II–Agricultural Labourers, III–Livestock, forestry, fishing, plantation of orchards and allied activities, IV–Mining and quarrying, V–Mfg. processing, servicing and repairs, a–Household industries, b–other than household industries, VI–Construction, VII–Trade and commerce, VIII–Transport, storage and communication, IX–Other services.

politics and gained stronghold in local bodies. One such follower, S.B. Chavan a Congress man remained in the State and National politics over a period of five decades and brought the name of Marathwada on the political map of India. Another group of politician led by Kamal Kishor Kadam dubbed as a man of Sharad Pawar had great influence in Maharashtra (Pawar, 2002: 29).

Status of Atrocities in the Region

Marathwada region is not only known for its socio-economic backwardness but also comes into public discussion because of caste tensions, atrocities on Dalits in the post independence period. The series of incidents of killings and physical assault on Dalits by high caste Hindus in Marathwada region take place from time to time. Most notably, the cases of atrocities have been in much discussion that include *Sirasgaon, Bamangaon, Tembhurni and Sugaon* and in recent times, *Bhutegaon*. Day-to-day discrimination of Dalits at public places, work places has become the regular feature in this region.

The study of atrocities on Dalits here may be divided into two periods; from 1950 to 1978, and from 1978 till date. The first phase of atrocities on Dalits in Marathwada may be discussed on how the caste regime of Hindus have been threatened by the Constitutional system in Independent India. In the new regime Dalits have been provided not only reservations in education and jobs but also given protections from the caste Hindus.

In the second phase, atrocities against Dalits need to be examined in the light of the renaming of Marathwada University after Dr Babasaheb Ambedkar and also hatred that has been perpetuated by the social structures of domination over Dalit progress.

The First Phase

N.D. Kamble's study (1981) highlights the issue by compiling the incidents of atrocities on Scheduled Castes all over India for the period from 1947–1981 based on newspapers, reports and weeklies, reports of Commission for Scheduled Castes and Committees on untouchability. In the absence of proper documentation of the incidents of violence against Scheduled Castes by government agencies the Scheduled Caste Commissioner and other central and state agencies, this study provides significant clues in terms of the cause, place, incident and remedy on the violence against Scheduled Castes. This study also provides significant insights regarding the nature of the violence against Scheduled Castes in Marathwada region, right from 1947 to 1978. The following Table 3 throws light on the violence committed on Dalits.

Table 3 *Under UOA and PCR from 1955–1977 in Marathwada Region*

S. No.	*Social Situation*	*No. of Cases*
1.	Untouchability	32
2.	Land Dispute	13
3.	Denial of performing traditional occupation	12
4.	Teasing and molestation of Dalit women	13
5.	Hatred and dislike, Caste abuses	18
6.	Defacing statues of Lord Buddha and Dr Ambedkar	4
7.	Caste clashes occurred on account of work denial	2
8.	Entering into Hindu temple	1
9.	Insult of SCs while taking food with others	1
10.	Progress of SCs not liked	9
11.	Other reasons – boycott, suspected theft, poverty, sacrifices, starvation.	20

Source: N.D. Kamble, *Atrocities on Scheduled Castes*, Ashish Publishing House, New Delhi, 1981.
Commission for Scheduled Castes, Marathi daily newspapers, Marathwada, *Maharashtra Times*, *Loksatta*.

It reveals from information presented in the above Table 3 that the cases of untouchability, land dispute, denial of performing customary occupations by Dalits, hatred and dislike of teasing and molestation of Dalit women are identical issues on which atrocities are committed. The number of cases must have been more than the reported cases. The simple reason of non-reporting was that the UOA was enacted in favour of the protection of Dalits which was not at all welcomed by caste Hindus. On the contrary, they used pressure on Dalits not to take advantage of this against them. Moreover, Dalits have to sustain their life in the dominant structure of the village. The very small numbers that we found in the table do not mean that atrocities have not been committed in large numbers. Whatever may be the number, but issues that have provoked violence by caste Hindus are eye-opening. In Marathwada region, caste structures, *Baluta* system and all other structures of domination were so rigid or intact, but for the first time challenged by new social legislations. Dalits took the advantage of new opportunities and denied performing the traditional occupations like carrying dead animals, playing music, cleaning the village, etc. The caste Hindus forced them to carry on the occupations which they (Dalit) have been doing over the years. Secondly, the caste Hindus, particularly the landed peasantry, provoked violence against Dalits on the issue of grazing land and land ceiling Act. Caste Hindus consider that grazing land is the common property of the village and it should not be given to Dalits. The Government version is that the barren land should be brought under cultivation and it should be distributed among the landless. In Marathwada there is a large number of disputes on grazing land that involved violence. Thirdly, Mahars began to assert and challenge the hegemony of caste Hindus and particularly landed peasantry which produced dislike and hatred against Mahars in Marathwada region and violence committed against their women. The number of these cases might be more than those reported. Obviously, for the reason that things should be settled in private instead of making it open for public discussion. Moreover, perpetrators of violence represent dominant caste. In the absence of social support to Dalit, law remains useless. Some cases reported accounting for violence against Dalit women are self-explanatory.

Sirasgaon

Immediately after the formation of Maharashtra State, the first case of atrocity against Dalit women was recorded in Sirasgaon, Gangapur taluka of Aurangabad district on 22 December 1963. The incident was preceded by a quarrel between Vithal Amrita Sirsat's youngest son Kishan, an agricultural worker and his employer Yadu Kale. In this case Laximibai Vithal Sirsat and her three daughters-in-law – Sonabai, Kondabai and Sacrabai were stripped and paraded naked in the village in broad daylight. Yadu Kale, along with other upper caste people went to the house of Vithal Amrita on 21 December 1963; armed with sticks with an intension to hit Kishan. Yadu Kale acted like this because Kishan misbehaved with his wife. It was the allegation made by Yadu who physically beat Vithal. Kishan saw the crowd at his house and ran away. Laximibai was beaten as well, and her sari was removed by Asaram Dada Agale, while Tukaram Bhika Kale and Tukaram Dashrath Sirsat removed Sonabai's sari. These two naked women were forcibly paraded throughout the streets in the village in an indecent and cruel manner. These women desperately covered their private parts with their palms. They were brought in front of Yadu Kale's house enabling Shevantabai (Yadu's wife) to witness (Rao, 1999).

The cause of the incident mainly resulted in a quarrel between Vithal Amrita Sirsat the son Kishan and his employer Yadu Kale. Nearly, six months before this incident, Kishan's wife Sonabai went to the field to provide breakfast to Kishan. While going to the house, Yadu Kale touched her sari and made unwanted gestures. Sonabai explained everything to her mother-in-law Laximibai about the behaviour of Yadu Kale. Kishan discontinued to work with Yadu Kale and complained to Shevantabai and asked what she would have done if this had happened to her. This dialogue was communicated to Yadu Kale which became the cause of the incident (ibid.).

A series of cases followed in a number of places in Marathwada region, committing rape and molestation against Dalit women. A fourteen-year-old Indu Katare in Georai, District Beed, was raped by caste Hindu when she went to the house of a person to collect money for sold mangoes. Her father launched complaints in the police station; the Police Inspector also raped her keeping her in police station for two days, Saturday and Sunday. Similarly a shopkeeper called Khawaja raped a thirteen-year girl, Sulbai and locked her up inside the house for two days in 1965. Similar is the case of is the Satcharabai, a SC woman from Kalam Dist. of Osmanabad – four employees of Tahsil office molested her in 1964. A minor girl, Kevlabai from Muli taluka, Gangakhed was lifted by Topa Kondiba, Basurao Hanmantrao and Gangaram Narain taken to the field and they raped her for four days continuously. She was in serious condition thereafter. In 1968, a SC woman, in the area of

Jayakwadi project, Paithan, Dist. Aurangabad was raped by a supervisor working on the project.

Similarly, this study found out that the atrocities have been committed on Scheduled Castes in Marathwada during this period due to untouchability, dispute of grazing land, dispute of surplus land, denial of traditional occupation by Dalits, upward mobility of Dalits by taking advantage of reservation policy, supply of water and caste hatred (Kamble, 1981).

Brahmangaon

An incident of atrocity happened in 1972 in Brahamangaon against two Dalit women which focused attention on the whole Maharashtra. The two women from the village of Brahamangaon, both Buddhist, went to collect firewood in the field and they felt thirsty. So they went to the nearby wells that belonged to Trimbak Shinde and Laxman Shinde, high caste Hindus. But they abused them in a filthy language for collecting firewood. Afterwards they started removing their cloths. With great efforts, these women could escape from them and took shelter in hutment of a Buddhist person, which was there nearby.

It is evident from the fact that for the first time, structured inequalities on the basis of caste in this region have been challenged by the democratic system after the independence. Though the wisdom of the Constitution makers reflected providing favour to the Scheduled Castes in various ways, the supporters of caste, however, opposed it using violence. The policy of reservation incorporated in the Constitution of free India in the field of education, services and legislature has provided a lot of opportunities to Scheduled Castes in this region. Land reform policy was introduced which benefit Dalit in terms of acquiring grazing land, a surplus land. The State intervention in the interest of Scheduled Castes has been contested by the high castes in this region in the form of violence, wherever it is possible, at public as well as private spheres. The caste hierarchies in this region have been maintained in the State of Hyderabad and Scheduled Castes remained the worst victims of this. The liberal values – liberty, equality and fraternity introduced in the Constitution have damaged the old structure of inequality which goes against the interests of high caste Hindus. In the initial years after independence Mahars' conversion to Buddhism has challenged the Hindu's social order. The Mahars or Neo-Buddhists in these days began to celebrate Dr Ambedkar Jayanti and Buddha Jayanti and because of this the incidents of throwing stones on the procession of Jayanti were found throughout the region. Mahars had availed large number of reservation benefits in the field of education and services and pushed themselves into better economic position. The high caste people in the field of region did not like this, and for one reason or the other, they were targeted, victimized and badly treated. Most importantly the Scheduled Castes began to deny the traditional occupation which they have been doing in the interest of caste Hindus. The Mahars were the first to use the protection provided to them in UOA and PCRA and they have not hesitated to register the cases in police stations. Hence, they were targeted by caste Hindus by violence against them.

Second Phase of Atrocities

The decision of the Maharashtra Government of renaming Marathwada University after their leader Dr Babasaheb Ambedkar resulted in widespread atrocities, violence on Dalits and destruction of public property, loss of lives throughout the villages of Marathwada region, towns and district places in the year 1978. Accumulated anger and agony of caste Hindus against Scheduled Castes which they developed over the years, triggered off because of their upward mobility in the field of education, services, economic and cultural condition. The caste Hindus resorted to physical assault, raping their women and killing social activists. Hence, the issue of renaming the university had long lasting consequences on the development of atrocities after 1978. However, this is no longer an issue at present. But it is being referred directly or indirectly in the matters of violence against scheduled castes.

It is evident from the following Table 4 that violence erupted in Marathwada region; in general the situation worsened particularly in Nanded. More instances of violence were reported at *Kandhar, Biloli, Mukhed* and *Nanded*. Cases of violence were also reported from Parbhani, particularly from *Gangakhed, Wasmat,* and *Kalam*. In all parts of Marathwada there were riots between the helpless/poor Scheduled Castes and aggressive *Savarna* population. The students association controlled by Congress and *Purogrami Yuvak Sanghthan* of peasants and workers party (PWO) have openly declared their support to the agitation. This has added fuel to the raging fire of the riots. The hard earned properties of Dalits have been destroyed. At the same time, upper caste agitators also turned to destroy public property. It has been reported that almost 40 government offices were targeted and set on fire. Similarly, 32 government jeeps were also set on fire and railway bogies, railway tracks were destroyed and fishplates were removed. Dalit hutments were set on fire and property destroyed on the event of renaming of Marathwada University after Dr Babasaheb Ambedkar (1978) in Marathwada region (Shakir, 1978).

Table 4 *Estimated Loss of Property of Dalits During Marathwada Riots*

S.No.	Name of the District	No. of Hutments Set on Fire	No. of Cases of Physical Assault	Estimated Loss of Property
1.	Parbhani District	141	31	1,06,931
2.	Aurangabad	41	–	2,81,335
3.	Latur and Osmanabad	35	–	
4.	Nanded	747	40	20,31,651
5.	Beed	Not reported		Not reported

Source: Report of Parliamentary Committee, September, 1978.

Punalekar's study of Marathwada riots on the renaming issue pursued the objective of why violence occurred in Marathwada region by asking various questions with regard to number of villages affected due to riots. This study revealed that a deep resentment had grown among the upper castes due to self-reliance, resoluteness and the modest improvement in the social and economic situation of the Mahars. All the resentment got built up over many years in the districts under the jurisdiction of the University (Mendelsohn and Vicziany, 2000: 74). Without studying the two incidents of killing of Dalits during the period of anti-renaming stir, the height of casteism of caste Hindus cannot be understood. Dalits in this region are not able to forget these incidents even today. Let us briefly focus on two cases which happened in village of *Tembhurani* (Nanded) and village *Sugaon* (Nanded) which itself explains the intensity of casteism and cruelty of caste Hindus in the region of Marathwada.

Tembhurni Case

An incident of throwing Pochiram Kamble to the burning hutment in the village of Tembhurani at Biloli Taluka, District of Nanded in 1978 has shocked everyone in the Dalit world. Violence erupted with the background of renaming Marathwada University after Dr Babasaheb Ambedkar.

Village Tembhurni had a population of 1,982 in the year 1978 out of which Neo-Buddhist population was 158, Matangs were only 33. The majority of the people live on dry farming but the *Barul* irrigation canal has more or less changed the face of the village specially when some part of the land was brought under irrigation. Dalits also took the benefit of bringing their land under irrigation which they acquired under land reform policy of the government. Among Dalits, Shankar Mariba Kamble, a Buddhist and Pochiram Mariba Kamble, a Matang remained at the forefront in organizing social activities mainly Ambedkar Jayanti celebrations every year. A unit of Dalit Panther Organization was established by Shankar in 1973. Pochiram Kamble was also active to the extent of becoming a member of Gram Panchayat. A majority population was presented by Dada Patil and Anna Patil both Marathas who were considered to be important in the sense of controlling and moving the village as per their directions. Social relation between Marathas and Dalits had a track record of conflict, particularly at the time of Ambedkar Jayanti celebrations.

In the backdrop of this situation Pochiram Kamble was mercilessly murdered by anti-renaming protesters in the village. Dhondabai, wife of Pochiram narrated the incident sequentially. The protestors first of all entered the *Buddhawada* with sticks, axes, iron chains, *Mashals (*torches*)* and set the houses on fire. Then, they turned to the house of Pochiram who was actually the main target of attack. He was awakened from his sleep by

Sadullah and Annwar. Pochiram anticipated the possible dangers coming from caste Hindu protestors. He, therefore, was not prepared to go out his house, but both Sadullah and Annawar happened to be his friends and they promised full protection from any danger from the protestors who were led by Dadarao Patil. Pochiram was brought up to the hutment of Baba *Mahar*, away from the main locality, where a mob of 500 protestors was waiting. It is unthinkable that Pochiram was forcibly pushed into the hutment filled with dry grass and then hutment was set on fire. Dhondhyabai witnessed the dramatic situation with her own eyes of her husband burning in front of the mob of hundreds. The body of Pochiram was burnt hundred per cent and he died on the spot (Gavane, 1995: 123–127).

The police Patil, named Laxman Vibhute Patil reported this matter after a lapse of twenty-four hours, though the Police Station, Narasi is just close to Tembhurni. It was said that Laxman Patil was the supporter of the protestors. The Police Inspector being an upper caste Hindu had all sympathy for the protestors and, therefore, moved the case in their interest.

There are certain important aspects associated with this incident. In the first place, the police Patil revealed that Pochiram Kamble was not in good terms with Maratha people. Dr Ambedkar Jayanti procession was stoned by some Marathas in 1975. The cases were registered against the few Marathas which later on with great efforts were compromised outside the legal procedure. Marathas since then considered Pochiram Kamble was the enemy of Maratha people. Secondly, the differences widened between the caste Hindus and Dalits on the issue of grazing land. It was not at all liked by caste Hindus that Dalits were making economic progress with the help of grazing land. Pochiram was one of those who was improving upon his economic condition as he brought his land under irrigation and he produced food grains and cash crops. Thirdly, Pochiram Kamble being Hindu Dalit he claimed for entry into the Hanuman temple. He poured water on the statue of Hanuman as a mark of his devotion. This attempt had created a tremendous sensation and tension in the village, because even Dalit Hindus are not allowed to enter the temple of Hindu gods or goddesses. Fourthly, the police Patil in his report stated that there is no instance to be quoted in which

Pochiram was involved in theft or sexual affairs. However, he clearly mentioned that Pochiram was targeted because of his social activities. His role in Dr Ambedkar Jayanti was highly disliked by the village Marathas. An anti-renaming move of caste Hindus provided great opportunity to the protestors to design the plot for the killing of Pochiram Kamble (ibid.).

Sugaon

Janardan Jaydeo Mawade, a Buddhist young man aged 35 years from a village of Sugaon, in the vicinity of Nanded Municipal area, was murdered by caste Hindus in their attempt of opposing the renaming of Marathwada University after Dr Babasaheb Ambedkar.

The population of Sugaon was 957 of which Buddhists were 564 and Matangs were 4. Because of the majority of Dalits and also because of the support of *Lingayats* (OBC), Vithal Vaidya became Sarpanch of the village. This created a rift between Marathas (all Bhosales) and Dalit-Lingayat combine. Neighbouring villages of Sugoan like Limbgaon, Waghi, and Chudava have been dominated by Maratha population. All these villages have been highly influenced by Congress leadership of Padamashri Shamrao Kadam and Kamal Kishor Kadam. These two leaders have played a significant role directly or indirectly mobilizing the Maratha aspirations against the renaming of the University. Undeniably, there is a great impact of *Varkari Sampradaya* (Bhakti cult) on Marathas. They engaged themselves in *bhajans* and *kirtans*. At the same time there has been large number of followers of *Mahanubhav* cult in the area. The canal of Purna project has improved upon the economic condition of Limbagaon area including Sugaon village (ibid.: 107–115).

In the background of the village profile, preplan of the killing of Janardan Mawade was made by Pralhad Patil. He invited all active Maratha Patils from neighbouring villages of *Waghi, Bhugaon, Borgaon, Pathri, Pimpalgaon, Dhoki, Bhanpur, Daryapur,* and *Waregaon* on account of celebrating '*Mawanda*' (Feast served to the people in the name of God-Vithala). The invitations were given with an intension of attacking Dalit *basti* with the help of the people who joined to grace the occasion of '*Mawanda*'. For the whole night *bhajan* and *kiratans* went on. Early in the morning after having rung the bell in the temple of *Maroti* (Hanuman) and slogans were made of *Shivaji Maharaj Ki Jay,* they turned to the Dalit locality with *lathis*, axes and bringing *mashals* (torch). Dalits thought that all Marathas are involved in *bhajan* and *kirtan* which they used to do regularly, and were sleeping by that time. But the voice of a mob of 500 people and aggressive slogans with attacking mood of the caste Hindus awakened the Dalits. First of all, protestors attacked Janardan Mawade's house, he was always at the forefront in organizing Dalits of Sugaon, celebrating Dr Ambedkar Jayanti and also actively participating in renaming of Marathwada University after Dr Babasaheb Ambedkar. Taibai, wife of Mawade asked for the help to overcome the situation. But violent crowd of hundred people took Mawade into their own custody and attacked him with *lathi* and axes and questioned him, 'would you now take the name of Babasaheb Bhimrao? Then finally, he was killed. The mob celebrated the killing of Mawade by shouting *'Shivaji Maharaj Ki Jay'* (Long live the king Shivaji). At the same time other group of protestors set the houses of Dalits on fire. As a result around 73 houses were destroyed (ibid.).

Versions of the Plot

Sudhir Gavane a journalist reports that there are many versions associated with the killing of Mawade. One dimension that has been in the discussion at that point of time is a political one. In Sugaon village, a Maratha person called Ramrao Bhosale replaced Vithal Vidya, a Buddhist as a Sarpanch. A Dalit's becoming Sarpanch was intolerable to all the Marathas in the village. In the second term Mawade played a significant role in making Deorao Himgive, a *lingayat* person as a Sarpanch replacing Bhosale. In the second place, there was much discussion that Mawade was characterless, involved in teasing and molesting the village women. It was also told that he was involved in theft, dacoity and there were many complaints pending in the police station against his misconduct. The people were fed up with him. Sugaon high caste Marathas were in search of an opportunity to teach a lesson to Mawade. The situation of renaming of University came as an opportunity to them. But it was not possible for them without the help of the Marathas in the surrounding village of Sugaon. Third version of the Dalit is equally important one. They say that Mawade has not done any wrong in the village. On the contrary he was helpful to everyone across the caste in the matters of everyday human relations. Of course, he used to be aggressive when upper castes committed injustice against Dalits in Sugaon. They also say that it was Ramrao Bhosale who spoiled the harmony of the village instigating caste biases. Bhosale also took the issue of Sarpanch to the political leader, Kamal Kishor Kadam and poured oil on the simmering differences (ibid.).

Limboni Massacre

The Limboni massacre was the third massacre of the Scheduled Castes in Marathwada, carried out by the landed Maratha peasantries after 1980. Limboni is a village situated in the interior parts of *Ambad* Tahsil of Jalna District. On 28 July, 1987, two Dalits were shot dead by a mob of 300 upper caste Hindus. The cause of this incident was that the grazing land around 100 acres was occupied by 24 Scheduled Castes people since 1968. This illegal encroachment was important for making it regularized and providing ownership. But *Talathi* had not recorded encroachment deliberately in order to deny the claims of Scheduled Castes in spite of the fact that these people continued to cultivate the land. The revenue officials also said that there is no record of encroachment or penalty paid on illegal possession of the land with the Scheduled Castes. Hence, they refused to make regularization of their possession on land. Contrary to it, the Scheduled Castes people showed the record that they were penalized on account of violating the rules and regulations. According to the legal procedure, this was sufficient evidence to make the extra-legal possession of land regularized. The village upper caste youth mobilized their anger against the Scheduled Castes giving them a social boycott. The hutments of Scheduled Castes were set on fire. Last of the entire rift turned out into caste conflict and two Scheduled Castes persons lost their life (Waghmare, 1987).

Atrocities in Marathwada and Other Regions

Among all other divisions in Maharashtra, Aurangabad division (Marathwada) stands first in committing atrocities. This could be substantiated from the statistics provided in Table 5.

Table 5 *Divisionwise Case Reported Under Prevention of Atrocity Act.*

Division	*1998–99*	*1999–00*	*2000–01*	*2001–02*	*2002–03*	*2003–04*	*Total*
Mumbai	9.39	9.88	7.38	3.82	6.90	5.50	42.87
Nashik	38.66	20.27	14.18	31.04	33.55	30.20	167.90
Pune	82.58	72.36	19.97	10.77	19.98	25.83	231.46
Amravati	11.84	17.45	12.39	19.10	16.40	26.00	103.18
Nagpur	48.32	51.65	20.53	14.98	17.43	16.00	167.91
Aurangabad	59.06	36.27	22.23	45.34	50.27	54.52	267.69
Total	249.85	207.88	96.68	125.05	144.53	158.05	982.04

Source: Yeshwantrao Chavan Development Administrative Academy, Govt. of Maharashtra, Pune.

Historically, this region was under the rule of the State of Hyderabad for a pretty long time. The feudal and caste tendencies had been developed in this state to a great deal, in which Dalits have continued to be exploited; humiliated Dalits had virtually served the entire caste Hindu population without adequate remuneration. The other regions of Mumbai and Nagpur were under Constitutional Governments during British India and were exposed to liberal values which also benefited making conducive environment for social cohesion. For instance, during British India, quotas were allotted for the first time to the Scheduled Castes in educational institutions and government services. As early as 1892, networks of schools were reserved and established. The British pursued these programmes till 1947. Mahatma Jotiba Phule's *Satyashodhak* movement founded in Bombay Presidency, in the late nineteenth century, was not a caste movement but was *bahujan samaj* (masses) movement which pursued anti-caste ideology. Phule discovered the notion of liberty and equality in the age of 'Reason and Human Rights' (Jaffrelot, 2003: 153). No such movements were launched in the bringing up of Marathwada region.

Aurangabad division, after independence, experienced a liberal situation created by law. But laws are not being supported by the society. Although Dalits are trying to come up socially and economically using the government laws, the caste-ridden society vehemently opposes the laws as their interests come under question.

However, the picture differs from district to district. It reveals from the information collected from Divisional Social Welfare Department that the cases registered during the period from 1995 to 2005 show highest number of cases of atrocities committed against Dalits in Nanded district, followed by Parbhani and Jalna district.

Table 6 *Districtwise Statement of Cases Registered Under Prevention of Atrocity Act 1989 in Marathwada Region from 1–4–1995 to 31–3–2005.*

S.No.	District	From Apr 1995 to Mar 2005	Police Cases	Convicted Cases	Acquittal Cases	Pending Cases	Finalised Cases
1.	Aurangabad	253	5	4	37	171	36
2.	Jalna	451	8	13	115	247	68
3.	Beed	317	2	13	190	80	32
4.	Parbhani	525	2	5	239	221	45
5.	Hingoli	298	7	5	44	213	29
6.	Nanded	619	7	7	183	340	82
7.	Osmanabad	162	1	4	53	93	11
8.	Latur	373	1	6	230	90	45
	Total	2,980	33	57	1,081	1,448	348

Source: Divisional Social Welfare, Aurangabad.

Teltumbade's study reports that among the eight districts of Marathwada, Jalna tops with 19 of the total 46 crime cases involved are of attack on Dalits registered in the last six months (Teltumbade and others, 1989).

The cases are registered in lowest number in Osmanabad district. This is because of the fact that Nanded and Parbhani and Jalna districts fall under Godavari basin. Having fertile land plus irrigation facility provided due to Jayakwadi irrigation project, upper Penganga irrigation project and Vishnupuri lift irrigation the landed peasantry in these two districts maintained a stronghold over the society in general and was able to bring Dalit population under its surveillance. At the same time, Dalits have come forward in the public life – though education, gainful employment, political institutions and by appropriating the fruits of reservation policy. They also enjoyed the surplus produce in the agriculture with the help of irrigation facilities available in these districts by way of putting labour in it. Consequently, Dalits in these two districts are assertive in every field and aware about their rights. They are able to fight back the pressures of caste Hindus and do not hesitate to register the complaints against Hindus.

Subcaste-Wise Atrocities

As Mahars were more assertive and forward among all other Dalit castes: Mangs, Chambhars and Dhors, and were targeted by high caste Hindus, particularly more so, in Marathwada region. As pointed out that the caste Hindus have shown resentment to the Mahars in the form of committing violence on them because of the progress that they have made in every aspect of their life. It is a common attitude among the caste Hindus to pull back the Mahars from any advancement. The castes Hindus differentiate the Mangs from Mahars, though both are ex-untouchable castes. The caste Hindus understand and recognize that Mangs are obedient and submissive and they also follow the tradition of the village (Punalekar, 1981).

However, it is evident from the statistics presented in Table 7 show that Mangs (Matangs) have also been targeted in the recent years (1995–2006) as they began organizing themselves in the name of great revolutionary novelist, poet Annabhau Sathe who belonged to their caste and also began to talk about injustice made by caste Hindus against them in the same way as Mahars.

Dalit Women

It reveals from the study of Manisha Tokale that Dalit women have been targeted in Marathwada region. The treatment that has been given to Dalit women is very inhuman and unwarranted. The following Table 8 reflects upon the incidents of rape against Dalit women.

Table 7 *Subcaste-wise Cases of Under Prevention of Atrocities Act, 1989 from 1995 to 2007.*

S.No.	Caste	Total No. of Cases	Year											
			1995 1996	1996 1997	1997 1998	1998 1999	1999 2000	2000 2001	2001 2002	2002 2003	2003 2004	2004 2005	2005 2006	2006 2007
1.	Mahar	218	26	52	35	24	09	12	07	11	05	13	23	01
2.	Chambhar	22	03	06	03	02	02	-	02	-	-	01	02	01
3.	Matang	123	21	24	16	14	07	04	05	10	09	03	07	07
4.	Mochi	01	01	-	-	-	-	-	-	-	-	-	-	-
5.	Malajangam	01	01	-	-	-	-	-	-	-	-	-	-	-
6.	Dhor	06	-	02	02	-	-	-	-	-	-	-	01	-
7.	Mahadev Koli	01	-	-	01	-	-	-	-	-	-	-	-	-
8.	Kumbhar	01	-	-	-	-	-	-	-	-	-	01	-	-
	Total	373	52	74	57	40	19	16	14	21	14	18	33	05

Source: District Social Welfare Office, Latur.

Table 8 *Rape Cases on Dalit Women in Marathwada*

S. No.	*Year*	*No. of Rape Cases*
1.	1987	1,173
2.	1990	1,163
3.	1991	1,067
4.	1992	1,236
5.	1995	873
6.	1996	949
7.	1997	1,002

Source: *Manisha Tekale, Dalitachi Ajachi Stithi*, Ram Puniyane (eds.) Ash Samatechi, Mumbai.

Two incidents of crimes against Dalit women in Marathwada itself suggest that how the Dalit women in Marathwada are being treated in the fifty-five years of India's independence. The incidents also confirm the gender and caste bias of the society. In 2001, a college girl named Miss Anita Baswante was hanged to death after she was raped in broad daylight at Kandhar, a taluka place of Nanded district. Another incident of violence took place in Bhutegaon in Jalna district in which actually the upper caste youths misbehaved and tortured a Dalit girl named Miss Shendge. Deelip Shendge intervened in it and lost his life.

Bhutegaon Case

Let's throw some more light on these incidents. Bhutegaon is a small village having population of 1,800 and comes in Ghansangvi taluka of Jalna district. The village is dominated by Maratha Patils named as *Bhutekars*. The track record shows Jalna at the top among eight districts of Marathwada. Fourteen households belong to Buddhists, eighteen household to Matang. Most of them are landless and few own *Gayran* (grazing land). They depend on high caste Hindus for their earnings and livelihood. Untouchability has been practiced in everyday life. A few Dalit families have migrated to Mumbai way back in 1972, including the family of Deelip Shendge who was the victim of the incident of attack on Matang community. This family lived in Kandevali Damupada slum of Mumbai. Shendge brothers and the family had come to Bhutegaon for the marriage of Deelip which was to take place on 27 May 2003, since their house in Damupada was demolished by Bombay Municipal Corporation at that point of time.

Ramesh and his wife Nanda and Lata came to Bhutegaon and were involved in making the arrangement for the marriage of Deelip. Because of some work, Deelip came a month later on 13 May 2003 and the very next day on 14 May 2003, the incident happened over a dispute on collection of drinking water. There are 12 hand pumps available in the area of high caste Hindus. Two of them are working, one being in the area of high caste Hindus near Narayan Bhutekar's farm close to Scheduled Castes residences. This pump is used mainly by Scheduled Castes. However, since the wedding ceremony of Bhutekar was there on 14 May 2003 and the members of his family were collecting water from all available sources. As per the custom it was expected that when high caste Hindus are fetching water, the Scheduled Castes are not allowed to fetch it from the same source. The Shendge brothers and sisters, being brought up in Mumbai metropolis, not knowing the caste customs and practices, decided to take water from this common hand pump. A younger sister of Deelip Shendge called Lata, went to fetch water from the hand pump. She was in a queue with her vessel at the hand pump. Lata's turn came and she was stopped by Vithal and Datta from Bhutekar family. A verbal hot exchange took place between Lata and them along with taunting and teasing.

As soon as Deelip came to know of this, he went to the spot and got into physical fight with Vithal and Datta Bhutekar. Lata was badly beaten and was seriously injured and fell unconscious. However, Bhutekar were not satisfied with this. They claimed that Deelip Shendge insulted them by indulging in a physical fight. When the wedding ceremony in Bhutekar family was over a mob of some 20 people with sticks and axes went to Deelip's house. Apprehending the aggression of the mob, Shantabai, shut Deelip up inside the house. Shyam Bhutekar climbed on the top of the house and attempted to enter in but in the process his leg was broken. Around 13 people managed to bring out Deelip from house and beat him up badly. Whereas Ramesh Bhutekar, known as a highly educated person in Bhutekar family and teacher of Hindi in a college in Jalna, poured kerosene on Deelip and set him on fire. No person came forward to save him, in spite the efforts and resistance to the protestors from his mother Shantabai, sister Lata and brother Ramesh. Deelip died in the hospital on 19 May, 2003. Deelip made it clear in his death statement the name of the culprits but the police have not recorded it. It is told that police did so as per the directives of their political boss from Jalna, in order to make the case weak and in the interest of Bhutekars. For namesake, the police arrested 13 people, all Bhutekars including the master mind, the so-called Professor Ramesh Bhutekar. Now all of them have been released from jail after completing the procedure of trial.

Post-incident politics began. *Dalit Mahasangh, Samajik Nyay Manch* and leaders from Matang community namely Laxamanrao Dhobale and others protested against Bhutekars who were responsible for the killing of Deelip Shendge. At the same time, *Akhil Bhartiya Chhava* and *Maratha Mahasangh* also took out processions and claimed that the incident was a fake. Bhutekars went to the extent of saying that Deelip Shendge was a patient of Aids and he burnt himself (Teltumbade and others, 1989).

Practice of Untouchability

The trends in untouchability practices and civil rights violation cases at all-India level show substantial increase from 1975 to 1976 and show progressive decline later over the years. The number of registered cases has gone down in the recent years (2004) (Venkatesan, 2006). The National Commission for Scheduled Castes and Scheduled Tribes (1989) in its fourth report points out that the offences under the PCR Act are declining in Maharashtra State. However, this report also accepts that even after 50 years of Independence, untouchability has not been abolished as per Article 17 of Indian Constitution. The incidents of atrocities continue to occur. The causes of untouchability are the same as they were in the long past such as; the deep rooted caste system, illiteracy, lack of awareness among SCs, rigidity created by religious literature, carrying on of unclean occupation by the Scheduled Castes (NCSCST, Fourth Report, 1998: 232–235). Educated class considers that untouchability is a dead issue and, therefore, there is no interest among the intellectual community to attack untouchability (Galanter, 1997: 212). However, a recent sample survey on Maharashtra discerned that 50 per cent villages in the State, strictly observe untouchability with regard to Dalits' entry into a temple. Still worst, is the scenario in Marathwada region of the State where, in 75 per cent villages, Dalits are prohibited temple entry. Around 50 per cent villages in Maharashtra have a separate arrangement of drinking water for Dalits and also separate cremation grounds for Dalits (Action Aid, 2002: 9–11).

In the private sphere, Dalits have less chance to participate equally in the marriage parties, at the dinning in the villages, even though they are invited. The Matangs are musicians and their role in marriages is important to play music but due to the practice of untouchability they are not allowed to have food with caste Hindus. However, in the recent years they have also professionalized their Band Parties and they just play music and do not stay back for food along with caste Hindus.

Seeds of Violence

Among all other factors, the social and historical factors have played significant role in the perpetuation and continuation of violence in Marathwada region. The structures of inequalities have remained altogether different in Marathwada. The western Maharashtra and Vidharbha were exposed to modern values in terms of providing opportunities to all the sections, because of Constitutional laws and democratic system in British India, while authoritarianism prevailed over the state of Hyderabad. The people in general protested against the misrule of the Nizam of Hyderabad. In contrast, this State provided certain amount of educational facilities to *pasatakhom* (untouchables). In Hyderabad region B.S. Venkatrao, a Mala-Mahar leader was at the forefront of the social movement. Hence, Mahars in Marathwada had a natural advantage and accompanying benefits. When Nizam of Hyderabad faced a crisis situation created by the democratic forces (Hyderabad Mukti Sangram) with the support of Government of India demanding abolition of Hyderabad State. Nizam established a private army with the help of Kashim Rizivi called *Razakars* for the protection of the State of Hyderabad as a separate State. In this situation it is no wonder that one section of Mahars remained loyal to Nizam against Hindu tyranny and that small section joined his private army.

Taking the advantage of the support of Nizam's rule, Kashim Rizavi committed atrocities against Hindus in general, and women in particular, in all parts of Marathwada. It was more or less a communal war between the Razakars and the Hindus. Lastly, the Hyderabad State was demolished with the help of Indian army operation. The five districts were merged into Maharashtra unconditionally. However, the caste Hindus are directly or indirectly of opinion that Dalits or in particular, Mahars were sympathetic to Nizam, while Dalits are of the opinion that caste Hindus are oppressive.

Dalits loyalty, to some extent, to the state of Hyderabad was a sort of protest against the Hindus but unfortunately it was politically exploited. Dr Ambedkar also cautioned Dalits in Hyderabad State to keep away from Nizam's misrule. Dr Ambedkar said: 'The Scheduled Castes of Hyderabad should under no circumstance side with Nizam and Ittchad-ul-Muslimeen. Whatever the tyranny and oppression which Hindus practice on us, it must not warp our vision and swerve us from our duty. The Nizam deserves no sympathy in opposing union with India. In doing this he is acting against his own interest. He does not realize that his own dynasty would be much safer if they were guaranteed by the Union constitution which would have the sanction of 90 per cent of Hindus of India than they would be if he relied on the Ittehad-ul-Muslimeen. I am anxious that no person from the Scheduled Caste bring disgrace upon the community by siding with one who is an enemy of India (Government of Maharashtra, 1982: 350)'.

Unfortunately, caste Hindus were not able to understand the real faith of Dr Ambedkar and his followers in Marathwada. On the contrary, they exploited the issue on the basis of few Mahars and committed atrocities against Dalits in general and Mahars in particular.

Dalits' conversion to Buddhism is most important attribute associated with provoking violence against Mahars in Marathwada region. A large number of Mahars in Marathwada region abandoned Hinduism and embraced Buddhism in 1956 as a response to the call of their leader Dr B.R. Ambedkar. Consequently Dalits threw away Hindu gods and goddesses from their homes and also left *gaowki* (traditional occupation) in all parts of

Marathwada. This created a new enthusiasm among Dalits to lead life differently with new values of Buddhism. *Buddvandana, Trisharan, Panchshilla,* songs of Buddha have replaced Hindu *bhajan, kirtan* in everyday life of Dalits in every village of the Marathwada. The portraits of Dr Ambedkar and Lord Buddha were fixed in every house of ex-Mahars; they felt it as solace of liberating themselves from centurys of humiliation in Hindu caste fold. The caste Hindus had also reacted to this move strongly by perpetuating hatred and agony. Though conversion to Buddhism was the phenomena all over Maharashtra, the caste Hindus had seen such movement prevailing for the first time in Marathwada. The other parts of the Maharashtra – western Maharashtra and Vidharbha have witnessed various movements: pre-Ambedkar movement and Ambedkar movement since the last decade of nineteenth century. The caste Hindus used to have slightly liberal democratic perception in the treatment of Dalits.

For the caste Hindus in Marathwada region Mahars' conversion to Buddhism was a strong development which they never imagined. Mahars such spontaneous response to Buddhism conversion prevailed all over the Marathwada, even in the smallest of the small villages. Consequently, caste Hindus perpetuated anti-Dalit and anti-Mahar feeling strongly, which was expressed in everyday life in the form of taunting, teasing, humiliating Dalits in the streets and in the farms. N.D. Kamble's (1981) work substantiates the fact that number of incidents of atrocities against Dalits have happened here more than other parts of the State, even though the Untouchability Offence Act (1955) was enacted.

In the third place, violence suffered by Dalits represents a bitter outpouring of resentment by landed peasantry to the various policies adopted by the Government. The role of the Government appeared to be significant after 1960, in terms of bringing socio-economic change in the interest of Scheduled Castes. In persuation of land reform policy, tenancy act, ceiling and redistribution of surplus land acts have been enacted. This State sponsored actions which benefited the landless labourers, mainly the Scheduled Castes. However, this has created heart burning amongst landed peasantries mainly the caste Hindus. Most of the clashes in the name of grazing land, erupted between Scheduled Castes beneficiaries and landlords for instance, in the year 1987–88 as many as 5,310 people had acquired 6,460 Hectare of land in Nanded district followed by Aurangabad district where 4,708 people acquired 4,984 Hectare of land (Sonkamble, 1992). Such kind of development has gone against the interest of caste Hindus as the grazing land was the common property of all the people across the castes. The caste Hindus had been rearing their cattles – cows, she goats on grazing land over the years. The Government decision of bringing the grazing land under cultivation by distributing it among the landless people has led to conflicting interest between the caste Hindus and landless Scheduled Castes. This can be substantiated from cases that we have cited in this study. Harassment, caste abuses, they are very commonly faced by Scheduled Castes population all over Marathwada region. Limbhoni massacre and Pochiram's murder have the context of grazing land, being the bone of contention.

Fourthly, regional identity of Marathwada has come into question because of the renaming of Marathwada University after Dr Babasaheb Ambedkar which became the major cause of perpetuation of atrocities in Marathwada after 1978. It is evident from the data presented earlier, that tremendous violence was committed against Scheduled Castes in all parts of Marathwada as soon as the announcement of renaming was made in 1978. As a consequence, the decision was kept pending till recent times. But renaming issue demarcated clearly the line of differential perception between caste Hindus and Dalits. The caste Hindus across their ideologies, social affiliation have never liked the decision of renaming of University after Dr Babasaheb Ambedkar. The caste Hindus are emotionally attached to the name of the region. The leaders such as Govindbhai Shroff, Anant Bhalerao, Balasaheb Pawar, Narhar Kurundkar, Shamrao Kadam, Kamal Kishor Kadam and so many others have shown their resentment against renaming, though few of them were actually sympathetic to the issues of Dalits. Marathwada has certain regional identity stronger than Vidharbha. This was partly because of the fact that this region has passed through bitter experiences during Nizam's rule. The people of Marathwada feel that they are ignored and deprived of opportunities even after their unconditional merger into Maharashtra. As an expression of deprivation the agitation by *Marathwada Andolan Kriti Samiti* in 1972 spread all over Marathwada, destroying public property and putting forth certain demands for the development of Marathwada. Though the agitation was politically motivated, it was not inspired by any particular group (Sadhu, 1978). The people of Marathwada have consolidated their identity by having social, cultural and educational institution in the name of the region. All these local inspirations have been asserted against the renaming of Marathwada University and undermined the contribution that was made by Dr Ambedkar in the development of the region. Milind College established by Dr Ambedkar was the first college in the region and remained as a great educational centre for all the students across the castes. The fact cannot be ignored that anti-Dalit feelings was perpetuated more among caste Hindus in Marathwada than on anybody elsewhere, because of various facilities and concessions which Dalit students received and the advantage they got in the recruitment to various services. This has given rise to frequently occurring fierce clashes. Under the pretext of renaming, accumulated resentment was expressed in Marathwada and it comes out as and when there is a chance to commit violence against Dalits, particularly women.

Lastly, urban-rural divide has given rise to conflicting sensibilities between Dalits and caste Hindus in Marathwada region. Historically, Dalit's mobility in the field of occupations and jobs is a result of their migration to cities during the period of British India. However, Dalits in Marathwada began to migrate to cities only in the post-independent period. Most of the population of poor Dalits migrated to Mumbai in search of their livelihood and stayed in slum areas. Osmanabad, Latur and Beed districts of Marathwada have faced drought situation over the last twenty-five years and Dalit population had no other alternative but to shift to big cities like Mumbai for their survival. However, they developed and adopted cosmopolitan culture and sensibilities in terms of social relations, dress, food habits and also looking at things differently. It is seen in the number of incidents of atrocities, that they are a result of the clash of their social behaviour with rural caste Hindus when they have returned from cities to their native place (village) with refined manners and dress sense. The caste Hindus in Marathwada are not exposed to modern secular culture. For example, in the Bhutegaon case the caste Hindus wanted Deelip Shendage to behave as per the code of conduct in the traditional village. Because he violated the code with a modern behavioural pattern which were developed in a liberal city like Mumbai, the caste Hindus – Bhutekars burnt him alive in broad daylight. There are many more cases in every village where Dalit people come from Mumbai slums to the villages and they are taunted, looked down upon at the public places; streets, spots of water supply, village bus stops, etc.

Dalit Assertion in Marathwada

Dalit's social political activism began to gain momentum in Marathwada only after 1930. Along with Malas and Madigas of Telugu speaking area Mahars of Marathwada followed the emerging Dalit leadership of Hyderabad state. B.S. Venkatrao (1890–1953), engineer by profession, having a powerful and magnetic oratory skill, known as the *Hyderabadi Ambedkar* was supported by large number of activists in Marathwada region. J. Subbia was another leader of the Scheduled Castes Federation (SCF) who became Ambedkar's man in Hyderabad. But he was unpopular among the Dalits, described by Venkat Swamy as dictatorial and opportunistic like P.N. Rajbhoj. Shyam Sunder on the contrary, most openly praised and considered him as a real friend of the *depressed classes*. Contestations focused on pro-Muslim versus adjoining Hinduism. Venkatrao himself began to side the pro-Muslim position and he established Hyderabad State Depressed Classes Association (DCA) known in Urdu as *Pashta Qaum*. Most of the Dalits from Marathwada region were found to be more influenced by Venkatrao's DCA, than the pro-Ambedkarite SCF. Among them were Sopanrao Dhanve (Latur), Ganpatrao Waghmare (Parbhani), Govindrao Gaikwad (Aurangabad), Hanmantrao More (Nanded) and Madhavrao Nirlikar (Parbhani). Both the DCA and SCF have used the name of Dr Ambedkar in Marathwada. However, the DCA's pro-Muslim attitudes and propaganda gained momentum from the point that Nizam had actually implemented some policies of distributing grazing land. This issue became the main source of conflict in Marathwada (Omvedt, 1994: 295–298).

After the merger of Marathwada into Maharashtra, Dalit leaders from Congress party have appropriated electoral politics to take over the power. However, the Republican Party led by B.K. Gaikwad and P.N. Rajbhoj was considerably supported by Dalits in Marathwada in various *satyagrahas* organized by the party for distribution of land and other demands. Yeshwantrao Athawale, Mama Yeole, B.H. Gaikwad were the leaders of Republican Party of India (RPI) from Marathwada and had some say in B.K. Gaikwad's alliance with Congress. In 1967 RPI was fractured into many groups: B.C. Kamble's group, B.D. Khobragade's group, Gawai group, etc. This has had a large impact on the social and political activities in the region of Marathwada.

Making use of reservation policy and other protections provided in the Constitution of India, the first generation of Schedules Castes began to participate actively in the democratic processes in Maharashtra in 1970s. The Dalit literature contributed in emulating the educated youths among the Scheduled Castes against the ruling classes for securing justice. The literary movement turned into action oriented programme in the form of Dalit Panther under the leadership of Raja Dhale and Namdev Dhasal. Their programme was based on the ideology of Dr B.R. Ambedkar (Deliege, 1995: 169–170). Dalit Panther started a statewide struggle against the upper castes and the rich. In fact, Dalit Panther was created in Mumbai but the real militant support that was provided came from Marathwada. Many Panther leaders and activists from Marathwada namely, Gangadhar Gade, S.M. Pradhan (Nanded), Ratankumar Pandagale and others have mobilized Dalit masses by organizing many demonstrations in every corner of the region. They protested against mishappenings in Sirgaon, Bamangaon, Antawelli, and Limbonihatyakand. While RPI and Dalit Panther failed to represent the socio-economic aspirations of Dalit masses, Prakash Ambedkar, a grandson of Dr Babasaheb Ambedkar established Bhartiya Republican Party on 27 November 1984 with a view to address the problems of Scheduled Castes, Tribes, *Vimukta Jatis*, landless people, peasants and workers. The leaders such as B.H. Gaikwad Shantaram Pandire, Avinash Dolas and Dadasaheb Gaikwad have mobilized Dalit population in Marathwada region on the issues of land and water resources (ibid.).

Another social organization called *Dalit Yuvak Aghadi* formed by S.K. Jogdand, Avinas Dolas and other activists had mobilized the Dalits in Marathwada region in 1970s for securing their rights. These youths had taken a lead to establish the branches of the front actors in the Marathwada. Additionally, other party organizations and party fractions of Republican Party of India have also worked in Marathwada region in the interest of Dalit masses. However, no leader from Marathwada region has been widely acknowledged. The party leadership has been accepted only from western Maharashtra.

Summary and Conclusion

Although Maharashtra State has been regarded as a progressive state, as it is pursuing the modern projects of Mahatma Jotiba Phule, Chatrapati Shahuji Maharaja and Dr Babasaheb Ambedkar in terms of providing special protections to Dalits for improving their life situations, very often caste riots occur and violence is committed in Marathwada region. This tarnishes the image of the State. This study has thrown light on region-specific violence against Dalits with special reference to Marathwada region which was once a part of State of Hyderabad. Initially, this study has probed in details as to why and how an outpouring of violence occurred in Marathwada, in spite of the fact that the protections such as UOA, PCR and Prevention of Atrocities Act are implemented in favour of Dalits.

Historically, Marathwada region has its unique social, economic and political background. The region is rocky and dry with low and uncertain rainfall. Irrigation facilities in the region are markedly low as compared to western Maharashtra and Vidharbha. The literacy percentage also remained below the State literacy percentage. Being the region ruled by Nizam for a pretty long time till 1948, the social situation remained feudal, casteist and undemocratic, deprived of proportionate share of benefits in post-merger of Marathwada into Maharashtra State. The lower segments of the society such as small peasants' movement and Dalits continued to be more exploited in Marathwada region than in other parts of the state.

In order to study the violence on Dalits, the two phases of violence were worked out. First is from 1950–1978 and second is from 1978 till recent times. The number of incidents of atrocity inflicted on Dalits in the first phase has been mainly identified as important issues that included the cases of untouchability, the cases of denial of performing customary occupations by the Dalit, the cases of hatred and dislike, the disputes over wasteland and defacing of the statues of Lord Buddha and Dr Ambedkar (*Putalyachi Vithambana*). Unfortunately, there is no proper documentation of the cases of incidents of violence and therefore, less number of cases is reported in the first phase. However, the caste Hindus provoked violence on account of their resentment to mainly three issues: the protections provided to Dalits in the form of Reservation Policy, the social legislation UOA and PCR and the land reform. It is found that two segments Mahars and Women were set as targets of violence since the merger of Marathwada into Maharashtra state. The cases of *Sirasgaon*, *Bamangaon*, and others substantiate the fact. Among all Dalits, Mahars are at the forefront as they have rare courage of acting openly against the tyranny of caste Hindus. The caste Hindus provoked violence against them and that particularly became responsible for their conversion to Buddhism.

In the pre-merger period, the fact needs to be acknowledged is that Nizam adopted a policy of distributing grazing land to Dalits, while Congress and Arya Samaji's were not able to do anything in their economic interest. As a result, Dalits in Marathwada responded to pro-Muslim leader Shamsunder and B.S. Venkatrao who were identified with *Razakars*. In the post-merger period, the caste Hindus unleashed violence and State used the occasion to take back the land given to Dalits in Nizam's regime. After 1960, the land reform policy had effectively begun to be implemented on the directions of Central Government as well as by the pressure brought up by RPI's *dharna* and *morcha* under the leadership of B.K. Gaikwad which was subsequently resisted by Hindus in the form of committing violence on Dalits.

In the second phase, the event that provoked greatest violence in the year 1978 was the act of renaming of Marathwada University after Dr Babasaheb Ambedkar. The decision of the Maharashtra Government resulted in widespread violence. The Mahars particularly were targeted by the protestors because they disliked Mahars' advancement in every field. Thousands of houses of Dalits were set on fire and their property was destroyed. Public property was also set on fire. Two Dalit activists called Pochiram Kamble and Janardan Mawade were killed by the Hindu protestors. This study found that there have been strains caused by disputes over land ceiling, wasteland, celebration of *Bhim Jayanti*, access to water, etc. The cases such as Tembhurni, Sugaon, Limbhoni and Bhutegaon substantiate the fact. It is also evident from this study that in the recent years Mang community has been fixed as the target by caste Hindus for committing violence because the Mangs also began to follow the footsteps of Mahars in terms of organizing an unrest in the community against the caste Hindus. They do not hesitate to come out openly against the Hindus in the matters of dispute over water, grazing land and other issues. For example, Deelip Shendge a young person of Mang community in Bhutegaon behaved with great courage. This study has probed into the details and found out the root cause of such an outpouring of violence against Dalits in Marathwada. In brief, Dalits in Marathwada in order to overcome their problems, remained pro-Muslim under the leadership of B.S. Venkatrao and Sham Sunder in the State of Hyderabad. But caste Hindus in Congress and Arya Samajis after independence, appropriated this issue of identifying Dalits with the Nizam and violence erupted on many occasions. Secondly, Mahar's conversion to Buddhism has not been recognized and accepted by caste Hindus. Thirdly, the caste Hindus have a lot of resentment to the reservation policy as well as land reform policy. Such overall attitude of caste Hindus exists strongly in Marathwada region. Fourthly and finally, feelings of regional identity is very strong in Marathwada and even opposed renaming of their University after a great man, Dr Babasaheb Ambedkar.

To sum up, we may arrive at the conclusion that atrocities all over India has been committed against Dalits on the basis of caste along with the other factors. In Marathwada region, the nature of atrocities has been deeply rooted in the historical background of the region. Secondly, most of the violence against Dalits is committed over grazing land. Thirdly, the structures of dominations in the villages of Marathwada have been greatly challenged by the reservation policy as well as social legislation of UOA, PCRA and prevention of Atrocity Act. Hence, caste Hindus provoked violence. Involving the civil society efforts and private initiatives along with effective implementation of social legislations may be the only remedy of prevention of atrocities against Dalits in India.

Note

1. Article 17 not only forbids the practice of '*untouchability*' but declares that 'enforcement of disabilities arising out of *untouchability* shall be an offence punishable in accordance with law'. Article 35 provides that 'Parliament shall have, and the Legislature of a State shall not have, power to make laws ... prescribing punishment for those acts which are declared to be offences under this part' [i.e. the Fundamental Rights section of the Constitution]. Parliament is specifically directed to 'make laws prescribing punishment' for acts declared offences in Part III 'as soon as may be after the commencement of this Constitution'. Until Parliament discharged this duty, existing laws prescribing punishment for such acts were continued in for 'until altered or repealed or amended by Parliament'. Thus, existing State (i.e. provincial) law was continued in force, but was frozen in its then-existing form, beyond the power of the state legislatures to modify or repeal.

   In 1955, Parliament exercised this exclusive power and passed the Untouchability (Offences) Act (UOA), which remains the culmination of anti-disabilities legislation to the early 1970s. The UOA outlaws the enforcement of disabilities 'on the ground of *untouchability*' in regard to, inter alia, entrance and worship at temples, access to shops and restaurants, the practice of occupations and trades, use of water sources, places of public resort and accommodation, public conveyances, hospitals, educational institutions, construction and occupation of residential premises, holding of religious ceremonies and processions, use of jewellery and finery. The imposition of disabilities is made a crime punishable by fine of up to ₹ 500, imprisonment for up to six months, cancellation or suspension of licenses of public grants.

References

Abhange, G.V. (1995), 'Sinchan Vikasachi Watchal', in S.M. Garge (ed.), *Marathwadyacha Vikas, Dish Ani Gati*, Pune.

Action Aid (2002), *People's Report on the Status of Untouchability in Maharashtra* (Executive Summery), Mumbai.

Deliege, Robert (1995), *The Untouchables of India*, State University of New York Press, New York.

Deshpande, V.L. (1984), 'Maharashtra Legislative Assembly', unpublished dissertation submitted to Marathwada University Aurangabad for the award of Ph.D., Aurangabad.

Galanter, Marc (1997), *Law and Society in Modern India*, Oxford University Press, Delhi.

Gavane, Sudhir (1995), *Marathwada Ek Shodh Yatra* (in Marathi), Aurangabad.

Government of Maharashtra (1982), *Source Material on Dr Babasaheb Ambedkar and Movement of Untouchables*, Mumbai.

Human Development Report, Maharashtra (2002), Mumbai.

Ingole, V.N. (1984), 'Regional Pressure Groups: A Case Study of Marathwada Janta Parishad', unpublished dissertation submitted to Marathwada University, Aurangabad as a partial fulfilment of the M. Phil. degree.

Jaffrelot, Christophe (2003), *India's Silent Revolution*, Hurst, London.

Kamble, N.D. (1981), *Atrocities on Scheduled Castes*, Ashish Publishing House, Delhi.

Mendelsohn, Oliver and Marika Vicziany (2000), *The Untouchables: Subordination, Poverty and the State in Modern India*, Penguin, New Delhi.

Omvedt, Gail (1994), *Dalits and the Democratic Revolution: Dr Ambedkar and Dalit Movement in Colonial India*, Sage Publications, New Delhi.

Pawar, M.C. (2002), 'Social Welfare Administration in Maharashtra: A Case Study of Nanded District', dissertation submitted to Dr Babasaheb Ambedkar Marathwada University, Aurangabad for the award of Ph.D.

Punalekar, S.P. (1981), *Aspects of Class and Caste in Social Tension: A Study of Marathwada Riots*, Centre for Social Studies, Surat.

Rao, Anupama (1999), 'Understanding Sirasgaon: Towards Conceptualizing the Role of Law, Caste and Gender in a Case of Atrocity', in Rajeshwari Sunder Rajan (ed.), *Signposts: Gender Issues in Post-Independent India*, Kali for Women, Delhi.

Sadhu, Arun (1978), 'Behind Violence in Marathwada', *The Times of India*, 7 August.

Shakir, Moin (1978), *Weekly Sunday*.

Sonkamble, A.C. (1992), 'Jamin Sudharana Dhoranachi Nanded Jillyatil Amalbajavani Ek Abhyas', dissertation submitted to Marathwada University, Aurangabad for the award of M. Phil. degree.

Teltumbade, Anand, Akram Siddique and others (1989), *Violence against Dalits in Marathwada: The Caste Cauldron of Maharashtra*, Mumbai.

The National Commission for Scheduled Castes and Scheduled Tribes (1998), Fourth Report, Vol. I, New Delhi.

Venkatesan, S. (2006), 'Crime against Dalits: Civil Rights Violation and Atrocities in India', *One World South Asia*, 3 April.

Waghmare, B.S. (1987), 'Limbhoni Massacre', an Occasional Paper, Aurangabad.

8 Beholder and Public Domain

The Other Side of Spectatorship

Y.S. Alone

It is an undoubted fact that active selectivity is the basic trait of vision[1] but when the visual objects/monuments go beyond its makers, the spectatorship in a public domain becomes an important phenomenon, for the fact that it involves the shaping of mind, which is shaped by its own cultural space. Shaping of a mind-set is deeply rooted in a typified socially constructed space and the image-building becomes an object of perception. Its complexities involved are addressed within the peripheral boundaries of a social group as well as the way certain propagation of mythical discourses are in a public domain. The object of perception assumes a considerable dimension of its cultural specificities. While excavating the minds of public, the objectives as set by the maker may not, all the time, fulfil the desired set. Historical reconstruction of the past has gone into the making of pictorial representations in the public domain as a part of political projects. Historical consciousness is constructed as a matter of self-imposed legitimacy. 'Which historical time?' is a big problem as even hundred or two hundred years are designated as *prachin,* i.e. ancient. There are numerous signboards on the roadside where temples are marked as *prachin* despite not having any specific visible evidence to showcase its ancientness. Thus, realization of the historical context becomes an agency to build something around such a notion which can be validated through the conscious mind of the beholder. The historical past acts as an agency as well as entry point for a beholder where his/her thoughts are loaded with the hierarchy of the present.

The element of shock has been involved in the spectatorship of a cultural construct but the way it has been argued under the wisdom of political and social conditions, it appears that representation of the pictorial signs also have inherited hatred towards certain representations. In India, when the education system was introduced, the biggest beneficiaries have been the upper caste society and with the entry of the lower caste masses into the system, there has always been hue and cry. Politics of *Swadesh* was located in the hegemony of the upper castes as a convenient political tool to address their own power which was getting replaced with the civil and administrative judicial system with the conviction that it would remain an exclusive domain, as for the fact that civil liberty rights of the lower caste masses remained a much cherished dream. However, study of India's past remained a subject of elites and therefore the Brahmanical past of the country becomes the dominant mode of historical inquiries. Many copper plate inscriptions[2] that are found in India describe donations to the Brahmin community, thus making the task easier to locate one's hegemony in the process of historical development. As a result of such interventions, *revivalism* and its political cultural projects have been instrumental in historicizing the Brahamanical past without questioning the idea of sacredness and the sacrosanct nature of its religious practices. Therefore revivalism needs to be critiqued and intervened from the perspectives of *for whom, by whom and of whom* in order to address the issues of public domain and the spectatorship. The ritualistic practices of the Indian society were further strengthened to ensure that Brahmanical values are nurtured and become as a standard of 'viewing' and the criterion by which a public sphere can move, remain the idea of greatness of tradition as well as of great historical past loaded with the notion of 'spirituality' as the greatest philosophical defense.[3] The revivalist agenda of the Arya Samajis and its percolation in the Congress politics systematized the homogeneity as cultural project and at the same time the factor of *others* as an integral part of the public domain. The political project of the Tilak and its catalyst service provider in the form of Gandhi in later times, systematized the idea of *others* so well that the category of *others* not only encompasses the other religious groups but also the lower caste masses.

The idea of martial race has been in circulation until recent times as it was associated with the caste pride. It is the caste pride that goes in the making of the spectatorship. At the same time the idea of rulers of the country in the immediate past became a potent weapon to inculcate not only the idea of ruling race but also the idea of hegemonizing the historical past through the edifices of the past relics, thus, monumental legacy received a different dimension. But nevertheless, the monumental legacy as a relic of the past became the site of living present and was contextualized as a dead past to inscribe the names of the present visitors, and the trend continues even today. On the other hand, the religious dogmas, indeed, were in practices that shaped the spectatorship on the lines of the political project of Tilak and Gandhi. The religious cultural nationalism of the revivalist and Arya Samajis had a tacit connection with the political project of the Congress party.[4] Excavated histories through archaeological past has been used as a tool in the public domain to define the agency of perception of the beholder. Communalism in the public sphere was deemed as a conflict of pride about past existence. 'Conflicts' in the arena of public domain circulated as an object of 'existence'. Once, the existence is objectified, it percolates as a missionary strength to justify the cultural construct through the element of spectatorship, where hierarchical ideals are nurtured and nourished as a convenient political tool regardless of the categories of spectatorships. The best examples in this regard is the issue of the Babri Masjid in which extensive excavations are carried out for determining its historicity, but when the same yardstick comes in the other cases such as the Bodhagaya[5] or the Jagannath temple at Puri (as present-day Puri in Odisha is identified as ancient Dantapuri where a stupa on the tooth relic was constructed), the response becomes no response. As a matter of fact, when the Archaeological Survey of India (ASI) was involved in the excavation of the Buddhist site of Ratnagiri (in Odisha State), a temple was situated there. It was a small Shaivite temple being worshipped by the villagers where the typical *panda* interventions were conspicuously less and became convenient for the ASI to shift the temple close to the existing site and the Buddhist remains under the temple were excavated. It was indeed a unique thing to have happened, but the way resistance to such a move was built up during that time, shows how minds were governed by the idea of *possessive* relic of past as shaped by the cultural nationalism. The *pandas* took up the battle to thwart the ASI intervention as an attack on their exclusive *public domain*. The other good example would be the site of Pavani located in Bhandara district of Maharashtra where a Buddhist Stupa was excavated[6] but a relatively modern Hindu temple was built on the stupa site and excavation was not allowed. It is still a site of conflict. Thus, the agency of perception is firmly grounded in the ideas of social power relations that have religious sanctions. Another example would be the site of Shelarvadi cave. It is the Buddhist cave located on the highway between Pune and Lonavala in the state of Maharashtra. The stupa in the cave is transformed and worshipped as *Shiva-linga*.

The place is converted into a sacred religious Hindu site. Similarly the Buddhist caves in Jakhinvadi group of Karad caves in the western Maharashtra have similar history to an extent that one of the Chaitya (Buddhist shrine) cave is converted into the *Vitthal-Rukmai* shrine and there is no initiative neither on the part of the government nor on the part of caste-Hindu community to withdraw any claim from these sites, thus the religious thinking and belief goes in the making of public sphere. It may be observed that the icons of goddesses are eulogized and are re-contextualized despite the scientific advancement and intervention in the knowledge system. *Mariamman*, who was once venerated as the goddess of smallpox, has been reinvented as the *AIDS-Amma*, or the 'mother who will cure AIDS', in the state of Karnataka.[7] Such transformation is a deliberate attempt on the part of the caste-group that finds creating such idols as a very self-satisfying means to control the public sphere which further grows around the icons and are circulated as a sacred contemporary.

Modernity in India enters in the backdrop of British rule, fierce argument about the notion of Indian sensibility is debated and undoubtedly, the mythical past has always hovered on the minds of the Indians which have always been in the interest of the Brahmanism/the present-day Hinduism. Despite the hybrid nature of pictorial language during the British rule and with the acceptance of academic realism, the Indian painter's sensibility to dwell into the themes of the Sanskritic poetries and the mythologies remain the standard subjects of pictorial representations.[8] Thus, when revivalism as a cultural project of pictorial modernity evolved, for those high caste painters who were producing images that were being addressed as Indian, by employing the Ajanta and Mughal tradition to their fellow caste-walls, it became the most convenient mode of articulations and was easily acceptable. Appropriating the historical tradition was a political project of revivalism to oppose the academic realism initiated through art-school education. Besides, the idea of 'village India' became a highly preferred theme of pictorialization as it would satisfy the political project of Congress as well as the imperial rulers. Exoticism of village India continued in the post-independent India, where there is no room to think of the societal problems, by many contemporary painters. Rather, the depiction of the village as a community and village as a site of pictorial contestation could not be the reference point, as for the fact that exoticism of village as romantic admiration forbids to see the other side of the village, and Gandhian notion of village never allowed to look into society as a problematic site, as the self of the artist was located in the caste hierarchy that had a very flat perception of homogeneity, greatness, spiritual, sacred and divine. Partly, it was structured into the projection of *rural* in opposition to the *urban*. The painters from rural background too could not come out of their romantic admirations and their emotional attachment worked as a site of revisit through pictorial conventions of their own. Elements of modernity, thus, reduced to the formal structure of painting but not to the structured existence of village community into a divided group of communities and their complete opposition to the cultural modernity.

The pictorial modernity in India is projected as a great achievement of high creativity in their formalistic engagements as well as eulogized through the academic textual narratives where 'high regard', 'great mind/creativity' has become standard lenses of investigations. The pictorial modernity in India as and when it is questioned, it is observed that it always functioned through the lenses of caste perception as it remained within the caste-hegemonic ideas and principles. The idea of great past, exoticism, adherence to mythical tradition, non-critical evaluation to religion and religious and social practices, and acceptance of the so-called national leaders are some of the important facets of the Brahmanical/Hindu caste-modernity. Many painters were part of such a political project. Neither the painter like K.K. Hebbar could resist himself to appropriate the formalistic modernity without any injunction of the graded social structure in the image-making practices nor could the painter such as Gade come out of the animated human figure against the rural backdrop.[9] Caste-atrocities, support to the civilian rights of the lower caste, critiquing of religious and social practices hardly had any place among the many modernist painters as their minds were loaded with their social caste-power that had a tacit sanction from the Arya-Samjis, the Congress, and many. The visual productions in the contemporary context are no different than what the pictorial modernity has involved its spectatorship during the colonial rule. While the colonial legacy was instrumental in enforcing change in the status of the gallery artists as new class, the post-colonial condition managed to strengthen the process to determine every kind of criterion and the resultant judgments in the new democratic open public space without disturbing its central characteristic of power equation. The post-colonialists are busy in defending and eulogizing Gandhi and his social and religious agenda in the theoretical paradigm of post-modernism where singular nature of the persona of Gandhi and his political progenies are deliberately interpreted in multiple meaning trajectories.[10] How is it possible that the post-colonialist and post-modernist scholarship in the country would like to read nationalism and its aftermath within the lenses of 'Congress and Gandhi' and there is complete disregard for the other icons like Ambedkar, Phule, Birsa Munda, Uddhamsingh, etc? Ambedkar and Gandhi debates[11] are extremely important in this context to see how perception governs and what are the intricate connections it has in shaping the beholder's mind? It may be recalled that Ambedkar had proposed the mandatory condition of not following the untouchability to join the Congress which Gandhi refused to accept, thus indicating the nature of perceptions of realities, Gandhi even was too vehement to accept the political rights of the untouchables. The caste-Hindus remained strong opponent of Ambedkar and remained great admirers of Gandhi, thus making a strident choice of their public spectatorship within the frame-work of Brahmanism. Spectatorship too centred on such political project and oppositions to Ambedkar's statues in the country are many and function within the syndrome of *others*. The fierce hatred generated in the spectatorship in the public domain shows how caste-perception governs the spectatorship and neither the modernist and the so-called post-colonialist and the post-modernist wish to accept these facts and address in the pedagogy as a part of intellectual project because, pedagogy in the country is so caste-centric that even the word of 'Ambedkar' became the sign of hate, thus reducing the public spectatorship into the Brahmanical viewership. In the contemporary media when the chief-minister of Uttar Pradesh Smt Mayavati unveiled or opened the Ambedkar memorials and parks, the event is addressed as 'statues of dalit icons have been erected and inaugurated by the chief minister sushri Mayavati ...' etc. thus making it apparent that the statues of Ambedkar, Phule, Buddha, etc. are not the *national icons* but are the community/caste centric icons. The choice of the words is careful selection of the caste-idea that goes in the perception process of category of 'others'. While addressing other figures no such choices occur in the print and electronic media, nevertheless the category of Dalit is gaining currency in the academic circuit as a framework of difference, and a systemic opposition to the Brahmanical/Hindu perceptual categories.

The image of Gandhi has been the essential project of Nehruvian-Congress nationalism without offering its critic. The same is observed in the pictorial representations of M.F. Hussain, Akbar Padamsee and the contemporary or the so-called post-modernist like Atul Dodhia. Atul Dodhia created series of images of Gandhi-like picture post-cards or popular calendars where he preferred to paint certain events of the so-called freedom struggle of India. The persona of Gandhi is a protagonist who cannot be introspected by posing a simple question related to certain events or the action because information that has been percolated right from the childhood is that of a hero who singularly fought with British rule and the caste Hindu population could easily identify themselves with such projections as Gandhi is considered as their own fellow Hindu brother. It may be noted that the very emergence of Congress as political party was from the Hindu Mahasabha where the political project of *swaraj* was articulated as a systemic tool to bypass the social reforms. Like Atul Dodhiya, Jitesh Kalat, Sudhanshu, etc. ultimately addressing their images to the high-caste spectators for whom the image of Gandhi is the most powerful symbol of nationalism but refuse to acknowledge that the religious nationalism of Gandhi was deeply structured in the fold of Brahmanism. Atul's work rather makes a candid statement that despite strong opposition to Gandhi which is generating with the new understanding has no meaning because Atul Dodhia and others are the protectors of the Brahmanical culture of nationalism and their caste perception is so strong that it does not allow any criticality towards Gandhi. The image is so powerful and strong in the minds of the artists that they abjectly surrendered to the unilinear projection of the cultural nationalism through the perception of the political constructs which is grounded in the Hindu nationalism. In the larger public domain, the image of Gandhi became an essential part of the pictorialized corporeality to teach the viewers and hammer their minds as to how the freedom movement has been achieved through the idea of *karma* of the Mahatma who had no sensitivity towards the change of the society rather than who always conceived the *sanatan* Hinduism as the supreme form of the living ideals.

However, the only first exception to offer the pictorial critic of image of the Gandhi was Ramkinker Baiz, who dared to put the human skull under the feet of large Gandhi statue; it is the most powerful critic of Gandhi where Ramkinkar, ventured in hitting the sentiments of public spectatorship (Figure 1, 2). He minces no duality in his image making process, the towering image of Gandhi walking with his stick is a very generic figure but as no one cares while walking what is beneath the ground, Gandhi too did not care as to see the problematic domain of sacredness and religion, thus representation of the human skull by Ramkinkar becomes significant for his critical understanding of the image of Gandhi and his persona. The skull represents a voiceless human who is being crushed by the grand narrative of Gandhi. Young painter, like J. Nandakumar considered very differently and conceives Gandhi in his painting Gandhi after Pune-karar (Figure 3) as a dictator who was instrumental in crushing the Scheduled Castes and Scheduled Tribes by forcing Ambedkar to accept the Poona pact. J. Nandakumar's Gandhi is constructed after reading the text of *Pune-Karar,* i.e. 'Poona-Pact' which is a widely circulated text in

Figure 1 *Gandhi by Ramkinker Baiz in Shantiniketan, West Bengal*

Figure 2 *Detail of the Figure 1 above.*

Figure 3 *Gandhi After Pune-Karar (by J. Nandakumar)*

Figure 4 *Burhanpur (Orrisa) Devi Temple*

Marathi. Gandhi's image has been constructed not in accordance with the nationalist meta-narratives of nationalism. He dismantles the generic notion of Gandhi and preferred to address Gandhi as destroyer of the rights of the *untouchable* communities in India, for which he converted Gandhi into a *multi-head persona* and his walking stick into the lance and trident, piercing into the body of a Dalit on which Gandhi is trampling. Such images are found to be volatile. J. Nandakumar refuses to be part of caste-Hindu narratives of Congress party. When Mayavati constructed the Ambedkar parks, there was a big hue and cry through the media. Why does spectator's response become so violent and outright reactionary? It is evident that caste becomes an important agency in the public sphere of spectatorship as it is the inherent character for opposition and resistance to certain pictorial symbols. The idea of religious spectatorship when it comes to certain forms of the public monument, be it among the learned as well as the non-learned beholder, the image of a female in the nude forms completely set aside the values that are being practised and the values that are being nurtured pictorially when it comes to image representations. Nude images have been opposed in the sphere of religious sentiments but nude images of woman on the temples become part of the public spectatorship (Figure 4), because the nude image of a woman is that of *Jogini* who is from a lower caste and not from the high caste or caste-Hindu community, indicating the politics of behaviour of the spectator is deeply rooted in their social positioning of 'caste' hierarchy.

Acknowledgement

Gandhi by Ramkinker Baiz photograph courtesy: Dr Sanjoy Mallik, Kalabhavan, Shantiniketan (West Bengal).

Notes

1. Rudolf Arnheim, *Visual Thinking*, University of California Press, Berkeley and Los Angeles, 1969, p. 20.
2. For example, see V.V. Mirashi, 'Inscriptions of the Vakatakas', in V.V. Mirashi (ed.), *Corpus Inscriptionum Indicarum*, Vol. IV, Archaeological Survey of India, Hyderabad. There are numerous such examples and are abundantly found all over India.

3. For development of early interpretations on Indian art see Partha Mitter, *Much Maligned Monster*, Clarendon Press, Oxford, 1977; for later development see Parul Pandya Dhar (ed.), *Indian Art History: Changing Perspectives*, D.K. Printworld, New Delhi, 2011; for discussion on spirituality see A.K. Coomaraswamy, *Transformation of Nature in Indian Art*, Harvard University Press, Cambridge, 1934.
4. For detailed discussion see B.R. Ambedkar, *Pakistan or the Partition of India*, now published as *Dr Babasaheb Ambedkar: Writings and Speeches*, Vol. 8, edited by Vasant Moon, Department of Education, Government of Maharashtra. The book illustrates the history of partition as well as issues of nationalism and its genesis; for further reading on partition of India see Bimal Prasad, *Pathway to India's Partition, Vol. I: The Foundations of Muslim Nationalism*, Manohar, Delhi, 1999 and *Pathway to India's Partition, Vol. II: A Nation within a Nation, 1877–1937*, Manohar, Delhi, 2000; for critic of nationalism see G. Aloysius, *Nationalism without a Nation in India*, Oxford University Press, Delhi, 1997.
5. For discussion on Bodhgaya temple see Jacob N. Kinnard, 'When is the Buddha Not the Buddha?', *Journal of the American Academy of Religion*, Vol. 66, No. 4 (Winter 1998), pp. 817–839.
6. S.B. Deo and J.P. Joshi, *Pauni Excavation 1969–70*, Nagpur University Press, Nagpur, 1972.
7. Meera Nanda, *The God Market: How Globalisation is Making India More Hindu*, Random House, Delhi, 2009, p. 89.
8. For historical development of modern Indian art see Ratan Parimoo, *Studies in Modern Indian Art*, Kanak Publications, Delhi, 1975; Yashodhara Dalmia, *The Making of Modern Indian Art*, Oxford University Press, Delhi, 2001; and also see Partha Mitter, *Triumph of Modernism*, Reaktion Books, London, 2007.
9. For discussion on Gade's painting and changing pictorial conventions see Yashodhara Dalmia, *The Making of Modern Indian Art*, Oxford University Press, Delhi, 2001, pp. 173–183.
10. Leela Gandhi, *Post-Colonial Theory: A Critical Introduction*, Oxford University Press, Delhi, 1999 and Akeel Bilgrami, 'Value, Enchantment and the Mentality of Democracy: Some Distant Perspectives', in Akeel Bilgrami (ed.), *Democratic Culture: Historical and Philosophical Essays*, Routledge, New Delhi, 2011, pp. 23–63. Both the authors are engaged in eulogizing Gandhi without making any critical intervention under the nomenclature of anti-imperialism and the post-colonialism, their analysis has been centred around the persona of Gandhi where Gandhi's neither political nor rational positions are investigated and

Bilgrami eloquently discusses the moral principal and percepts of Gandhi but failed to understand the deep-seated Hindu syndrome of graded inequality which Gandhi envisaged when Gandhi describes his position and admiration for the Sanatani Hindu religion, his dictum during non-cooperation movement where Gandhi appeals not to cooperate with British but to follow all obligations to the native landlords. Thus, making it obvious that such issues are conveniently bypassed by the post-colonialist.

11. See B.R. Ambedkar, *What Congress and Gandhi have Done to the Untouchables*, Thacker & Co., Bombay, 1945; *Annihilation of Caste*, now published in *Dr Babasaheb Ambedkar: Writings and Speeches*, Vol. I, edited by Vasant Moon, Department of Education, Government of Maharashtra, Mumbai; also see Eleanor Zelliot, 'Gandhi and Ambedkar: A Study in Leadership, in Michael Mahar (ed.), *The Untouchables in Contemporary India*, University of Arizona Press, Tuscan, 1972; and Valerian Rodrigues, 'Between Tradition and Modernity: The Gandhi-Ambedkar Debate', in A.K. Narain and D.C. Ahir (eds.), *Dr Ambedkar: Buddhism and Social Change*, B.R. Publishing Corporations, Delhi, 1994, pp. 137–161.

9 The Exclusion in the Context of Inter-caste Marriages

Jagan Karade

The modern young India is changing rapidly because of the new means of transportation and communication and the development of cities has brought in a degree of economical, cultural and social change. The institutions and organizations emerged or were established on the western style such as universities, scientific laboratories, hospitals, business firms, factories, political institutions and parties, law courts, etc. But these institutions and organizations are established as 'a hierarchy' but do not depend on 'purity and pollution'. Therefore, people began to migrate to the cities in search of work or job as well as modern education. The barriers of caste began to break down slowly. The Indian caste system was one of the harsh systems of hierarchy to be found in the world. Each caste found its place in the hierarchy in accordance with the rules of 'purity and pollution'. Occupations, food materials and even persons were ranged on a scale from the purest to the most impure. For instance, occupations that involved contact with bodily or other waste – scavenging, leather-work and the like were considered deeply polluting.'[1] Meanwhile economists say that, India is called as *Young India* and in next few years India will be leading the world for development' as in the contemporary period, educated young Indians' expectations about development as well as ideas about the cultural changes have changed.

India is a home to many religions and thousands of castes. Although inter-religious marriages are not very frequent in our society (as they are met with fierce protests from the families). As a result, inter-caste and inter-communal marriages are performed by the couples secretly or in a law court, since parents do not allow such commitments.

In the past, caste system imposed many restrictions on the principles of marriage. Each caste and sub-caste is known as an endogenous group and the members have to marry within their own caste. At that time inter-caste and inter-communal marriage was strictly prohibited in the Hindu society. Culturally, modern India shows several contradictory developments. Today, marriages are preferred not only within castes but within sub-castes also. In Haryana and Rajasthan, for instance, the *khap* (caste council) gives orders to kill young lovers for marrying outside their caste. Such inhuman killings are glorified as *honour killings.*

In this research paper I try to analyse the cultural lacuna concerned with caste and marriage institutions. Only upper caste people have accepted the marriage in horizontal community but the upper caste communities do not allow marrying a person of lower caste communities. The majority of the marriage advertisements, the upper caste communities mention, 'we are ready for inter-caste marriage, but Scheduled Castes and Scheduled Tribes (here after SCs and STs) are excluse' It means this statement has proved that the discrimination is continuously going on.

Caste and Marriage

After independence, 'the democratic aspiration of Dalits could be met partially in the sense that they could participate as equal citizens in the political process of the country. They also benefited from the process of democratization of bureaucratic structures through reservations and, more importantly, through the adoption of universal adult franchise. Through these opportunities, legal, administrative and institutional, Dalits were able to establish some amount of control over time and acquire some kind of secular space in a "civil society" that was forced to become, if not more tolerant, then at least more benign. They could now seek to change their occupations. They could attempt to get into more secular occupations in the tertiary sectors. They could send their representatives to decision-making bodies at all levels, local, regional and national.'[2]

But on sociological point of view they have not been involved in the cultural field or institution, especially that of marriage.

'Undoubtedly, due to multidimensionality and complexity of the *caste* system ... . There are two prominent views about caste: (1) the structural aspect of *caste*, which is explained by accepting it as a general principle of stratification; and (2) *caste* as a cultural system, which is understood in terms of prominence of ideas of pollution-purity and notions of hierarchy, segregation and corporations. The structural view explains that stratification is a universal reality, and caste is, therefore, an aspect of the reality. The culturological view perceives caste as a distinct phenomenon found in Indian society in particular.'[3] And on this point Yogendra Singh mentioned that, 'sociologists who look across the cultural view of *caste* have right from the beginning associates with an autonomous principle of stratification. The basis of which is institutionalized inequality closer to social system in respect of social mobility, an elementary level of division of labour, legitimized on ritual bases of reciprocity and emphasis on quality (ritual purity or racial purity) rather than performance. In other words, caste is associated with an autonomous form of cultural system or worldview'.[4] V.K. Sharma mentioned that 'Caste has its own distinct customs, traditions, belief, rituals – both social and religious, occupations and taboos'.[5] The caste-based discrimination has ruined the Indian society and created differences amongst the people belonging to different castes and the relation between caste and marriage is much closer. Marriage is a sacred institution especially in the context of Indian customs. The caste system which was intervening among different castes but which within gotra or clan is prohibited. This rule of exogamy is observed strictly in villages and in urban society also as well as marriage is closely related to endogamy group. Even though the world has advanced a lot, the Indian people still follow strictly the caste rules and customs. For years, the Hindu society has been divided on the basis of caste. The problem of caste system was deep rooted; 'Even today, India is struggling to come out of this social menace. History reveals that efforts have been made by various social reformers and other individuals to make India free from the clutches of caste system, untouchability and caste discrimination.[6]

Among the social reformers Dr Babasaheb Ambedkar is a leading personality. He struggled for human rights of all the backward classes and for the first time, he raised many questions connected with the caste. First, he rejected the defense of caste on the basis of division of labour and argued that, 'Caste system is not merely a division of labour which is quite different from division of labour – it is a hierarchy in which the divisions of labourers are graded one above the other.'[7] He concluded that, 'the real method of breaking up the caste system was not to bring about inter-caste dinners and inter-caste marriages but to destroy the religious notions on which caste was found'.[8] Now the social scientists agree with him.

In last six decades the anthropologists and sociologists have focused on the caste system and its change. The sociologist, Béteille (1991), argues, 'caste and sub-caste have ceased to play an active part in the reproduction of inequality, at least at the upper levels of the social hierarchy where they are no longer important agents of either social placement or social control'.[9] In this way, the caste system has been a rigid part of Indian customs. It is an evil that has made the rules and regulation of Hindu tradition and unfair discrimination based on the caste, which created differences among the people belonging to different castes. In contemporary period some persons say that, caste has been destroyed in contemporary period but in Hindu religion, each and every person remembers his/her own caste at the time of school admission, searching for a job in private or public sector, also if he/she starts a business and lastly if he or she wants to marry.

The institution of marriage is found since the early periods in all human societies. According to Dharmshastra, 'marriage is one of the sixteen *Sanskaras* or (the most significant event of person's life) or stage through which the individual enters *grahasthashram* of the stage of married life'.[10] In the villages two kinds of marriages are found: endogamy and exogamy. In the Indian villages, marriage between cousins is a taboo. As regard hypergamy (*Anuloma*) and hypogamy (*Pratiloma*); the cases of hypergamy are more frequent than those of hypogamy because of the Dharmashastra. The people restricted marriages in their own caste. Inter-caste and inter-communal marriages in India were a taboo for most people in the earlier days. The social inequality was dependent on family and marriage because these two institutions are forwarding the identities of the society, since marriage relates to social customs and tradition. They had a conception that marriages are only possible in the same community and caste.

Generally, in villages, marriages are prearranged and nothing is left to the choice of the boy or girl. The marriages are arranged by elder members of the family who normally are the grandfather, father or uncle. The parents attach great importance to the property consideration. Every parent naturally wants that, the girl should go to a well-to-do family so that she may have an easy and happy life. The majority of the marriages in rural areas are between different clans and different villages; they are nonetheless between the same castes.

Srinivas pointed out, 'rituals and the observance of caste rules never entirely disappear. While caste may recede from certain areas of life, it remains in others and even thrives'. The scholars have written about the capacity of modern Indians to compartmentalize their lives. In this context, it is interesting to remember what one informant said to a well-known anthropologist: 'When I put on my shirt to go to the office, I take off my *caste*, and when I come home and take off my shirt, I put on my *caste*'.[11] In this way every person who belongs to Hindu religion, he or she is forwarding his/her caste identity.

While the provisions are made in the Constitution to abolish untouchability and the Central and State Governments have been providing educational and economical facilities for social and economical upliftment of SCs and STs, but we have not actually achieved social equality as was expected at the time of independence. Some questions emerge concerned with education: if educated people forward the paradox, especially about the marriage activity, then the question is how to create social change through education?

Present Scenario

Rowena Robinson mentioned that, 'There is an increase in the age of marriage and women increasingly have an opportunity to get education and work before and after marriage. While more girls enter careers nowadays, this is sometimes because men want educated and employed brides. However, there is also a sharp increase in women working because they want to carve out independent careers. Men and women meet and try to discover areas of compatibility, even when marriages largely continue to be arranged by family members. However, there is also an increase in inter-caste, inter-religious marriages, especially among the urban, educated elite. Among such groups, the income, lifestyle and education of the partners often count for as much if not more than just caste position.'[12] When we are thinking about Marxist perspective, it is correct because in the contemporary period men want educated and employed brides, therefore girls have been achieving education and getting jobs. It is a change but when we are thinking on subaltern perspective, then the ratio is so less compared with others because in India one still does not welcome the concept of inter-caste marriages; even today people are very rigid in the matter of marriages. They prefer that, their sons and daughters should marry in the same caste and community. We know that, each and every caste has economical and social identity. Beyond these, it has a cultural identity which is based on caste; therefore, we can say that, the caste and religious institutions are barriers for progressive modern India. Many sociologists pointed out that, 'Indians had an orthodox mindset. They couldn't imagine inter-caste marriages. They had a conception that marriages are only possible in the same community and caste.'[13] Even they know that, the biological advantages are there. Physical fitness counts a lot because as per the genetic theory, the chances that an offspring will be better are highest when the mating species do not relate to each other.

We have to agree that there is the impact of certain powerful factors such as modern education, industrialization, urbanization, rapid development of transportation and communication, social reform movement, political movement, religious movement which force caste system to undergo drastic changes in modern India. And we know, the Constitution of India lays down that, untouchability is abolished and its practice in any form is forbidden. The enforcement of disability arising out of untouchability shall be an offence punishable in accordance with law,[14] at the same time, the 'Dalits continue to face wide-ranging economic, social disadvantages, and day-to-day humiliation and degradation, denial of justice and violent atrocities in India'[15] and majority of the atrocity cases related with inter-caste marriages. Inter-caste marriages can also lead to large scale attacks on lower castes for example, in January 2012, Mulgaon village in Satara district of Maharashtra. The evidence is a lower caste boy having an affair with high caste girl, but ego problem emerged from upper caste family and they have beaten the boy's mother. After that, girl's uncle warned the concerned lower caste family as 'you should go anywhere but not allowed in this village'.[16] In this case the economic position of upper caste family is the same as that of the lower caste family but they have caste ego.

Many educationalists view that, 'Education has broadened the periphery of thinking and helped people develop their analytical powers. It has not only altered their perception about life, but also about social concerns such as marriage and relationship;' because it serves as a beacon light for social equality in order to break the perils of caste-system, it has become incumbent that there should be inter-caste marriages. And marriage is mostly dependent on true love and feeling and once this is achieved, caste and religion factors become secondary issues.

The social reformers said that 'education is a main instrument for social change' therefore, many people have educated themselves and though they changed their economic position, they have not changed in the cultural level. And they carry the customs and religious practices which are so strict, even sometimes the boy and girl have been hacked to death by their own family members (due to the pressures from the society) which is called 'honour killing' because, these persons are afraid of the society or social norms. According to them people will punish in the social terms and will suffer a loss in their social and cultural status. The parents prefer that, their sons or daughters should marry in the same caste and community. The SCs or STs students who are highly educated and who get good jobs in government and semi-government services and in private sector, want to marry a girl from the other community. But caste endogamy has been thrust upon them and they are under pressure or they get inferiority complex when restrictions are imposed within the field of their marriage.

In this matter, the media is promoting caste system and paradox. It has supported discrimination because many a time media has introduced cultural components such as caste and sub-caste. For example, media has been giving more space to an event against the marginalized communities. In the recent period, various newspapers published marriage advertisements inserted by individual or inserted by marriage bureau. The newspapers highlight on caste of bride or bridegroom. Generally, the daily newspapers in Maharashtra state, have published marriage advertisements and discriminated against the lower castes. They specially mentioned as 'we are ready for inter-caste and inter-communal marriage but excuses for SCs and STs'. In this point of view, the upper caste people and also newspapers focused on caste and discriminate against the SCs and STs.

For the analysis of discrimination against SCs and STs the data has been taken from the daily newspaper *Loksatta*, which is dominated by upper caste in Maharashtra state (paper dated Sunday, 5 June 2011, Page No. 9, 10 and 11). In Maharashtra, majority of the educated people have a holiday on Sunday, and, therefore, they read the papers carefully and majority of marriages are organized in the month of May and June. In this newspaper was published a total of 260 marriage advertisements; among this 187 (71.92 %) marriage advertisements were accepted only by same caste candidates. And 33 (12.69 %) were accepted from any caste, that means they are allowing marrying with any caste. About 40 (15.38 %) marriage advertisements accepted inter-caste marriage but they clearly mentioned, 'excuse for SC and ST candidate or communities'. Therefore, these 40 cases have been taken for analysis; these discriminate SCs and STs.

Caste, Gender and Marriage

Modern India has increased in special mobility of the people, and thereby, put an end to the geographical isolation, which was a favourable condition for the creation of caste system in India. But the majority of the caste or religious groups have been carrying the paradox which is seen everywhere. We know that, Indian society was divided into four categories, e.g. *Brahmins, Kshatriya, Vaishya* and *Shudra*. Members of these groups do not marry members of other groups. Therefore, the caste system is rigid and complex. Afterwards, sub-castes were created within the caste. In the recent period, each caste has developed an ethnic identity, therefore, the system is increasing in complexity. In this way the upper caste and lower caste also follow the ethnic and cultural identity. The society was more restricted before independence. If anyone went against any religious activity then the upper caste persons punished them. We know that education is a main instrument for social change, but nothing was done in this regard for SCs, and STs before independence. Dr Babasaheb Ambedkar, struggled against the caste discrimination and he suggested to his followers 'educate, agitate and organize'.[17] The positive results of this effort has been achieved by many people through education and gaining of higher posts in government, semi-government and private sector services but upper caste communities still do not allow them to marry a person of higher caste. Even if the upper caste persons are illiterate or are economically poor, they still discriminate against SCs and STs.

Table 1 *Caste and Genderwise Distribution*

Name of the Caste	*Gender*		*Total*
	Male	*Female*	
Bhavsar	1	1	2
	10.0%	3.3%	5.0%
Brahmin	6	7	13
	60.0%	23.3%	32.5%
Gurav	—	2	2
	—	6.7%	5.0%
Kshatriya	—	2	2
	—	6.7%	5.0%
Mahadev Koli	—	1	1
	—	3.3%	2.5%
Marathas	2	7	9
	20.0%	23.3%	22.5%
Rajput		1	1

Cont'd...

...Cont'd

	—	3.3%	2.5%
Teli	—	2	2
	—	6.7%	5.0%
Vaishyavani	1	1	2
	10.0%	3.3%	5.0%
Other	—	6	6
	—	20.0%	15.0%
Total	10	30	40
	100.0%	100.0%	100.0%

Note: Name of the caste arranged alphabetically.

The Table 1 shows that, out of 40 marriage advertisements, those concerned with male are only 10 (25%) and those concerned with the female are 30 (75%). The ratio of male marriage advertisements is more than female because the relation is very close between age of marriage and girls' education. On this issue Rowena Robinson mentioned that, 'There is an increase in the age of marriage and women increasingly have an opportunity to get education and work before marriage. While more girls enter careers nowadays, this is sometimes because men want educated and employed brides. However, there is also a sharp increase in working women because they want to carve out independent careers. Men and women meet and try to discover areas of compatibility, even when marriages largely continue to be arranged by family members. Among such groups, the income, lifestyle and education of the partners often count for as much, if not more, than just caste position.'[18] Three decades ago, the age of marriage on an average was 18 for the girl and 21 for the boy but now the average age of marriage has increased. In the city area, every person wants security or they require economic stability in the society. For that purpose, education and skill development are more important and as a result the age of marriage has increased.

As caste and marriage are linked we have seen earlier, that the restrictions, imposed by religion are followed by the members of society as part of custom or culture. The Table 1 also shows that, the majority of the communities are *Gurav, Marathas, Teli, Vaishyavani* and others. These communities fall under Other Backward Classes (OBCs) and an important point is that, even *Mahadev Koli* 1 (2.5%) which is under the Scheduled Tribes community gave excuses against SCs and STs; which means that this lot also discriminated against their own community.

Education, Gender and Marriages

The awareness of development has increased more after independence in the society. The result is that the girls have achieved higher education and higher posts in government, semi-government and private sector jobs. Therefore, they are aware that without economic stability they cannot marry therefore the number of girls with higher education is more than the boys. After 1991, Indian government has been following the pattern of globalization and its impact is on every sector – especially educational sector – the traditional education is declining day by day and modern professional education is expanding everywhere, with such courses like BBA, MBA, BCA, MCA and IT. Therefore, in these professional educational courses the girls have enrolled themselves.

Table 2 *Education and Genderwise Distribution*

Education	*Gender*		*Total*
	Male	*Female*	
Graduate	1	12	13
	10.0%	40.0%	32.5%
Post-graduate	1	7	8
	10.0%	23.3%	20.0%
Professional	8	10	18
	80.0%	33.3%	45.0%
HSC	—	1	1
	—	3.3%	2.5%
Total	10	30	40
	100.0%	100.0%	100.0%

The above Table 2 shows that, out of 30 female candidates, 29 (99.96%) are highly educated. Among these 7 (23.3%) candidates have achieved post-graduate and professional education has been undertaken by 10 (33.3%) candidates. Even modern education is based upon secular principles and domestic values and so it is playing a big role in diminishing the importance of caste system in India. On the one hand, it gives importance to the democratic ideas like equality, liberty and fraternity and on the other, it develops a scientific approach towards any event. Modern education is usually imparted in the co-educational institutions. It encourages inter-caste marriages, based on love, among the educated young generation. It acts as a very powerful force against castes in India. But this data shows that, while they are highly educated, these persons are also discriminated if they belong to SCs or STs. If this situation continues time and again then how can we say 'education is a master key of social change? And what type of change is expected from an educated person? This table also proves that, many brides and grooms are highly educated, due to the progress of science, industrialization and modern education. The present-day educated women are against gender bias and discrimination by castes. They have generally succeeded in their struggle for equality with men, specially in educational and professional fields. However, when it comes to marriage, discrimination by castes still prevails, which is a dichotomy in our society.

The Marital Status and Caste

In the earlier period, the parents were taking the decision of children's marriage between 18–20, but now the age of marriage is

Table 3 *Gender and Marital Statuswise Distribution*

Gender	*Marital Status*		*Total*
	Unmarried	*Divorced*	
Male	9	1	10
	25.0%	25.0%	25.0%
Female	27	3	30
	75.0%	75.0%	75.0%
Total	36	4	40
	100.0%	100.0%	100.0%

increased in the society. The Table 3 shows that, out of 40 candidates, 36 (90%) candidates are unmarried and 4 (10%) have taken divorce. In Indian society generally the status of person (who wants to re-marry) is considered to be lower than the status of an unmarried person. In this matter the 4 (10%), candidates want to re-marry but these candidates are also discriminated against, on the basis of caste.

City, Gender and Marriage

Urbanization is the direct result of industrialization. As city is the collection of different people irrespective of caste, religion, *Varna*, language and so on, it is difficult to practice caste restrictions. In a city, people do not know the identity of the other person. Due to the impact of urban civilization, the idea of pollution by touch, by casting of a shadow, etc. is gradually vanishing from the minds of the urban people. Due to the industrial development, the different types of modern means of transportation like buses, trains and so on, it is impossible to observe caste rules, with regard to food, drink and social intercourse.

Table 4 *Gender and Citywise Distribution*

Gender	*City*			*Total*
	Mumbai	*Abroad*	*Not Mentioned*	
Male	9	1	–	10
	30.0%	25.0%	–	25.0%
Female	21	3	6	30
	70.0%	75.0%	100.0%	75.0%
Total	30	4	6	40
	100.0%	100.0%	100.0%	100.0%

The Table 4 shows that, out of 40 candidates for marriage, 30 (75%) candidates are living in Mumbai. Out of these, 9 (30.0%) candidates are male and 21 (70.0%) are female. And out of 40 candidates, 4 (10%) are living abroad, they have a good job and they are living in a casteless society. But these candidates also still discriminate against the SCs and STs. This means their mindset has not changed even though they have gone world over.

This table also shows that, out of 30 female candidates, 21 (70%) candidates are living in Mumbai city and 3 are (10%) living aborad and generally people say that, a person cannot follow the caste restrictions in the city areas. But here we found that, the *upper caste* communities have followed caste restrictions concerned with marriage, which is followed not only in Mumbai but even abroad.

Conclusion

The broad conclusion that could be drawn here is as follows:

Those who think rationally about marriage, realize that a successful marriage is not dependent on factors, such as same caste and religion but it depends on the built-in aspects of mutual understanding and compatibility. It is based upon how well you understand each other's needs and how you feel for your life partner. It is not necessary that, a person has to belong to the same community or caste to understand his/her spouse better. But here, we found that each caste is a separate identity as well as even those who are more educated in the upper castes or communities also discriminate against the SCs and STs.

On the social and economical ground there are no problems for the upper caste community, as *upper caste* people allow dominating in the social, political, religious and educational level; they have no problem. But where the culture, especially of marriage is concerned the relation is not good, as they are not allowing the marriage in the *lower caste* even if either person is educated or economically well settled in the society.

The basic cultural practice has not undergone changes at all. However, if there are changes then these changes are on a limited scale. In various cases, the law has its limited effect. It is a common practice in the society to insult SCs and STs but this uncivilized act has not yet disappeared and various legislative measures such as the Protection of Civil Rights Act, 1955, and the Scheduled Castes and Scheduled Tribes (Prevention of Atrocities) Act, 1989, have proved to be virtually worthless because of the lack of political will to implement them. Even if the SCs and STs person holding M.Sc. Ph.D. or M.D. in medicine or M.S. in chest diseases or even if they have good jobs in government or semi-government service or private sector , but such education has no significance when it comes any change in their mindset when related to the issues like marriage.

Notes

1. Rowena Robinson, *India: Culture and Society*, www.ufmg.br/cei/wp-content/plugins/download.../download.php?id=10, dated 27 August 2011.
2. Guru Gopal, 'Dalits: Reflections on the Search for Inclusion', in Peter Ronald deSouza (ed.), *Contemporary India*, Sage Publications, New Delhi, 2000, p. 62.
3. K.L. Sharma, *Indian Social Structure and Change*, Rawat Publications, Jaipur, 2007, p. 172.
4. Yogendra Singh, *Social Stratification and Change in India*, Manohar Publications, New Delhi, 1977, p. 6.
5. V.K. Sharma, *Caste, Class and Society*, Book Enclave, Jaipur, 2007, p. 163.
6. Ibid., p. 165.
7. *Dr Babasaheb Ambedkar: Writings and Speeches*, Vol. 1, Education Department, Government of Maharashtra, Mumbai, 1989, p. 47.
8. Dr B.R. Ambedkar, *Annihilation of Caste*, Samata Prakashan, Nagpur, 1944, p. 60.
9. Robinson, op. cit.
10. P.V. Kane, *The History of Dharmshastra*, Part 1, Bhandarkar Oriental Research Institute, Poona, 1941, p. 194.
11. M.N. Srinivas, *Social Change in Modern India*, Orient Longman, Hyderabad, 1988, p. 123.
12. Robinson, op. cit.
13. V.K. Sharma, op. cit., p. 165. Kolenda and others. (complete this reference)
14. Constitution of India, Part III, Fundamental Rights, No. 17.
15. The Report of Planning Commission on Development Challenges in Extremist Affected Areas, Government of India, New Delhi, April 2008, p. 4.
16. Author's collected data when he visited the village on 18 February 2012 at 2.30 P.M.
17. Shankarrao Kharat (ed.), *The Letters of Dr Babasaheb Ambedkar*, Indrayani Sahitya, Pune, 1990, p. 6.
18. Robinson, op. cit.

10 Marginalization Through Citizenship

A Glimpse of the Exclusion of Scheduled Castes in Manipur

Vishal Jadhav

This paper examines how the ideology and the classificatory policies of the Indian state such as cataloguing the nation on the basis of identities – forward and backward caste, upper and lower class, forward and backward region, majority and minorities in religion, urban and rural areas – leads to the construction of a rather rigid framework through which citizenship operates. This paper argues that by this practice of recognizing group-based and territorial-based identities and spaces, the State creates ambiguities and thus derecognizes large sections of the Scheduled Castes individuals who find it difficult to identify with this state classificatory schema. In this paper, the plight of the Scheduled Castes individuals and communities of Manipur vis-à-vis the State is examined. The Scheduled Castes population of Manipur in 2001 Census totals 60,037 individuals, which constitutes 2.8 per cent of the total population of the State. The State has registered 61.8 per cent decadal growth of Scheduled Castes population in 1991–2001. There are seven notified Scheduled Castes (SCs) communities in the State: Lois (86.1%), Patni (5.6%), Namasudra (5.5%), Yaithibi (0.9%), Sutradhar (0.2%), Dhupi (0.1%) and Muchi (0.1%).[1] The SCs population of Manipur is primarily Hindu. Of the total of 60,037 SCs in 2001 Census, 60,007 are returned as Hindus, 24 Sikhs and only 6 Buddhists. The Lois and the Yaithibi are the only two Scheduled Castes communities that originally belonged to Manipur. The rest of them are migrant communities from adjoining States (Laisram, 2004).

Manipur is administratively divided into nine districts, namely, Bishnupur, Chandel, Churachandpur, Imphal east, Imphal west, Tamenglong, Thoubal and Ukhrul. The population of Manipur in 2001 Census has been 2,166,788. Of this 741,141 are Scheduled Tribes (STs), which constitutes 34.2 per cent of the total population of the State.[2] Besides the Scheduled Tribes and Scheduled Castes there is another marginalized community, i.e. the Muslim community which constitutes almost 8 per cent of the total population of the State. They are labelled as *Pangals* in Manipur and most of them are refugees who settled here after the 1971 war. Of the total STs in Manipur, *Thadou* is the largest with 1.8 lakh population representing 24.6 per cent of the State's total STs population, followed by *Tangkhul* (19.7%), *Kabui* (11.1%), *Paite* (6.6%), *Hmar* (5.8%), *Kacha Naga* (5.7%) and *Vaiphui* (5.2%). Among other major tribes, *Maring, Anal, Zou, Any Mizo* (*Lushai*) tribes, *Kom* and *Simte* are having percentage between 3.1 and 1.5. The STs population in Manipur is predominantly rural with 95.3 per cent rural and 4.7 per cent urban population. Of the thirteen major STs, *Kacha Naga* (99%), *Anal* (98.5%), *Maring* (98.2%), and *Simte* (98.1%) have returned to majority (98–99%) of their population in rural areas. Ukhrul, Tamenglong, Churachandpur and Chandel are predominantly tribal districts having more than 90 per cent of the district's population as Scheduled Tribes.[3] Senapati has recorded 78.5 per cent of its population as Scheduled Tribes. These five districts together hold 92.4 per cent of the State's total STs population. The rest of the four districts of Manipur have negligible percentage of STs Population (Census 2001, http://censusindia.gov.in/Tables_Published/SCST/dh_st_manipur.pdf).

It is no secret that the tribals in central and western India are one of the most marginalized communities in the country, but this would not hold true at least in the north-eastern parts of the country and, therefore, in Manipur. The Indian State has divided the tribal population in the country on the basis of physical space and geographical location. It has not taken account of the differential historical trajectories of these disparate tribal communities and has instead continued viewing them through the colonial lens as a monolith category who are mainly forest dwellers practising animistic religions. Also it assumes that the tribals are socially and culturally primitive. Rather than distinguishing these communities in terms of their socio-economic attributes, the State has located them in spatial terms; these places being identified in terms of the proportion of tribal population in residence. Thus, it has designated some parts of the country as tribal territory and also has made special efforts to develop these regions through tribal sub-plans. But this was not so in case of the Scheduled Castes communities and there exist no such sub-plans for this community. Why is this so, and does this threaten the livelihood chances of the Scheduled Castes individuals in Manipur?

The tribal communities in Manipur predominantly belong to the Christian denomination and display a high level of literacy. The high literacy level and a fair level of westernization have allowed many of these individuals to get placed in Central and State services. Besides, as most of the grant-in-aid and special packages such as tribal sub-plans, tribal area development plans, special drives amongst many others, have empowered these tribal groups/communities (unlike their counterparts in the rest of the country). In the central and western regions of India where the tribal population is concentrated, the Indian State has encouraged exploitation of natural resources, inauguration of large-scale projects (Special Economic Zones, Reserved forests, hydel and thermal power projects among others) which has not only displaced many of the tribal communities but also culturally uprooted them from their moorings.

There is however another problem that is plaguing the State of Manipur and other States in North-East India – the menace of insurgency which initially had its beginnings in separatist movements. Currently, this region is placed under the Armed Forces Special Powers Act (AFSPA), which confers special powers on military and paramilitary forces. There have been several civil society mobilizations in these 'disturbed areas' (in the States of Arunachal Pradesh, Assam, Manipur, Meghalaya, Mizoram, Nagaland and Tripura) to draw attention of the nation to the gross human rights and human dignity violations. The North-East in many ways invokes a sense of a *distant* land in the minds of most

Indians. So much so that since the post-independence period, the Indian State lacks the imagination and the necessary will to improve the political economy of this region. Just providing grant-in-aid and subsidies has really not sufficed in bringing this region at par with other States of the country, at least in terms of the development model that the Indian State has embarked on (Baruah, 2005; Chatterjee, 1993, 1997, 2004).

In recent times, the State of Manipur has been the site of the most violent unrest. There are more than 29 insurgent groups that represent various ethnic groups in the State.[4] In a situation where the citizen is caught between the conflict involving the armed forces and paramilitary forces on one hand, and the insurgents on the other, it becomes a desperate situation. The case of *Sharmila* whose plea to reign in the extraordinary powers of the state and the cries demanding justice seems to be fading from our memories, only goes to show how indifferent we, as a nation, have become towards such instances of State violence occurring in the North-East (Nag, 2002; Sharma, 2000).

The incongruity of the misassumption of the State possibly stands out rather starkly in this case – on the one hand the State believes that insurgency can be controlled if not ended through the AFSPA, and on the other, the State doles out sizeable resources through its grant-in-aid system and also encourages the local government institutions to vigorously pursue the scheme.

Of much significance is the fact that there exists a parallel State in Manipur. Fieldwork indicated that the insurgents have taken over as the negotiators, i.e. the link between the common citizen and the State. Thus, for instance, a citizen who needs to procure a license to sell petrol or kerosene, a motor driving license, domicile certificate, permission to open and operate a school/shop/enterprise, marriage certificate, birth certificate, job cards for MNREGA, getting pension sanctioned, public contracts, etc. approach insurgent groups who provide these facilities at a commission. The insurgent groups work hand in glove with State officials (either by invoking fear or by bribing) and ensure that the individuals who can afford such transactions (having requisite social, cultural and symbolic capital) get benefits. Such kind of interactions involves operationalization of primordial identities such as tribal and ethnic identities. As the Scheduled Castes (SCs) communities constitute only around 2.8 per cent of the total population in Manipur, they hardly have any negotiating power to access their citizenship rights. Moreover, as the State is predominantly upper caste Hindus (66%) and tribals (34.2%), the reservation quota is generally accessed by the tribal communities. In such a context the Scheduled Castes individuals remain excluded and marginalized.

As the State is placed under the martial law, the common people are caught amidst the conflict involving the armed forces and paramilitary forces on one hand, and the insurgents on the other. This conflict has affected the civil administration which has almost collapsed. For instance, the supply of electric power is sporadic and intermittent and sometimes does not reach the citizens for days together. The State is also not evident when it comes to collecting sales tax and property tax. Most of the time, it is the insurgent groups that collect these taxes on behalf of the State or keep it for themselves (Baruah, 2005; Nag, 2002; Sharma, 2000).

The SCs population of Manipur is primarily concentrated in Thoubal district (Kakching block), which accounts for 56.6 per cent of the total SCs population of the state. Other two districts have sizeable proportion of SCs population like Imphal West (22.1%) and Imphal East in *Sekmai block* (17.3%). One can also locate sparsely populated SCs pockets in the district of Bishnupur (Thanga and Leimaram village). With the advent of colonialism their traditional way of life was completely destroyed as modernity and industrialization began to replace the traditional system. Currently, the SCs communities are predominantly urban based, i.e. 65.3 per cent reside in urban areas and find their source of livelihood in these areas (2001 Census).

The *Lois* which is the largest SCs community in the State has the highest urban population with 74.5 per cent. It is followed by the *Yithibi* community that has 37 per cent amongst them, being urban based. The *Namasudra* and *Patni* communities on the other hand, have maximum membership based in rural areas – their percentage is (96.1%) and (99.9%) respectively. What is also interesting is that the SCs population in the State exhibits a high proportion of literacy level.[5] According to 2001 Census, in Manipur

72.3 per cent of the SCs population is literate, with the *Namasudra* recording the highest literacy rate of 73.4 per cent, followed by the *Lois* (72.5%) and *Yaithibi* (70.5%). The *Patni* is the least literate (65.9%) among the four main SCs communities. The 2001 Census has also documented another interesting facet, i.e. statistics regarding higher education. Manipur is one of the leading states having 12.8 per cent of its total SCs literates having graduate and above educational level. The *Lois* with 14.4 per cent is significantly ahead of other SCs such as *Yaithibi* (5.5%), *Namasudra* (0.6%) and *Patni* (0.4%).

According to the 2001 Census report, the percentage of Scheduled Castes workers to total population stood at 51.4 per cent, which is higher than the aggregated figure for SCs at national level (40.4%). The breakup of these SCs workers reveals that 67.4 per cent have been recorded as main workers and 32.6 per cent as marginal workers. Another interesting facet worth mentioning here is that the female work participation rate (WPR) stood at 47.5 per cent. The *Lois* community has recorded the highest work participation rate which stood at around 53.1 per cent. A noteworthy fact is that among *Lois*, men and women contribute more or less equally to the household economy, i.e. the work participation rate is 55.4 per cent and 50.8 per cent respectively. The *Yaithibi* has recorded comparatively a low WPR at 47.9 per cent. However, their female WPR (48.4%) is higher than that of their male (47.5%). The WPR is quite low at 35.5 per cent among *Namasudra,* followed by *Patni* (36.6%).

Most of the Scheduled Castes individuals are bereft of land and mostly work as agricultural labourers. They possess small patches of land especially in hilly terrains. As a percentage of the total work force amongst the SCs 35.3 per cent of them have been reported to be employed as cultivators (marginal cultivators, who only produce rice) and 12.3 per cent as agricultural labourers. Together, the largest chunk of the SCs workers is employed in agricultural activities, i.e. 47.6 per cent. According to the 2001 Census report, between the four main SCs communities in Manipur, *Patni* has recorded the highest 49.4 per cent of their total main workers as cultivators, closely followed by *Namasudra* (48.6%), while it is only 37.4 per cent among *Lois*. The *Yaithibi* has recorded the lowest at 8.8 per cent. They, however, have recorded the highest, 32.5 per cent agricultural labourers. Thus, one can also notice stratification amongst the SCs population. The *Yaithibi* is the most marginalized among the seven notified Scheduled Castes. As employment is seasonal in agriculture-related occupations, they migrate to the nearest district headquarters or urban areas to search for a livelihood. All the communities are predominantly found to be employed in the unorganized sector such as at construction sites, road making, and rock quarrying, making and selling illicit liquor amongst many other such occupations. Their women are also to be found in large numbers in prostitution and selling of narcotic drugs (Interviews conducted by the researcher in 2011).

The traditional occupation of the *Lois* was handicraft and cottage industries in the 19th century. The various sub-castes among this community were also specialists in the art of carpentry, blacksmith, weaving, jewellery, pottery and others. Some of the villages in which the *Lois* population was predominant had become famous during the colonial period, such that during the census exercise the British had unknowingly catalogued these *Lois* village names as sub-castes of the *Lois* community for instance, the Sekmai village in East Imphal was known for producing high quality alcoholic liquor (made from rice) and the *Lois* residing here came to be known as *Sekmai*. Similarly the villages Khurkhul, Leimaram and Phayeng which were sites of fine quality of silk yarn soon came to be recognized as groups of people. Also the Andro, Chairel and Thongjao villages known for its artistic pottery came to be sub-castes of the *Lois*. Waikhong village which was famous for its high quality rock salt came to be congruent to a sub-caste of the *Lois* (Laisram, 2004).

Though the Constitution of India recognizes citizenship at two levels, i.e. at an individual level and the other at a community level, it was only the communitarian identity that has been highlighted until now. The following section will try and assess some of the implications of such a bias by the Indian State. For one, in Manipur, where the tribal population is predominant, most of the reservation quota and other developmental benefits inherently go to these communities. In such a case the Indian State should make the necessary amendments to ensure that the marginalized among other communities also get a fair chance in accessing resources of the State.

Citizenship Through a Communitarian Identity

To comprehend how community identities got reinforced and routinized as a way of accessing State sponsored welfare programmes, it becomes necessary to understand how the Indian State conceptualizes citizenship in India. The paper argues that it is the State practice of classification that has inherent exclusionary manifestations. The Indian State recognizes individuals as citizens through the dual lens of formal and communitarian citizenship. Thus, the birth certificate, domicile certificate, election card, ration card among such other identity providing documents enables the individual to claim formal citizenship. However, this formal citizenship is not substantive in nature and, therefore, leaves the poor and the destitute to fend for identity, livelihood and social security all by themselves. At another level, the State also recognizes another level of citizenship, especially, when disbursing resources, i.e. communitarian citizenship. For instance, the State language recognizes group identity rather than formal individual identities when it recognizes social categories such as religious and linguistic minorities, backward regions, forward castes, Other Backward Classes (OBCs) and SCs, STs and other tribes, urban and rural spaces, forward and backward States (such as the BIMARU) among others. Many a times these categories and individuals do not superimpose and this leads to marginalization of the most powerless and the poor.

This section of Manipur people do not possess the kind of social networking that other 'citizens' can access through the State recognized communitarian framework. Moreover, many of the poor have shifting identities, especially the poor migrant labourers who sometimes do not even have a residential proof. The State demands certain set of bureaucratic procedures, to claim formal citizenship. Many cannot even obtain these and are non-existent for the State.

The Indian State and Its Classificatory Policies

In the early decades following independence, it was realized by the nationalist political actors that Indian society was markedly manifest in deep inequalities – at the social, cultural, political and material levels. These disparities and differences were partly inherited during colonialism and partly exaggerated due to the processes of electoral democracy in the post-independence era. With India adopting a democratic model, these differences, which were social and cultural markers, were translated into political identities. Identities such as caste, religion, language and ethnicity became important conduits through which political power was organized. This was because the Indian State in its Constitutional framework followed a classificatory policy – such as cataloguing and recognizing the nation on the basis of religion, caste, tribe, class, region, language and also on the basis of rural and urban settings. The then political leadership, led by Nehru, believed that the only way to 'modernize' India was to have a centralized top-down planning approach. It was in this context that the Planning Commission was inaugurated which continues to plan and decide for the whole country even today. Though this classificatory policy did help in mapping and reducing poverty, it also created stereotypes that have led to exclusion of many at individual level.

By constructing such classifications to enable better targeting we argue that the Indians oversimplified sociabilities. We contend that it is high time that the State began to derecognize these imaginary categories as representations of homogenous group of individuals. This, of course, is not true. For instance, the Constitution of India states that there is a Hindu majority religion and the rest are minority religions. Even within the minority religion it makes a distinction between the larger denominations and 'others'. Islam, Sikhism, Christianity, Jainism and Buddhism as one category and Judaism, Zoroastrianism, Bahaism, together with animistic forms of religion falls in the latter category. Hinduism itself, is not a homogenous category and, therefore, certainly not a community. So it is with other religious denominations. A special scheme has been inaugurated by the State for the minorities but that does not cover the most deprived Dalit castes and tribal denominations, as they are clubbed as a denomination within Hinduism or other religions. Additionally, the State does not recognize culturally deprived status such as SCs status even amongst the Muslims and Christian denominations. It is acknowledged that many of the Muslims and Christians are Scheduled Castes converts from Hinduism. Moreover, what happens when an individual does not want to be identified by any religious identity or by an identity that is not legitimated by the Indian State?

Similarly, in the post-independence period, the States were reorganized on the basis of administrative territories which were demarcated on linguistic grounds. Further, these linguistic States were catalogued in terms of forward and backward categories and attempt was made to 'create temples of modernity and development' in backward States. Even within linguistic States, areas were notified as backward and forward. Therefore, some States such as the BIMARU States have always received larger grants-in-aid from the Centre. It is pertinent to note that the North-Eastern States have always been high on literacy level. But this does not mean that they are highly developed.

A similar exercise in categorizing the tribal population was also undertaken. The total tribal population constitutes approximately 8 per cent of the total population of the country. The Constitution recognizes 573 communities as Scheduled Tribes and the rest as other tribes. The former groups of tribals enjoy the Constitutional benefit of reservations in education and employment, the latter do not. But even within the former group the benefits accrue only when the individual is applying for reservation within the geographical region in which the tribe is recognized as part of Scheduled Tribes or when applying for a Central Government employment. In other administrative regions or linguistic States the individual belonging to the Scheduled Tribes is considered as a general category individual. Certain areas within the linguistic States were also given special status – Tribal areas and Scheduled areas which have a special tribal plan grant in each Central and State budgets.

Similarly, the Indian State recognizes 18 official languages, but in all, there exists over 300 languages most of them tribal languages which over the time have been marginalized to such an extent that most of them do not have a script. They are practised and transmitted orally or sometimes scripts of other 'mainstream' languages are used. The idea that linguistic groups consist of homogenous individuals, and are communities, is itself misleading. This kind of categorization of linguistic groups has led to construction of loaded stereotypes. These stereotypes then become exclusionary mechanisms in time. These tribal languages do not get the same attention from the State as some dominant languages do.

When it comes to categorizing castes, the task becomes rather impossible as there are innumerable 'jatis' specific to a region or territory in India and also because caste-based census was given up after 1931. Based on cultural (erstwhile untouchable jatis) and educational backwardness index, the Constitution acknowledged a special category called the Scheduled Castes. Again, this category was tied to territorial spaces/linguistic States. It was also acknowledged that there was a high correlation between caste and class (Omvedt, 1982). This led to inauguration of a new category called the Other Backward Classes (OBCs) which was based on the criterion that these communities were backward due to reasons of cultural exclusion. Scholars, however, have demonstrated that this is not a homogenous community and is stratified in terms of *haves and have nots*. In many States, it is a section of this category that actually constitutes the political elite for instance the *Reddys, Kamma, Lingayat, Yadav, Kurmis, Jats* and *Vokkaligas* among others (Brass, 1990; Frankel and Rao, 1990; Harriss, 2003).

To conclude, this paper has endeavoured to shed light on the faulty premises under which the Indian State functions and operates. The Scheduled Castes in India, even to date, face stigma in the form of untouchability and discrimination in public facilities, residence choice, eating places, temples, fines, imprisonment among others. According to Thorat and Newman (2010) they also face discrimination in the form of caste-based labour. In Manipur too, the Scheduled Castes individuals when compared to individuals of forward castes, are denied employment, are paid less than others, are overworked and are made to remain unskilled. According to official statistics, the Scheduled Castes constitute 14 per cent of the total population of the county of which 90 per cent live in rural areas and are, in some regions, still bound by a modified form of *balutedari* or feudal system (Government of India, 2010; Shah et al., 2006).

Deshpande (2011) has calculated the occupational levels of household heads of major States into four categories, i.e. Scheduled Caste, Scheduled Tribes, Other Backward Classes (OBCs) and Forward Castes, based on the NFHS-III data. According to her calculation, the Scheduled Castes as a percentage of their total population are found to be in the following categories: (a) not working 4.94 per cent, (b) manual labourers and farmers 67.54 per cent, (c) clerical workers, sales workers, service workers and merchants 14.03 per cent, (d) creative workers and artisans 9.77 per cent, (d) professional, technical and administrative managers (low level) 3.44 per cent, (e) professional technical and administrative managers (high level) 0.28 per cent. These statistical figures demonstrate how marginalized and deprived this section of society is and that despite Constitutional safeguards, individuals from this community face discrimination and are also subject to stigma and labelling. The case study that follows, illustrates the condition of the individuals belonging to the Scheduled Castes. The situation is no different in the North-Eastern States. In Manipur, the Scheduled Castes communities do not enjoy the Constitutional provisions meant for them and this is a major concern.

What this paper reflects on, is whether the classificatory policies of the Indian State need to be revamped so as to become sensitive to the issues of the Scheduled Castes and other Dalit members of society. We need to ensure that classification amongst themselves do not exclude exercising of citizenship.

Notes

1. Census of India, 2001, Data Highlights: The Scheduled Castes of Manipur. The figures in the parenthesis indicate the percentage of each community as a ratio to the total numbers of Scheduled Castes in Manipur as notified by the Constitution.
2. According to the 2001 Census there are 33 Scheduled Tribes in Manipur - *Aimol, Anal, Angami, Chiru, Chothe, Gangte, Hmar, Kabui, Kacha Naga, Koirao, Koireng, Kom, Lamgang, Mizo, Lushai, Maram, Maring, Mao, Monsang, Moyon, Paite, Ralte, Sema, Simte, Suhte, Tangkhul, Thadou, Vaiphei, Zou, Poumei Naga, Tarao, Kharam and any Kuki* tribes. These tribal groups generally reside in the hill districts of Manipur. The *Mao* tribe is predominantly found in the Senapati district, the *Tangkhuls* in Ukhrul, the *Kabuis* in Tamenglong, the *Anals and Maring* in Chandel and *Thadous, Kuki and Paite* in Churachandpur district. According to 2001 Census, the Scheduled Tribes population was 7.41 lakhs (3.74 males and 3.67 females) as against 6.32 lakhs in 1991 Census. There are 7 Scheduled Castes communities in Manipur. They are *Loi, Yaithabi, Dhobi, Muchi or Rabidas, Namsudra, Patni and*

Sutradhar. The total Scheduled Castes population in Manipur was 60 thousand (30 thousand males and 30 thousand females) in 2001 Census.

3. Churachandpur is a hilly district and the two main ethnic groups that are predominant are the *Kukis* and the *Paites*. This district has been a site of ethnic clash in the 1997 (between the *Paite* and the *Kukis*) that in time spread to other parts of Manipur and even to adjoining States of Mizoram and Nagaland. Churachandpur is also a special case because this district falls under the constitutional provision, i.e. scheduled area under article 371. This provision entails that instead of 'normal' Panchayat system these areas have an institution called tribal councils which are also based on the principle of representation through election (Baruah, 2005).
4. The well known insurgent groups are Peoples Liberation Army (PLA), United National Liberation Front (UNLF), Revolutionary Peoples Front (RPF), People's Revolutionary Party of Kangleipak (PREPAK), Manipur Liberation Front Army (MLFA), Kanglei Yawol Khnna Lup (KYKL), Revolutionary Joint Committee (RJC), Kangleipak Communist Party (KCP), Peoples United Liberation Front (PULF), National Socialist Council of Nagaland (NSCN-K), National Socialist Council of Nagaland (NSCN-I/M), Naga Lim Guard (NLG), Kuki National Front (KNF), Kuki National Army (KNA), Kuki Defense Force (KDF), Kuki Democratic Movement (KDM), Kuki National Organisation (KNO), Kuki Security Force (KSF), Chin Kuki Revolutionary Front (CKRF), Kom Rem Peoples Convention (KRPC), Zomi Revolutionary Volunteers (ZRV), Zomi Revolutionary Army (ZRA), Zomi Reunification Organisation (ZRO), and Hmar Peoples Convention (HPC).
5. The literacy rate of Manipur is among the highest in India as well as in Northeast. The literacy has increased from 59.89 per cent in 1991 to 68.87 per cent in 2001. The male ratio is 71.63 per cent to 77.87 per cent while the female increased from 47.60 to 59.70 per cent.

References

Bajpai, R. (2011), *Debating Difference: Group Rights and Liberal Democracy in India*, Oxford University Press, New Delhi.

Baruah, S. (2005), *Durable Disorder: Understanding the Politics of Northeast India*, Oxford University Press, New Delhi.

Brass, P. (1985), *Caste, Faction and Party in Indian Politics, Vol. II: Election Studies*, Chanakya Press, New Delhi.

——. (1968), 'Coalition Politics in North India', *The American Political Science Review*, Vol. LXII, pp. 1174–1191.

——. (2004), 'Elite Interests, Popular Passions and Social Power in the Language Politics of India', *Ethnic and Racial Studies*, Vol. 27, No. 3, pp. 353–375.

——. (1991), *Ethnicity and Nationalism: Theory and Comparison*, Sage Publications, New Delhi.

——. (2002), 'India, Myron Weiner and the Political Science of Development', *Economic and Political Weekly*, Vol. 37, No. 29, pp. 3026–3040.

——. (1984), 'National Power and Local Politics in India: A Twenty-Year Perspective', *Modern Asian Studies*, Vol. 18, No. 1, pp. 89–118.

——. (1990), *The New Cambridge History of India, Vol. 4: The Politics of India Since Independence*, Cambridge University Press, Cambridge.

——. (2003), *The Production of Hindu-Muslim Violence in Contemporary India*, University of Washington Press, Seattle.

——. (2000), 'The Strong State and the Fear of Disorder', in Francine R. Frankel et al. (eds), *Transforming India: Social and Political Dynamics of Democracy*, Oxford University Press, New Delhi, pp. 60–88.

Brass, P. and Achin Vanaik (eds) (2002), *Competing Nationalisms in South Asia: Essays for Asghar Ali Engineer*, Orient Longman, Hyderabad.

Chatterjee, P. (1986), *Nationalist Thought and the Colonial World*, Zed Books, London.

——. (1993), *The Nation and its Fragments*, Princeton University Press, Princeton.

——. (2004), *The Politics of the Governed: Popular Politics in Most of the World*, Columbia University Press, New York.

Chatterjee, P. (ed.) (1997 and 1998), *State and Politics in India*, Oxford University Press, New Delhi.

Das, B. (ed.) (1963), *Thus Spoke Ambedkar*, Vol. 1, Buddhist Publishing House, Jalandhar.

Davey, B. (1975), *The Economic Development of India: A Marxist Analysis*, Spokesman Books, Nottingham.

Deshpande, A. (2011), *The Grammar of Caste: Economic Discrimination in Contemporary India*, Oxford University Press, New Delhi.

Government of India (2001), *Census Report*, Ministry of Home Affairs, Delhi.

——. (2011), *Census Report* (Provisional Population Figures), http://www.censusindia.gov.in/2011-prov-results/paper2/data_files/manipur/Manipur_Paper_2_Vol_12.pdf

——. (2010), *Report of the National Commission for Scheduled Castes*, Delhi.

Laishram, S. Bidhan (2004). 'Manipur and the Paradox of Security', Institute of Peace and Conflict Studies, http://www.ipcs.org/article/terrorismin-northeast/manipur-and-the-paradox-of-security-1456.html assessed on 19 September 2011.

Mahajan, G. (ed.) (2011), *Accommodating Diversity: Ideas and Institutional Practices*, Oxford University Press, New Delhi.

Nag, S. (2002), *Contesting Marginality: Ethnicity, Insurgence and Sub-Nationalism in North-East India*, Manohar Publishers, New Delhi.

Roy, A. (2010), *Mapping Citizenship in India*, Oxford University Press, New Delhi.

Shah, G., H. Mander, S. Thorat, S. Deshpande and A. Baviskar (eds) (2006), *Untouchability in Rural India*, Sage Publications, New Delhi.

11 Atrocities Against Dalits in Haryana

A Sociological Study

Desraj Sabharwal

Caste discrimination and caste oppression are not new in India. But what is extraordinary to the caste system and caste-based deprivation in the newer forms is that these oppressions and exploitations can take place in the everyday discourse and interaction. Interestingly, social segregation based on casteism is not only operative in the social sphere but is even more dominant in the political arena of modern state. After independence, abolition of untouchability has been brought under the jurisdiction of constitutional provisions. But 'untouchability' is practised in all the senses. Dalits who have been erstwhile 'untouchables' have eternally been subjected to exploitation and injustice. Discrimination and barbarity towards the Dalits are age-old phenomena. The dominant castes consider that it is their privilege and birthright to beat and butcher the Dalits and the downtrodden. When Dalits attempt to resist the unjust rules imposed upon them, retaliation by upper castes is swift and often violent. Dalits who try to assert their rights face the risk of social and economic boycott, and even physical intimidation, humiliation and beating. The act of brutal inhumanity such as rape and lynching are justified by upper castes who invoke the Hindu scriptures to seek moral legitimacy. One of the reasons why Dalits are forced to suffer extreme humiliation and violence is the traditional caste belief that regards Dalits as inauspicious. Not only their touch but also their shadow is treated as polluting. It is believed that Dalits cause drought and diseases. For instance, in one village in Gujarat, people believed that Dalits were the cause of a disease suffered by livestock in the village. They, therefore, went to a Dalit house and 'forced a woman and her daughter to go to the cattle and remove the curse upon them by stretching their hands over the beasts and eating an offering of coconut' (Mendelsohn and Vicziany, 1998: 46).

The Incidence of Atrocities and Dalits

Caste atrocities are not a new phenomena in Indian society. But the structure and the methodology employed in carrying out murderous attacks on the Dalits is something different. Significantly, even today, the Dalits are treated as the cancerous segment of Indian society. Forced by external forces, every Dalit child grows with this sentiment that he is an inferior being or not a full being or not a human being at all. This sense of being inferior or being a worthless creature generates a paralyse fear and dread towards the dominant castes.

While talking about the scavengers, this unprivileged social group is treated as 'impure' and consequently ritually avoided. They are socially ostracized because of their ritual impurity. As outcastes and the rejects of the Indian society, scavengers have suffered condemnable human indignities throughout the ages. They have been treated like dreaded, contagious disease calling for a disdainful distance and the most minimal social contact. Besides social backwardness, scavengers are economically backward too. Most scavenger families, therefore, live in situation of abject poverty (Pathak, 1998).

The incidences of atrocities against Dalits are increasing day by day because the dominant castes wants to reinforce their power and to assert their superior status. The whole phenomena has a greater significance as it generally occurs when upper castes feel threatened and when their status quo is being challenged by Dalits seeking basic human rights and equality. This paper discusses atrocities against Dalits and the legal and other avenues for preventing such violence.

It is pertinent to mention here that Haryana has not been an exception to such acts of brutality against Dalits. The ghastly tales of these atrocities of which Dulina tragedy was widely publicized became a part of the sociologists' concern (Gupta, 2002). In this tragic incident, five Dalits were lynched to death by the mob, which consisted of mostly the dominant caste people of the adjoining village of the Jhajjar district of Haryana. The nation was ashamed and stunned once again, this time by the merciless slaughter of five Dalit men within the boundary of a police station. On the evening of 15 October 2002, traditional leather-workers were skinning a dead cow close to the Dulina police station. With them were animal skin trader, Kailash, the driver, Tota Ram and conductor, Raju of the hired vehicle in which the carcass was transported. All of them were Dalits. A crowd of villagers gathered near the Dulina police station, infuriated by a rumour that a cow was being skinned alive. They attacked and gravely injured the Dalit men, who were later dragged to the police station. The policemen failed to evacuate the critically wounded men to safety and render medical attention even during the passage of four hours.

This barbaric incident took place when a tractor-load of young men, who were returning from Dussehera celebrations, converged on the Police post, and lynched the men in the presence of three magistrates and at least 60–70 police personnel who had been summoned by them. The assembled police force did little to save the lives of the five Dalits. Yet, not even a single teargas cylinder was fired. More importantly, the local unit of the Vishwa Hindu Parishad (VHP) immediately issued a statement in defense of killings, and demanded that no arrests be made. The police have since dragged its feet in making arrests and claim that it was too dark at the time of the incident to identify the murderers (Mander, 2003).

The VHP was not the only organization that defended the killings. Representatives of the local *gaushallas* and *gurukuls* also issued statements that amounted to saying that the life of a cow was more valuable than that of humans. They all demanded that no police action be taken against those involved in the killings. When the police rounded with a few villagers, the upper castes, particularly those from the locally dominant caste of Jats, held several protest meetings where the emotive significance of cow was repeatedly underlined. The killings were attributed yet against 'mistaken identity'. They repeatedly argued that the crowd of 'Hindus' was completely innocent because they not only believed that a cow had indeed been slaughtered, but also had no clue to the fact that those who were being lynched were Dalits and not Kasais (Muslim slaughterers). Apart from the VHP and local communal organizations who spoke in defense of the killings, fearing police action a section of the locally dominant Jats also began to organize along caste lines. Traditional caste institutions, such as the Khap Panchayat was revived to bring the Jats of the whole belt together. The local *gurukuls* and *gaushallas* that came up during that period, did popularize the cow as a symbol of an aggressive Jat Hindu identity. In the post-Dulina scenario also, these organizations played an active role in mobilizing locals in defense of the killings (Jodhka and Dhar, 2003). Similarly, the defense of the attackers was that the cow was alive while being skinned by the Dalits and it was this outrage of their religious sentiments that fuelled the mob fury. The state administration remained callous and indifferent.

After Dulina, it was the turn of the Dalits of Harsoula village of Kaithal district to face the ire of dominant Jat community. Dalits were beaten and their property damaged, i.e. first on 11 February 2003 and again on 20 March 2003 and were terrorized for celebrating Ravidas's Anniversary. The fact is that the incident happened in front of the police, who remained mute spectators and allowed such a brutal episode to take place, shows the state machinery's inept handling on matters relating to Dalit atrocities. About 200 Dalit families fled from the village after an attack by members of the dominant community. These Dalit families took shelter in the town and saved their lives. Dalits were first attacked on 11 February 2003 and the members of the community returned to the village following the intervention of the administration. However, the truce was broken on 20 March 2003, when the dominant community again attacked the Dalits. The root cause of the attack on the Dalits was a minor scuffle that took place between some Dalits and Jat youths as preparations were underway for the Ravidas Jayanti celebrations. The incident indicated that the two communities did not enjoy cordial relations in the past.

On the other hand, Dalits camping at Geeta Bhavan in Kaithal town said the conditions were not favourable for them to return to the village because only nine, out of 80 persons named by them, had been arrested. During this incident Harsola Sangharsh Samiti was constituted, which was headed by Mr Jogi Ram, a former MLA, and demanded that the cattle, being looked after by members of the Jat community in the village, be returned to their Dalit owners. The Dalits said that they were not provided any help by the administration during the difficult time and they were only looked after by voluntary organizations. During this episode, a large number of Dalits took the decision to give up Hindu religion and embrace Buddhism and other religions. The decision was taken on a call given by Mr Udit Raj, National Chairman, All India Confederation of Scheduled Castes/Scheduled Tribes Organization and Chairman Buddha Club, who was addressing a gathering of Dalits, at the Geeta Bhawan in Kaithal town. They urged them to give up Hinduism, which had failed to protect them from humiliation and atrocities by upper castes. These incidents show that greater awareness among Dalits about their rights has led to individual and collective assertions against the practice of caste discrimination. Dalits' assertion has been met with upper-caste repression.

The most visible and long-standing form of caste discrimination in rural India and also the most taken-for-granted aspect of untouchability in the public sphere, is the residential segregation of Dalit households. In yet another incident of caste discrimination on the eve of *Ghurchari*, a marriage party of Dalit was not allowed to pass through a street in a Rajput dominated village, Jatu Lohari, in Bhiwani district. On defying the decision of the dominant caste people, the entire Barat party was beaten up, insulted and their clothes were torn. Even the bridegroom and his guests were not spared. Dalits faced the anger of dominant Rajput community because they wore 'decent' clothes in the presence of Rajputs and their status is low in the caste hierarchy. The act of violence against Dalits was later justified by the traditional Khap Panchayat of Rajput community. Similarly in Nawada Aar village of Panipat district, Dalits who were allotted land in 1975 were beaten up by the hired hooligans of the dominant caste group. The idea was to terrorize them so that they leave the village and their land could be reclaimed by the dominant caste people. Several unidentified armed persons, brought by the influential persons of Kurad, Sanoli Kurad and Nawada Aar villages, descended on the village on two tractor-trailers and allegedly dragged the menfolk out of their houses. These armed men then 'ordered' the families to vacate their houses. The attackers went into the houses, breaking the household items. In fact, one of the houses was completely demolished and walls of several others were pulled down. Even as the terrified men were asked to line up outside the houses, the women who tried to resist were assaulted and, as a result, five women were injured. The helpless victims were tortured for occupying the Shamlat land (common land). During the past several years, the influential persons had been eyeing the prime Shamlat land, the prices of which had shot up. The Dalits were forced for a compromise by the police and administration. As a result, the Dalits had lived in constant fear. Even their valuable articles such as TV, and tape recorders, which were forcibly taken away by the attackers on 15 November 2003, had not been returned; while no case was registered by the police, it did work out a compromise between the two parties.

Rohtak district of Haryana, alone has been a witness to several incidents of Dalit atrocities. In Masudpur village of Kalanaur Block, Dalits were mercilessly attacked on 7 March 2003 by the members of dominant caste people. In this incident, four women and one Dalit youth was injured. Even pregnant women of Dalit community were not spared. These people were beaten up by the dominant caste people for not supporting their candidate in the last Panchayat election that took place in the year 2000. There is yet another reported incidence of a missing Dalit sarpanch, Karan Singh of Pehrawar village of Rohtak district since October 12, 2003. The mysterious circumstances resulting into disappearance has made his family members believe that he has been the victim of some conspiracy in which state government is allegedly trying to save the members of some high caste men involved in this act. Similarly, another reported incident on 12 March 2003 of gang rape of Dalit woman in Kharkara village of Rohtak district, recalls the scene of a Hindi film. In the presence of her husband she was kidnapped by six armed men of dominant caste of the village. Her husband was mercilessly beaten up. She was taken to an isolated place nearby village and was forced to drink wine. She cried for help but nobody came to save her. More than half a dozen kidnappers raped her one by one. The family members of the victim registered a complaint with the police against the kidnappers but nobody was arrested.

This brutal act crossed all limits of oppression when dominant caste people asked for the proof that she was raped.

In another horrible tale of atrocities, Dalit youths of Bhegwatipur village of Rohtak district were attacked with sticks and sharp edged weapons by the youths of the upper caste. They used abusive language against the Dalits and humiliated on caste lines. They dragged several Dalits out of their houses and they were beaten up by the upper caste youths. During the scuffle, they tore the clothes of Dalit women and beat another woman, who came to the victim's rescue. In this incident, six Dalit youths were seriously injured. Moreover, when the victims reached the police station to register a complaint, the cops on duty directed them to reach a compromise. Similarly, in yet another incident of Gohana town of Sonepat district on 31 August 2005, can be recalled the act of brutality and terror. In this incidence Balmiki Basti (Dalit colony) was attacked by the people of a dominant caste. Aged people, women and children were mercilessly beaten up and many people were seriously hurt. This situation emerged when a youth belonging to upper caste was murdered by a Dalit youth. This incident created a situation of caste war between Dalits and Jat caste groups. More than two dozen houses of Dalits were burnt or demolished and their valuable items such as TV, refrigerator and furniture, etc. were either taken away or destroyed in the presence of the administration. All the Dalits of the locality were forced to leave their houses. Dalit families took shelter in various places to save their lives. Traditional Khap Panchayat of dominant caste of the area not only spoke in defense of this violence but also actually participated in this crime.

The atrocities committed against Dalits by the dominant caste have once again opened the discourse between the caste politics and electoral politics. Dalits being subjected to brutal and cruel atrocities in the past was not the point for debate. But the manner and the method in which these atrocities are being carried out in the last few years in Haryana, present a crucial fact here. In the past, all the political parties had used Dalits as a 'vote bank'. But now Dalits have started to assert their political rights by raising their voice against atrocities. When Dalits exercise their civil rights by stepping outside their 'given' oppressive role, they are humiliated, terrorized and even physically assaulted. For instance, in a village Jatu Lohari in Bhiwani district the entire Dalit barat party was beaten up because they dared to wear bright clothes.

The study shows a number of instances when Dalits refused to follow upper caste directives about voting for a particular candidate or party, they were socially boycotted and forced to migrate from the village. Even in case of a reserved seat, when a Dalit is elected as Sarpanch, he or she is often humiliated by other members of dominant castes. Most of the incidents show that when Dalits attempt to exercise their rights, they face physical and psychological violence. Dalits, who defy upper-caste norms, face not only physical violence but also they are victims of oppressive tactics such as social boycott. Dalits who challenge upper caste privilege find that their access to work, credit and public facilities may suddenly be cut off. Since the dominant caste controls the rural assets, it is difficult for Dalits to assert their rights. The state officials and police, who should be responsible for safeguarding the Dalit rights, are often closely allied with dominant caste groups.

There are a number of instances from different parts of the state where Dalit women have become the targets of upper-caste violence. Dalit women are especially vulnerable to caste-based exploitation and humiliation. Poverty compels Dalit women to work for upper-caste households, often in spaces where they are at high a risk of sexual and other abuse. Thus, conflict between men of different castes often results in attacks on 'their' women. In some reported incidents, Dalit women were raped by the people of dominant caste. When these women wanted to fight against violence, they were asked for proof that they were raped. Dalit women's bodies become the site on which caste violence is practiced.

State Responses to Atrocities Against Dalits

The Indian Constitution has made specific provision for the lower castes. Article 46 of the Constitution clearly and categorically spelt out that, 'The State shall promote with special care the educational and economic interests of the weaker sections of the people, and in particular, of the Scheduled Castes and the Scheduled Tribes, and shall protect them from social injustices and all forms of exploitation.' The Constitution guarantees certain rights to all citizens and places upon the state an additional charge: to protect and serve the interests of the weaker sections so that they may gradually attain liberty, the socially disadvantaged groups should be protected from any form of oppression and injustice.

Government of India implemented two key laws: the Anti-Untouchability Act of 1955 and the Scheduled Castes and Scheduled Tribes (Prevention of Atrocities) Act of 1989, to check crimes against Dalits. The Anti-Untouchability Act (renamed the Protection of Civil Rights Act in 1976) made it a criminal offence to practice untouchability. Any act of discrimination against individuals and groups on the basis of their caste identity was prohibited under this law. However, it was felt that the Anti-Untouchability Act was an ineffective instrument to check crimes against Dalits. In most of the cases, after the crime is registered with the police, cases tend to languish in police files, and the relative powerlessness of Dalits meant that offences against them rarely get investigated or pursued through the courts. This inaction has created a situation where Dalits have lost faith in the administrative and judicial system. In order to signal its commitment to social justice and to safeguard the rights of Dalits, the government promulgated the Scheduled Castes/Scheduled Tribes (Prevention of Atrocities) Act in 1989, which came into force in 1990. The Act defined the term 'atrocity' specifically and identified 22 acts by non-Dalits, non-Scheduled Tribes as offences under the Act. The POA Act also specified the administrative and judicial process to ensure that offences were investigated and offenders were prosecuted speedily. A case registered under the Scheduled Castes/Scheduled Tribes (Prevention of Atrocities) Act must be investigated by a police officer of the rank of Deputy Superintendent or above. The investigation has to be completed within 30 days and its report must be forwarded to the state's police officer, the Director General of Police. The victims of atrocities and their families are to be provided monetary relief as well as maintenance and travel allowances to support them during this period. The Act directs each state to establish a Scheduled Castes/Scheduled Tribes Protection Cell, appoint supervising officers and constitute vigilance and monitoring committee at the district and state level.

The official statistics for the decade 1990–2000 indicate that a total of 2,85,871 cases of various crimes against Dalits were registered, of which 14,030 were of the Prevention of Atrocities Act. This means that an average 28,587 cases of caste discrimination and atrocities against Dalits were registered every year during the 1990s. These include 533 cases of murder, 2,990 cases of grievous hurt, 919 rapes, 184 kidnapping/abductions, 47 dacoities, 127 robberies and 456 cases of arson, 1,403 cases of caste discrimination and 8,179 cases of atrocities. In other words, every hour, more than three cases of atrocities against Dalits are registered, and every day, three cases of rape and at least one case of murder are reported. The actual incident of atrocities is much larger in magnitude since many incidents are not reported to the police and remain unrecorded (Shah et al., 2006).

The present study shows that the reporting of crimes against Dalits under the untouchability and SCs/STs (Prevention of Atrocities) Act rarely results in conviction, showing the failure of the State to investigate and prosecute such offences. The administration and the police officials generally ignore the Act's provisions for conducting investigations. In most of the cases police and administration forced the victims for compromise with the offenders. It was also found that Dalits withdrew many cases under pressure of dominant castes. In other registered cases we found that due to sheer negligence of the police, administration and government prosccutors, the offenders are acquitted and go scot-free.

Conclusion

The iron grip of casteism, caste discrimination and deprivation are not new to the Indian social history. It is significant to note the fact that a section of the Indian population believed that the caste system is a passing phenomenon. But, in reality, caste atrocities and caste discriminations are not isolated phenomena. Caste practices and caste discriminations are ingrained in the very foundation of the Indian society, Indian culture, Indian political economy and finally in the very Indian mindset. Caste discrimination and caste related atrocities are the logical outcome of the historical hatred and social hierarchy. The discriminatory behaviours against the underprivileged castes are seen in the very way the dominant castes address the Dalits. We observed that even educated upper caste persons have fundamental aggressiveness and repulsion towards the Dalits. This ancient hostility in the day-to-day life gets converted into anger and the anger takes the form of violence. These horrifying incidences of violence lead to dreadful effects on Dalits.

The caste system has produced numerous rules that govern everyday interactions among different social groups in rural society. According to these rules, the people of lower castes are not allowed to use certain wells and hand pumps; they are forced to eat separately and these rules regulate all aspects of life for Dalits and constantly reinforce their sense of subordination. Also norms about maintaining caste boundaries apply to all castes and even upper-caste individuals may be socially boycotted by their caste members for violations. Dalits are most severely punished for violation. When Dalits attempt to resist discrimination and attempt to assert their rights, they have to face the risk of physical and psychological violence. The study shows that beside the physical violence, Dalits also face the risk of social and economic boycott, and even residential segregation. Even in ordinary day-to-day interactions, the upper caste people reinforce surveillance on Dalits. The National Dalit leaders reported that a woman from the Dalit community in Rohtak district, was beaten up ruthlessly and her clothes were torn by upper caste youth. But more deplorable than this act was that they abused her by calling her with caste name, which is derogatory. This goes to establish the fact that the upper castes are not satisfied in inflicting only physical pain but want Dalits to go through mental agony and social stigma. In most of the cases the dominant caste persons with tacit approval of the police and administration are engaged in criminal assaults on the Dalits and in some cases either their houses are burnt or destroyed, their valuable property or even men and women are burnt to death.

From the above presented facts, it can be argued that Dalits have been subjected to poverty, indignity, insult, humiliation, dishonour, and terror tactics within the inhuman caste system. Dalit labourers could be extended and expanded at the will of the upper caste. Dalit women were also subjected to physical assault and sexual abuse. Whether in agricultural operations, or during the household activities or while the women are collecting fuel or fodder, they could be teased, insulted and injured. Women were not spared from ill-treatment by the dominant caste even during festivals and religious ceremonies. Dalit community has to bear all these without mercy or any recourse to law. There are many more atrocities that go unreported, since the victims fear of further retaliation. The police administration, most often, does not register these cases and brushes them aside as insignificant.

Now, with the little awakening that has taken place among Dalits, they are trying, in a feeble and modest way, to resist the injustices and atrocities that have been heaped upon them in a most shameless manner. These oppressions and atrocities are such as can hardly be dreamt of in a civilized society and seem to grow in number and intensity. Guilty persons are hardly brought to book and punished because legal procedures are so lengthy and expensive. It can be stated here that all the atrocities committed against Dalits are not accidental incidents but well pre-planned conspiracy to uphold the hegemony and monopoly of the dominant castes. But Dalits have now become conscious of their legitimate place and they have begun to raise their voice against atrocities. Hence, as a reprisal the dominant upper castes are engaged in barbaric repressive measures against Dalits. As a consequence, dissent has been erupting among Dalits. Although the state has legislated elaborate measures to protect the rights of Dalits, these legal provisions are restricted by a caste-biased administration. Despite many hurdles, Dalits continue to mobilize against injustice, discrimination and are now demanding 'justice' and dignity.

References

Dainik Bhaskar, 11 April, 9 and 14 March 2003, Panipat.

——. 24 September 2005, Panipat.

Gupta, Dipankar (2002), 'Jats Close Ranks: A Maha Cover-Up in Jhajjar', *The Times of India*, New Delhi, 7 November.

Jodhka, Surinder S. and Murli Dhar (2003), 'Cow, Caste and Communal Politics: Dalit Killings in Jhajjar', *Economic and Political Weekly*, Vol. XXVIII, No. 3, pp. 174–176.

Louis, Prakash (2002), *Casteism is Horrendous than Racism: Durban and Dalit Discourse*, Indian Social Institute, New Delhi.

Louis, Prakash and Surinder S. Jodhka (2003), 'Caste Conflict and Dalit Identity in Rural Punjab: Significance of Talhan', *Social Action*, Vol. 53, pp. 335–359.

Mendelsohn, O. and M. Vicziany (1998), *The Untouchables: Subordination, Poverty and the State in Modern India*, Cambridge University Press, Cambridge.

Mander, H. (2003), 'Savaged by Traditions', *Frontline*, National Daily.

Omvedt, Gail (1994), *Dalits and the Democratic Revolution: Dr Ambedkar and the Dalit Movement in Colonial India*, Sage Publications, New Delhi.

Pai, Sudha (2001), 'From Harijans to Dalits: Identity Formation, Political Consciousness and Electoral Mobilization of Scheduled Caste in Uttar Pradesh', in Ghanshyam Shah (ed.), *Dalit Identity and Politics: Cultural Subordination and the Dalit Challenge*, Vol. II, Sage Publications, New Delhi, pp. 258–287.

——. (2002), *Dalits Assertion and the Unfinished Democratic Revolution: The BSP in Uttar Pradesh*, Vol. III, Sage Publications, New Delhi.

Pathak, Bindeshwari (1998), 'The Psycho-Social Scenario of Scavenger and the Role of Sulabh International', in N. Hasnain (ed.), *Weaker Sections: The Psycho-Social Perspective*, Gyan Publishing House, New Delhi.

Shah, Ghanshyam (ed.) (2001), *Dalit Identity and Politics: Cultural Subordination and the Dalit Challenge*, Vol. II, Sage Publications, New Delhi.

Shah, G., H. Mander, S. Thorat, S. Deshpande and A. Baviskar (eds.) (2006), *Untouchability in Rural India*, Sage Publications, New Delhi.

The Tribune, 13 November and 15 December 2002; 15, 17, 20 February and 21 November 2003, Chandigarh.

Index